PRAYING SHAPES
BELIEVING

PRAYING SHAPES BELIEVING

A Theological Commentary
on *The Book of Common Prayer*

Leonel L. Mitchell

MOREHOUSE PUBLISHING
Harrisburg, PA / Wilton, CT

Citations of Scripture (except for the Psalms) are to the Revised Standard Version of the Bible, Second Edition © 1971, by the Division of Christian Education of the National Council of Churches of Christ in the U.S.A., in conformance to the text in *The New Oxford Annotated Bible with the Apocrypha,* New York: Oxford University Press, 1977. Used with permission.

Citations of Psalms are to the Psalter of the *Book of Common Prayer,* 1979.

Morehouse Publishing

Editorial Office
78 Danbury Road
Wilton, CT 06897

Corporate Office
P.O. Box 1321
Harrisburg, PA 17105

Library of Congress Cataloging-in-Publication Data
Mitchell, Leonel L. (Leonel Lake), 1930-
  Praying shapes believing: a theological commentary on the *Book of Common Prayer*/Leonel L. Mitchell.
    p.   cm.
  Reprint. Originally published: Minneapolis: Winston Press, © 1985.
  Includes bibliographical references and index.
  ISBN: 0-8192-1553-8
  1. Episcopal Church. *Book of Common Prayer* (1979) 2. Episcopal Church—Liturgy. 3. Anglican Communion— Liturgy. I. Episcopal Church. *Book of Common Prayer* (1979)
  II. Title.
  [BX5945.M57   1991]   90-28624
  264'.03—dc20   CIP

Printed in the United States of America
by BSC LITHO
Harrisburg, PA 17105

To the memory of
my father, Leonel Edgar William Mitchell,
who taught me to love and celebrate the liturgy,
and Edward Rochie Hardy, Jr.,
who taught me to study it

Contents

Acknowledgments

Many of the themes contained in this book were worked out in lectures and conferences over the past several years. In particular an earlier and briefer form of many of the thoughts which I was developing for this work appear in *The Way We Pray*, published in 1984 by Forward Movement Publications, 412 Sycamore Street, Cincinnati, Ohio 45202-4195.

I am grateful to Seabury-Western for the sabbatical time to complete this work and to my colleagues there who offered encouragement and support at various stages of the project, and also to Howard E. Galley, whose intimate knowledge of the production of the 1979 *Book of Common Prayer* saved me from a number of errors in the interpretation of the material.

It also seems appropriate to acknowledge my gratitude to the Kaypro Corporation, manufacturers of the computer without which I never would have been able to complete the manuscript.

Introduction:
The Religion
of the Prayer Book

Probably more than any other contemporary religious group, Episcopalians are people of a prayer book. Not only do we use the *Book of Common Prayer* for the conduct of our public services; it is the guide for our private prayer and the source of most of our theology. The recent revision of the Prayer Book was more for us Episcopalians than simply the alteration of a service book. It called for a readjustment of the language of our relationship with God, and therefore affected that relationship itself. Traditionally this dependence of theology upon worship has been expressed in the Latin maxim *lex orandi lex credendi,* or more accurately *legem credendi lex statuat supplicandi,*[1] which means that the way we pray determines the way we believe. Anthropologists say, "Creed follows cult." Worship, religious activity in all of its aspects—what we do and how we do it, as well as what we say and how we say it—underlies religious belief.

Although these principles are equally true for all religions in the broadest possible sense, most religions (certainly most Christian churches) do not equate their worship with a liturgical book, nor do they see their identity bound up in their service book. The Orthodox Churches, for example, clearly see the liturgy as an experience in which they participate, rather than as a book. In this they are certainly correct. Episcopalians really believe this too, but we tend to express our beliefs

1

in terms of the Prayer Book. Ceremonial changes, for
example, which were mentioned in neither the 1928
nor the 1979 Prayer Book, were frequently cited by
churchgoers as objections to the revised Prayer Book.
Clearly it was the total experience of the liturgy, not
simply the text of the Prayer Book, to which they were
reacting.

In a real sense, then, we Episcopalians are liturgical
theologians. We read our theology out of the *Book of
Common Prayer* and the manner in which we celebrate its
services. Formally, the theology of the liturgy is called
primary theology, or *theologia prima*.[2] Theology is
"God-talk," and primary theology is the language we
use when we talk *with* God, not simply the words we
speak, but the entire liturgical act. Secondary theology,
which is often simply called theology, is the body of
statements or propositions based upon or derived from
reflection upon our interchange with God. It is talk
about God. The "Outline of the Faith" in the Prayer
Book is this kind of theology. It spells out the beliefs
which are proclaimed in the worship. In a sense, this
distinction between primary and secondary theology is
technical and academic, but the primary nature of the
language of worship is real and important. For example, it is not necessary for every Christian to understand
the doctrine of the Trinity as it is spelled out in the
Athanasian creed.[3] However, it is necessary for every
Christian to offer prayer and praise to the Father and
Creator of all through Jesus Christ in the fellowship of
the Holy Spirit, for such is at the heart of our faith.

Recently, in responding to an address by Geoffrey
Wainwright,[4] I commented:

> My view of the task before liturgical theologians is to
> reflect upon the worship of the church in the light of the
> dictum of Prosper of Aquitaine *Legem credendi lex statuat
> supplicandi,* considering the *lex supplicandi* or *lex orandi*
> which establishes our rule of belief as not simply the text

of the rite but the entire liturgical act in its multi-dimensional integrity. If we are serious about the priority of first-order language, or *theologia prima*, then it is from the liturgy itself that the principles of a secondary liturgical theology must derive.[5]

I further contended that we need to begin by reflecting on a specific liturgical tradition. In my case, that tradition is that of the *Book of Common Prayer* 1979. It is to this task that the present effort is addressed. What I plan to do in these pages is not so much to examine every item in the Prayer Book as to discuss the theology of the *Book of Common Prayer* as a theology which is faithful to the tradition of both the Catholic Church and the Anglican Communion, and as a theology which we can believe and teach to people today.[6] God does not change, and the Gospel which we preach does not change. It is the same Gospel which Peter and Paul proclaimed. But we change and the world changes, and we approach God with new problems and new questions. The language of theology must be able to hear and respond to these new experiences without changing its age-old witness to the Eternal and Unchanging God.

Chapter One:
The Service
of the Church

The Church is first and foremost a worshiping community. It is the *synaxis*, the gathering together of the people of God for corporate worship, which is the heart and soul of the Church's life. We say this in a great many ways. Massey Shepherd, writing in the original Church's Teaching Series in 1952, quoted the acts of the 4th-century martyrs:

> As if a Christian could exist without the Eucharist, or the Eucharist be celebrated without a Christian! Don't you know that a Christian is constituted by the Eucharist and the Eucharist by a Christian?[1]

Associated Parishes, an organization of the Episcopal Church dedicated to liturgical and parochial renewal, said it this way:

> Jesus Christ is the Lord of all creation and is the Head of the human race. Through Him, in the unity of the Holy Spirit, the Christian Church is called to worship God the Father, to await His kingdom, and to serve in His world. . . . The Holy Eucharist is the characteristic and representative action of the Church in the fulfillment of this vocation. . . . From the altar, God's redeeming and renewing power reaches out into every phase of life; to the altar every aspect of our existence is to be gathered up and offered to God through Christ in the fellowship of His Holy Spirit.[2]

Vatican Council II, in the second paragraph of the *Constitution on the Sacred Liturgy*, put it like this:

. . . it is the liturgy through which, especially in the divine sacrifice of the Eucharist, "the work of our redemption is accomplished," and it is through the liturgy, especially, that the faithful are enabled to express in their lives and manifest to others the mystery of Christ and the real nature of the true Church.[3]

We should not be surprised, then, to find the Prayer Book sounding this same note at its very beginning, in the section entitled "Concerning the Service of the Church" (BCP: 13):

The Holy Eucharist, the principal act of Christian worship on the Lord's Day and other major feasts, and Daily Morning and Evening Prayer, as set forth in this Book, are the regular services appointed for public worship in this Church.

We might follow this up with the statements of the catechism, An Outline of the Faith (BCP: 859f):

. . . the Eucharist, the Church's sacrifice of praise and thanksgiving, is the way by which the sacrifice of Christ is made present, and in which he unites us to his one offering of himself. . . . The benefits we receive are the forgiveness of our sins, the strengthening of our union with Christ and one another, and the foretaste of the banquet which is our nourishment in eternal life.

The Prayer Book lays out at its beginning the traditional Christian and Catholic format of the life of the Church. At its center is the Lord's Service, the Holy Eucharist, celebrated by the Lord's people on the Lord's Day, Sunday. The Holy Eucharist is our common gathering as the family of God, united with one another in Christ our head to celebrate his death and resurrection until he comes again. But the Sunday eucharist does not stand in isolation. Daily Morning and Evening Prayer provide the supporting framework of corporate and personal prayer for the Sunday liturgy.

This is the ongoing structure of the liturgical life of the Church which is the focus of the new life in Christ. It does not sit alone and isolated from the day-to-day business of living, but permeates it and offers it all—joys, sorrows, successes, failures, frustrations, anger, and love—to God. The psalmist sings not only "Have mercy upon us, O Lord" (Psalm 123:4) and "Hallelujah! Praise the Lord from the heavens" (Psalm 148:1), but also "Greatly have they oppressed me from my youth up" (Psalm 129:1), and "Happy is the one who pays you back for what you have done to us!" (Psalm 137:8). The prayer of God's children offers up *all* of life to God.

The Context of Liturgical Life

This ongoing life in Christ is set in the traditional context not only of the day, with Morning and Evening Prayer, and of the week, with the Sunday eucharist, but also in the context of the whole year as a liturgical expression of the work of our redemption. The liturgical year has its roots in the early centuries of the Church's life and turns the mystery of life in Christ like a fine jewel so that we see it reflected and refracted through different windows as we pass from Advent through Christmas to Epiphany and then from Lent through Holy Week to Easter and Pentecost and the season following. It is in this traditional "year," and especially in the celebration of the Good Friday-Easter sequence, that the work of our redemption is proclaimed and celebrated.

The initiation of new Christians has been the central act of this sequence since at least the fourth century. The Great Vigil of Easter was intended to be the clearest and fullest expression of the meaning of our faith and life, and this Vigil has been restored to a central position in our Prayer Book. This restoration, in turn, also restores focus to the Church year and gives a context to the sacraments of Christian Initiation.

Finally, the Prayer Book provides appropriate rituals for the important personal occasions of life—births, weddings, sickness, death—and for the ordering of the Christian community with rites for ordinations, consecrating churches, and beginning ministries. All of these are related to the central celebration of the eucharist and are ways of bringing the specific occasions of individual and communal life into the eucharistic assembly.

Liturgical Roles

The Prayer Book not only provides a framework for the liturgical life of the Church; it also provides for the full and active participation of the entire people of God in that life.

> In all services, the entire Christian assembly participates in such a way that the members of each order within the Church, lay persons, bishops, priests, and deacons, fulfill the functions proper to their respective orders, as set forth in the rubrical directions for each service. (BCP: 13)

The rubrics of the individual services naturally provide the specific directions for participation, but the principle of common participation by the entire assembly, a principle which stands at the very center of the Liturgical Movement of the 20th century, is there established. This is certainly not a novel idea for Episcopalians. It seems to be both a logical extension of the insistence of the Reformers that the people should be able to understand the worship they attend and a restoration of the earlier practice of the Church.

This participation is not to be without order, but all are to "fulfill the functions proper to their respective orders." This is made more explicit in the rubric which follows and describes the bishop and priest as the normal leaders of worship, but permits deacons and lay persons to preside at the Liturgy of the Word when no priest is available. The principle underlying this directive is the Pauline one of the many members of the one body, each having different functions (1 Corinthians 12).

The ordination rites and the general rubrics at the beginning of individual services will, of course, describe the different functions of the four orders in more detail, but the important point being made here is that <u>each order has its own liturgical functions</u> and should be permitted to fill them. At one level this has to do with the proper ordering of rites and making clear ritually the different roles of different orders, but there is also a theological dimension. If the theology of ministry is not manifested in the liturgical actions of the ministers, then there is a disparity between the *lex orandi* and the *lex credendi*. If this disparity is great enough, either orders of ministry will be seen as irrelevant to the actual worship of the congregation, or, more likely, the theology of ministry which is expressed in the liturgy will supplant the official theology in the minds of worshipers. It is difficult, for instance, to explain the theological importance of the diaconate in a parish in which the deacon's liturgical role is always filled by a priest, or to explain the role of the laity in the Body of Christ at worship if all liturgical functions are performed by ordained persons.

The Prayer Book speaks of "exceptional circumstances, when the services of a priest cannot be obtained" (BCP: 13) and permits the authorization of deacons to preside at other rites. The Canons also permit lay readers to preside at some services. These, however, are exceptional circumstances, and their effect is to subordinate the liturgical functioning of the

ordained ministers to the needs of the assembly of the
people of God. Generally speaking, Episcopalians have
not been willing to carry this principle to the extent of
permitting lay persons or deacons to preside at the
eucharist. We have traditionally seen a necessary theological connection between priestly ordination and
eucharistic presidency. In the same way, we have seen a
necessary connection between episcopal presidency and
ordination. Other Christians have not always seen these
liturgical roles as being required theologically, and they
have been willing to authorize lay presidency of the
eucharist or ordination effected by priests or
presbyters. The examination of the ordination rites will
give us an opportunity to explore this more fully, but
the Episcopal Church is clearly in the tradition of both
Anglicanism and the Catholic Church in these practices.

Liturgical Continuity

One further theological reflection should be made concerning the material in this section. It concerns continuity with the liturgy of the past. The classic
expression of this continuity has normally been found in
the preface to the Prayer Book of 1789, which has been
printed as the Preface of every succeeding American
Prayer Book. It contains this statement:

> . . . this Church is far from intending to depart from
> the Church of England in any essential point of doc-
> trine, discipline, or worship; or further than local cir-
> cumstances require. (BCP: 11)

In 1789, this was a clear discription of the doctrinal
and liturgical position of the fledgling Episcopal
Church. Its Prayer Book and other formularies could
be compared with those of the Church of England and
interpreted in their light. Since that time, not only has
the Church of England itself engaged in liturgical

reform, producing *Alternative Services 1980,* but the various churches of the Anglican Communion have adopted their own variants of the *Book of Common Prayer,* so that it becomes increasingly difficult to speak of the liturgical bond of the Anglican Communion. Certainly this is an issue of which the leaders of the various national churches are quite aware, and serious efforts are being made to assure that the liturgical continuity with the *English Prayer Book of 1662,* which was once the hallmark of Anglican unity, is not abandoned but brought up to date on the basis of common liturgical principles.[4] We need to recognize also that the Anglican Communion is a much more ethnically and culturally diverse body today than it was in 1789. Much of it does not worship in the English language, and much of it is African, Asian, or Caribbean in culture.

A more fruitful place for us to begin appears to be the provisions for the use of "previously authorized liturgical texts" when it is desired to sing music composed for them (BCP: 14). These provisions permit the continued use of classical Anglican liturgical music, as well as the great liturgical music of the Western Church which has formed a part of so much Anglican worship, and avoids the loss to liturgical celebration of the treasury of liturgical music that the Roman Catholic Church experienced in its recent liturgical reform. But there is more involved here than music. The provisions recognize that the worship of the 1979 Prayer Book is continuous with that of the earlier liturgical tradition, and they affirm that the services in the Prayer Book are the legitimate descendants of those in the earlier books.

The same point could also be made from the inclusion of the Rite One traditional language services in the Prayer Book, and the provision that other services may be conformed to the traditional language (BCP: 14). The continued use of the music *and* the texts from previous books, and the inclusion of much traditional

language material in the present Prayer Book, combine
with the continuity of title and authorization to ensure
that this liturgy is related to that previously used and
has, in fact, developed from it and its collateral relatives.

Chapter Two:
The Calendar,
Times and Seasons

The first major section of the Prayer Book, following its general introductory rubrics, "Concerning the Service of the Church" (BCP: 13-14), is the Calendar (BCP: 15-33). Closely related to it are the Collects (BCP: 159-261), the Proper Liturgies for Special Days (BCP: 264-95), and the various tables and lectionaries (BCP: 881-1001). Together they make up a substantial portion of the Prayer Book. We must therefore recognize that a concern with liturgical time, festival and season is an important part of our religious heritage, as it has been traditionally in Christianity and in most other religions. The establishment of a calendar of festivals has been an important function of most religions throughout history.

The most significant questions to be asked about the calendar have been well posed by Louis Bouyer in his classic work *Liturgical Piety.*

> Is the liturgical year to be understood merely as a kind of high evangelical pedagogy? Is it merely a psychological device invented to make us meditate in turn on all the phases, all the events, in the life and death of our Lord? Is it merely a system of readings, songs and prayers so arranged as to cause us to go more deeply each year into the meaning of the Word of God and enable us to understand it more fully?[1]

Certainly the liturgical year does all of these things; but are they all it does? Is there some real relationship between the celebration of Easter and the resurrection of Christ? Is there some reason beyond mere convenience for worshiping on Sunday rather than on Thursday? If the answers to these questions are not at least in some sense yes, then we may well ask with Bouyer, "Were not the Puritans really right after all when they rejected the whole liturgical year as being a baseless superstition?"[2]

Certainly, too, the liturgical year has frequently been presented as if it were a particularly successful lesson plan for churchwide Christian education. But such is a truly secondary consideration. Massey Shepherd has stated the traditional view with vigor and clarity.

> The Christian year is a mystery through which every moment and all the times and seasons of this life are transcended and fulfilled in that reality which is beyond time. Each single holy day, each single gospel pericope in the sequence of the year, is of itself a sacrament of the whole gospel. Each single feast renews the fulness and fulfillment of the Feast of feasts, our death and resurrection with Christ.[3]

Shepherd describes this view of the liturgical year as "sacramental." It is also called mysteriological. It sees a real relationship between the liturgical celebration and the reality being celebrated, such that the participants in the celebration become participants in the saving reality. We find this view implied if not actually expressed in the collects for various feasts, especially the three principal feasts of Christmas, Easter, and Pentecost.

The first Christmas collect speaks of celebrating "the yearly festival of the birth of your only Son." This declaration makes no greater demand than that we accept Christmas as the anniversary of Christ's birth. The second collect, however, goes beyond memorializing a birth date and says, "You have caused this holy night to shine with the brightness of the true Light" (BCP: 212). It identifies *this* night with the breaking forth into this world of the true Light which is Christ, and it identifies the celebration of the festival with the shining of the Christ Light into our lives. To celebrate Christmas, then, is in a real sense to participate in the event which it celebrates. The third Christmas collect speaks of Christ as "born [this day] of a pure virgin," again identifying the festival with the saving event it celebrates. The brackets surrounding "[this day]" make the point even more clearly, since they are to be omitted if the collect is used on a day other than Christmas.

This same identification is found in the second and third Easter collects (BCP: 222). The second, which is also the traditional collect for the Great Vigil, prays, "O God, who made this most holy night to shine with the light of the Lord's resurrection. . . ." The third speaks of celebrating with joy "the day of the Lord's resurrection." The point is made even more clearly in the Exsultet, the paean of praise sung at the lighting of the Paschal Candle at the Great Vigil. Over and over again the phrase is repeated, *"This* is the night. . ." [emphasis mine] (BCP: 286f), as the mighty acts of God in the Exodus and the resurrection of Christ are proclaimed. Both Pentecost collects also use the phrase "on this day" to describe the outpouring of the Holy Spirit upon the disciples (BCP: 227).

It appears that the Prayer Book considers its festivals to be more than just commemorations of great events in the history of our salvation. The contemporary philosopher-theologian Josef Pieper has appropriately observed:

> Memorial days are not in themselves festival days. Strictly speaking, the past cannot be celebrated festively unless the celebrant community still draws glory and exultation from that past, not merely as reflected history, but by virtue of a historical reality still operative in

the present. If the incarnation of God is no longer understood as an event that directly concerns the present lives of men, it becomes impossible, even absurd, to celebrate Christmas festively.[4]

Pieper's example is particularly relevant to our discussion. It is the opening of these events to our participation in them and their celebration as the constitutive events of our Christian life that give them their sacramental character and their proper significance. We instantly see the effect of Pieper's distinction if we turn from a consideration of the principal Christian feasts to the lesser commemorations of the calendar. The latter are merely "memorial days" for most of us, and we do not in fact celebrate them festively. The parochial celebration of Christmas is quite different from that of Mary and Martha of Bethany or of William White. By contrast, a Franciscan community might well see the celebration of October 4, the festival of St. Francis of Assisi, as a true community festival and celebrate it as such, setting the liturgy within the more general celebration of a *fiesta*.

The calendar presents us with three separate areas for reflection: the weekly celebration of Sunday, the seasons of the Church year, and the celebration of the festivals of the saints. We shall consider each separately.

The Lord's Day
and the Christian Week

The Lord's Day, is the principal Christian feast. According to the Prayer Book calendar, "All Sundays of the year are feasts of our Lord Jesus Christ" (BCP: 16), and only Principal Feasts take precedence over them. At the simplest level, this rubric explains what proper collects, psalms, and lessons will be used on a particular occasion; but, at a deeper level, it is the dignity of the Lord's Day which is being ritualized by the rubric. The collect for Sunday at Morning Prayers prays:

> O God, you make us glad with the weekly remembrance of the glorious resurrection of your Son our Lord: Give us this day such blessings through our worship of you, that the week to come may be spent in your favor. . . . (BCP: 98)

This makes clear the significance of Sunday: it is the "weekly remembrance of the resurrection." It is the day of worship which is to inform the coming week. The same message is given in the Compline collect for Saturday, which asks, "May our joy abound in the morning as we celebrate the Paschal mystery" (BCP: 134), and in the collect for Sunday Evening Prayer, which prays:

> Lord God, whose Son our Savior Jesus Christ triumphed over the powers of death and prepared for us our place in the new Jerusalem: Grant that we, who have this day given thanks for his resurrection, may praise you in that City of which he is the light, and where he lives and reigns for ever and ever. (BCP: 123)

When we look at the Sunday eucharistic celebration, we find that the second of three proper prefaces for the Lord's Day proclaims:

> Through Jesus Christ our Lord; who on the first day of the week overcame death and the grave, and by his glorious resurrection opened to us the way of everlasting life. (BCP: 377)

The eucharistic preface not only identifies Sunday with the day of the Lord's resurrection, but it also speaks of Sunday as "the first day of the week." This reminds us that Sunday is not the Sabbath, which is the seventh day of the week, our Saturday, but a specifically

Christian observance, a day of eucharistic worship in
celebration of our risen Lord.

The Lord's Day is at the center of our Christian celebration as the day of giving thanks for the Lord's resurrection. About this Sunday gathering for worship Justin
Martyr wrote in the second century:

> We all hold this common gathering on Sunday, since it is
> the first day, on which God, transforming darkness and
> matter, made the universe; and Jesus Christ our Savior
> rose from the dead on the same day. For they crucified
> him on the day before Saturday [the Sabbath], and on
> the day after Saturday he appeared to his apostles and
> disciples and taught them those things which I have
> passed on to you also. . . .[5]

Justin also mentions that God created light on the
first day of the week. This idea, too, is found in the
liturgy: the first of the proper prefaces for the Lord's
Day speaks of the Father as "the source of light and life"
(BCP: 377). A further identification of Sunday as the
day on which the Holy Spirit was given (Acts 2) is
implied in the third of the Sunday prefaces, which says:

> For by water and the Holy Spirit you have made us a new
> people in Jesus Christ our Lord, to show forth your
> glory in all the world. (BCP: 378)

We can expound neither the history nor the theology
of the Christian observance of Sunday here,[6] but we can
recognize that from the earliest times the Lord's Day is
and has been considered the primary Christian festival.
The medieval liturgy's displacement of Sunday by a
variety of lesser holy days evoked serious complaints
from both Catholic and Protestant reformers, and the
restoration of the Sunday celebration to its primacy in
the calendar has been a concern of both Anglican and
Roman Catholic contemporary liturgical revision.

The French theologian Yves Congar has written concerning the theology of Sunday:

Sunday is the day when the Church truly sees itself, sees itself as the heavenly City, and another world than this; it is the day of the royal and priestly people, of a new spiritual creation, of which the beginning is in us, of faith in the Word of God, and of which the reality is the whole body of Christ. Just as the other days are days of the earthly city, of the building of this world, Sunday is the day of the people of God, of that people who believe in eternal life and know that they are called to it, of that people consecrated and set apart to offer to God witness, worship, and praise.[7]

The Prayer Book expresses this traditional theology of Sunday in its calendar and more especially in its collects and prefaces for Sunday. There we clearly see the primacy of the Sunday observance shown forth in the liturgy itself. Statements such as that of Congar, important though they may be, are secondary to the expression of the joy of the Lord's Day found in liturgical prayer.

As we have seen, the Prayer Book expects the Lord's Day to be celebrated with the people assembled for the celebration of the Holy Eucharist. The very expression "Lord's Day" (*Kyriake*, in Greek) is apparently related to the phrase "the Lord's Supper," which includes the same adjective. Sunday is particularly the *eucharistic* day.   *cf Acts 20:7*

The Prayer Book mentions two other weekly observances which are dependent on the weekly celebration of the Lord's Day: Friday and Saturday. Saturday is, of course, the biblical Sabbath, and the collect for Saturday Morning Prayer refers to the Sabbath rest ascribed to God in the creation narrative:

Almighty God, who after the creation of the world rested from all your works and sanctified a day of rest for all your creatures: Grant that we, putting away all earthly anxieties, may be duly prepared for the service of your sanctuary, and that our rest on earth may be a

preparation for the eternal rest promised to your people
in heaven. . . . (BCP: 99)

We might describe this collect as a simple acknowledgment of Saturday as the Old Testament day of rest, but
it is more than that. The collect combines the eschatological understanding of Sabbath rest found in Hebrews
3 and 4 with the idea of Saturday as a day of preparation
for Sunday worship.

The collect for Saturday Evening Prayer speaks only
of the preparation for Sunday worship (BCP: 123). The
Jews referred to the day before the Sabbath as the Day
of Preparation, and the collect is a Christian parallel to
that usage. The prayer apparently does not intend to
establish any particular Saturday observance, but to
reflect devotionally on the themes of Saturday as the
biblical day of rest and as the day on which we prepare
to celebrate the Lord's Day.

Friday, on the other hand, appears in the calendar as
a Day of Special Devotion "in commemoration of the
Lord's crucifixion" (BCP: 17). The collect for Friday
Morning Prayer refers to the crucifixion (BCP: 99); that
for Friday Evening Prayer refers to Jesus' death (BCP:
123). Friday observance can be traced back to the first-
century *Didache*, which considers Friday one of two
weekly fast days (*Didache* 8). The *Didache* gives no reason for the Friday fast other than distinguishing the fast
of Christians from that of the hypocrites, who fasted on
Monday and Thursday [!]. The Prayer Book, however,
identifies all Fridays with Good Friday and with the
celebration of the Lord's death, and there is ample evidence that this identification was universally considered
to be the reason for Friday observance in the early
Church.

Earlier versions of the Prayer Book described Friday
observance as including "a measure of abstinence."

The current Prayer Book speaks of "special acts of discipline and self-denial" without further specifying what they might be. This is the same designation given to the weekdays of Lent. No special liturgical observance beyond the use of Friday collects at the Daily Office seems to be intended, but the significance of Friday as the weekly memorial of the crucifixion is included in the observance of the Christian week.

The Liturgical Year

It is generally believed today that the observance of Sunday as the Christian festival of the resurrection is older than any form of annual celebration.[8] The oldest annual festival is universally agreed to be the *Pascha*, a unitive celebration of the death and rising of Christ, which was apparently observed at the time of the Jewish Passover. The Passover, in turn, was recognized (from the testimony of the Gospels) as the occasion of the crucifixion. (Remarkably, English is one of the few languages in which the same word *Pascha* is not used for both the Jewish and the Christian festival.) By the end of the second century, the Christian *Pascha* was observed by Christians everywhere.

The *Pascha* forms the basis of the original cycle of the liturgical year. This cycle is described by the Prayer Book as "dependent upon the movable date of the Sunday of the Resurrection or Easter Day" (BCP: 15). The Paschal cycle consists of the seasons of Lent, Holy Week, and Easter.

The date of Easter is "movable" in our calendar because it is dependent on the date of the Jewish Passover, which is the 15th of the lunar month of Nisan in the Jewish calendar. Our Gregorian calendar is a solar calendar, and lunar dates vary over a nineteen-year cycle. These years are identified in the Prayer Book calendar by the Golden Numbers. Since Easter is today described as "the Sunday after the full moon that occurs on or after the spring equinox on March 21" (BCP: 880), the actual date of Easter will vary from March 22 to April 25 according to a 532-year Great Paschal Cycle. Theoretically this date will be the Sunday following the lunar date Nisan 14, but in practice the actual date may be a full lunar month earlier than the Jewish observance. We shall have occasion to note the identification of the Christian and Jewish Paschal celebrations when we consider the Great Vigil of Easter, but it is important to observe now that the actual dating of Easter manifests its dependence on the date of the Passover.

The fifty-day season of Easter was originally known as the Pentecost or the Great Fifty Days. It was considered to be an extension of the Sunday festivity throughout a fifty-day period. It corresponds to the seven-week period in the Jewish calendar which separates the festivals of Passover and the Feast of Weeks (Pentecost or Shavuot). Athanasius, in the 4th century, spoke of the seven weeks of the Holy Pentecost as spent "wholly rejoicing and exulting in Christ Jesus our Lord." (*Festal Letter*, 330 A.D.) The Prayer Book marks the seven-week Easter celebration not only in the Calendar but also in the Prayer Book's provisions for using special canticles and adding "Alleluia!" to versicles and responses during Eastertide. Eucharistic propers for every day of the Easter season are provided in *Lesser Feasts and Fasts*.[9]

Holy Week is the center of the Paschal celebration. Rooted in 4th century Jerusalem,[10] Holy Week's celebration resulted from the separation of the elements of the earlier *Pascha* into separate celebrations of the historical events surrounding the passion and resurrection of the Lord: the triumphal entry, the last supper, the crucifixion, the burial, and the resurrection. The *Pascha* celebrated both the passion and the resurrection. It was the annual commemoration of the *unity* of Christ's death and resurrection. This unitive element, including the celebration of the passion, seemed to distinguish the *annual* celebration from the *weekly* Sunday, which celebrated the resurrection only. The Friday before Easter was observed as the beginning of a two-day Paschal fast, in which the whole Church joined with those who were preparing for Easter baptism. The 4th-century Jerusalem Church also came to celebrate the historical events of the passion on those days of the week with which the Gospels associated them and at the places at which they were believed to have actually occurred. The triumphal entry came to be celebrated on the Sunday at the beginning of Holy Week with a procession into Jerusalem from the Mount of Olives, the crucifixion on Friday at the site of Golgotha, and the resurrection itself early on Easter morning at the *Anastasis,* the shrine surrounding the empty tomb. This celebration of Holy Week became popular with pilgrims and was soon exported throughout the world.

The Prayer Book provides for the celebration of Holy Week not only by furnishing proper lessons and collects for every day but also by providing special liturgies to be used on the most significant days of the week: Palm Sunday, Maundy Thursday, Good Friday, and Holy Saturday. In addition the Prayer Book provides for the celebration of the Great Vigil of Easter, which we shall consider separately.

In our calendar Holy Week is an eight-day week, beginning and ending with a Sunday. The first Sunday is called "The Sunday of the Passion: Palm Sunday"; the second is "Easter Day." The double name of Palm Sunday bears witness to its historical development. Originally the passion and resurrection of Christ were both celebrated at the Great Vigil, but eventually the celebration of the passion was moved back to the preceding Sunday so that the Easter festival could focus on the joy of the resurrection. The gospel reading at the eucharist on the first Sunday is always one of the synoptic accounts of the crucifixion. Its message is applied by the collect:

> Almighty and everliving God, in your tender love for the human race you sent your Son our Savior Jesus Christ to take upon him our nature, and to suffer death upon the cross, giving us the example of his great humility: Mercifully grant that we may walk in the way of his suffering, and also share in his resurrection. . . . (BCP: 272)

The central position of the cross in Christian theology and devotion hardly needs to be insisted upon. This central saving act is chiefly celebrated on the Sunday of the Passion. This is not to imply that not every celebration of the eucharist is a celebrat on of the crucifixion, but its historical circumstances are particularly considered in the Sunday liturgy on this day. Of course, the cross and passion are also the theme of the Good Friday liturgy.

The second title of this first day of Holy Week, "Palm Sunday," is derived from the historical extension of the passion events, an extension which began in the 4th-century Jerusalem Church. The synoptic chronology placed the triumphal entry into Jerusalem on the Sunday prior to the crucifixion, and the Jerusalem Church began to celebrate it on that day with a palm procession from Bethany to the Holy City. This procession gained a place in Christian devotion and eventually gave its name to the day. The blessing which the Prayer Book gives to be said over the palms before the procession explains its meaning:

> It is right to praise you, Almighty God, for the acts of love by which you have redeemed us through your Son Jesus Christ our Lord. On this day he entered the holy city of Jerusalem in triumph and was proclaimed as King of kings by those who spread their garments and branches of palm along his way. Let these branches be

for us signs of his victory, and grant that we who bear them in his name may ever hail him as our King, and follow him in the way that leads to eternal life. . . . (BCP: 271)

Here again we find a "sacramental" understanding of the liturgical celebration which involves our participation in the original saving event. Palm Sunday speaks of the proclamation of Jesus as King and recalls us to our proper role as his people. It speaks also of the great victory of his passion, thus tying the two foci of the Sunday together.

Maundy Thursday celebrates the institution of the eucharist at the Last Supper. Traditionally the eucharist has been celebrated in the evening on this day. The day's primary theme is the celebration in the eucharist of the Lord's death until he comes (1 Corinthians 11:26). Following the example of Jesus in the gospel reading traditionally assigned to this day (John 13:1-15), the Prayer Book also provides for the "Maundy" or "the ceremony of the washing of feet." The command to love one another is the theological content of the ceremony. This command, taken from John's Gospel and appointed to be sung during the foot washing (BCP: 276), is the source of the name "Maundy," from the Latin *mandatum*, "commandment." We imitate the action of Christ in order to share in the love of which it was the outward and visible sign.

Good Friday does not have a celebration of the eucharist. The special liturgy provided for the day is a Liturgy of the Word, with the reading of the Passion according to John, the Solemn Collects, anthems sung in honor of the cross, and optionally, the distribution of Holy Communion. The Good Friday celebration is the commemoration of the crucifixion, and its theme is well expressed in its collect: ". . . behold this your family, for whom our Lord Jesus Christ was willing to be betrayed. . ." (BCP: 276). The actual components of the liturgy come from Jerusalem, Constantinople, Gaul, and Rome. Although the Good Friday liturgy heavily emphasizes one aspect of the Paschal Mystery (crucifix- ion and death), it actually celebrates the unity and total- ity of the Paschal Mystery. The liturgy's most theologically expressive words—found in the first anthem in honor of the cross—make clear the unitive nature of the celebration:

> We glory in your cross, O Lord,
> *and praise and glorify your holy resurrection;*
> *for by virtue of your cross*
> *joy has come to the whole world.* (BCP: 281)

The anthem makes it clear that the crucifixion has not been separated from the resurrection, but that the liturgy sets before us the Paschal Mystery in its totality. Although there have been many advantages in extending the celebration of the events of the passion throughout the entire eight days of Holy Week, such extension also runs the risk of leading us to look only at the Paschal Mystery's parts. That is why texts such as the anthem above, which remind us of the entire Pas- chal event, are so important.

Like Good Friday, Holy Saturday does not have a eucharistic liturgy. The Prayer Book provides only a simple Liturgy of the Word which celebrates the burial of Christ. The Holy Sabbath is an empty day as the Church prepares for the celebration of the Great Vigil. The Holy Saturday collect sounds the themes of waiting upon God and hope in the resurrection:

> Grant that, as the crucified body of your dear Son was laid in the tomb and rested on this holy Sabbath, so we may await with him the coming of the third day, and rise with him to newness of life. . . . (BCP: 283)

The third season that is part of the Paschal cycle is the season of Lent, which is well described in the special liturgy for the first day of Lent, Ash Wednesday:

> The first Christians observed with great devotion the days of our Lord's passion and resurrection, and it became the custom of the Church to prepare for them by a season of penitence and fasting. This season of Lent provided a time in which converts to the faith were prepared for Holy Baptism. It was also a time when those who, because of notorious sins, had been separated from the body of the faithful were reconciled by penitence and forgiveness, and restored to the fellowship of the Church. Thereby, the whole congregation was put in mind of the message of pardon and absolution set forth in the Gospel of our Savior, and of the need which all Christians continually have to renew their repentance and faith. (BCP: 264f)

Thus, although Lent has its origins in the preparation of candidates for Easter baptism, it has also come to be a season of repentance and renewal for the entire congregation. The Prayer Book exhorts contemporary congregations to observe "a holy Lent, by self-examination and repentance; by prayer, fasting, and self-denial; and by reading and meditating on God's holy Word" (BCP: 265). The Litany of Penitence, which forms a part of the Ash Wednesday rite (BCP: 267-9), sets the penitential focus for the season. At the same time, the second of the two lenten proper prefaces demonstrates that Lent is also a season of renewal that prepares us for Easter:

> You bid your faithful people cleanse their hearts, and prepare with joy for the Paschal feast; that, fervent in prayer and in works of mercy, and renewed by your Word and Sacraments, they may come to the fullness of grace which you have prepared for those who love you. (BCP: 379)

The Prayer Book lists "Ash Wednesday and the other weekdays of Lent and Holy Week" along with "Good Friday and all other Fridays of the year" as Days of Special Devotion (BCP: 17). *Lesser Feasts and Fasts* lists propers for daily celebrations of the eucharist on the lenten weekdays.

Ash Wednesday, along with Good Friday, is given a special status in the calendar. Both are called "Fasts" and listed with the Holy Days as well as with the Days of Special Devotion (BCP: 17). The Prayer Book also furnishes a Proper Liturgy for Ash Wednesday (BCP: 264-9). Its central elements are the recitation of Psalm 51, the best known of the penitential psalms, and a Litany of Penitence. The ceremony which gives its name to the day, the imposition of ashes, is provided for the first time in an American Prayer Book, although its use is optional. The meaning of the rite is expressed both in the prayer said by the celebrant before the imposition and by the words used during it: "Remember that you are dust, and to dust you shall return" (BCP: 265). The prayer of imposition reads:

> Almighty God, you have created us out of the dust of the earth: Grant that these ashes may be to us a sign of our mortality and penitence, that we may remember that it is only by your gracious gift that we are given everlasting life. . . . (BCP: 265)

The rite reminds us that we stand before God as sinners doomed to die, and that it is only through God's gift that we can hope for anything else. This prayer combines with the other penitential elements of the Proper to produce a heavily penitential liturgy for a day which has been aptly called a Christian Yom Kippur, a day on which we confess our sins to God and ask for God's mercy. This is an appropriate beginning for a season of penitence.

Penitence, however, is not the only lenten theme. As we have seen, the second lenten eucharistic preface speaks of Lent as a time to "prepare with joy for the Paschal feast" (BCP: 379). Joy, love and renewal are as much lenten themes as are penitence, fasting and self-denial; and we need to remember that it is within the context of preparation for our participation in the Feast of feasts that the lenten penitence is expressed. Our penitence is not the penitence of those who have no hope of forgiveness, but of those who have been redeemed by the dying and rising of Jesus the Lord.

The seasons of Lent, Holy Week, and Easter comprise the first cycle (Paschal cycle) of the Church Year (BCP: 15). The second cycle (Incarnational cycle) centers around the "Feast of our Lord's Nativity or Christmas Day." The Incarnational cycle developed later than the Paschal cycle and probably was also originally a baptismal cycle: Advent prepared for the celebration of baptisms on the Epiphany, which was celebrated as the Feast of the Baptism of our Lord. The Prayer Book places this latter feast on the First Sunday after Epiphany.

As we saw earlier in the quotation from Josef Pieper, Christmas is more than the birthday of Christ. It is our participation in the mystery of salvation seen under the aspect of Incarnation. Epiphany, and the Feast of the Baptism of our Lord which must be taken with it, celebrate the manifestation of Jesus as the Christ to the world. In fact, the Baptism of Christ is the primary epiphany. In the gospel lesson of that feast (*Lectionary Year A*: Matthew 3:13-17; *Year B*: Mark 1:7-11; *Year C*: Luke 3:15-16, 21-22), Jesus is manifested as the Son of God by the voice of the Father, and the Holy Spirit is seen in the form of a dove. The Eastern churches consider the Baptism of Christ to be the primary theological meaning of the "Theophany"—as they call this feast

—for in it God is made known in the person of Jesus
Christ.

Perhaps the meaning of the Incarnational cycle is
best expressed in the ancient collect which the Prayer
Book assigns to the Second Sunday after Christmas:

> O God, who wonderfully created, and yet more wonder-
> fully restored, the dignity of human nature: Grant that
> we may share the divine life of him who humbled him-
> self to share our humanity, your Son Jesus
> Christ. . . . (BCP: 214)

This collect, with its roots in patristic Christology,
speaks clearly of our participation in the divine life of
the Incarnate One. It is that participation which is the
essence of the Incarnational cycle.

The Paschal and Incarnational cycles interconnect
each year both during the season after Epiphany and
during the season following Pentecost. These Sundays,
sometimes called "Green Sundays," are not simply filler
or "ordinary time." They are an integral part of the
year. The season after Epiphany binds the Incarnational cycle to the Paschal cycle, using the celebration of
the Transfiguration in the propers of the Last Sunday
after Epiphany as a transition to the lenten season. The
season after Pentecost continues the Paschal cycle from
the commemoration of the first Pentecost, when the
Holy Spirit came upon the Apostles, to the celebration
of the final Advent or "Second Coming," when Christ
will come in glory. The propers of the last Sunday after
Pentecost sound the Advent themes, and on the Last
Sunday after Pentecost the Advent theme of the reign
of Christ is stressed. This theme links the years one to
another in a circle. The final post-Pentecost Sundays
lead to the celebration of the second coming (Parousia)
on the first Sunday of Advent, which in turn modulates
into a celebration of the first coming, and the cycle

returns to its beginning. It is, of course, in these Sundays after Pentecost that we actually live—that is, in the period between the first and final coming (Advent); but in the liturgy, all of time, past, present, and future, is laid before us to be celebrated in the mystery of the liturgical year. In the words of Massey Shepherd:

> The Christian Year . . . makes present to us here and now all that is final and ultimate. The liturgy is not a discipline that prepares us step by step for some future goal and reward. The liturgy is at any time and in any place that goal present and real *now*.[11]

The Festivals of Saints

In addition to the weekly celebration of the Lord's Day and the annual cycle of the liturgical year, the Prayer Book calendar also includes the festivals of saints. These are described as "Major Feasts" and "Other Commemorations." An additional liturgical book, *Lesser Feasts and Fasts*, makes fuller liturgical provision for these "Other Commemorations." Traditionally, Anglicans have called the Major Feasts for which the Prayer Book makes liturgical provision "Red Letter Days" and the lesser feasts "Black Letter Days." This nomenclature follows the tradition of the calendar makers, who printed holidays in red ink and other days in black. Printings of the Prayer Book in two colors have followed this custom.

The Prayer Book itself does not provide any rationale for the inclusion of the saints' festivals, but *Lesser Feasts and Fasts* includes this rubric:

> Since the triumphs of the saints are a continuation and manifestation of the Paschal victory of Christ, the celebration of saints' days is particularly appropriate during this season [i.e., Eastertide]. (LFF: 56)

This theological statement is both traditional and significant, for it identifies the celebration of the festivals
∨ of the saints with the Paschal Mystery of Christ. Both
the biblical account of the martyrdom of Stephen (Acts
6-7) and the early Christian *Martyrdom of Polycarp* are
concerned to show the parallel between the death of the
martyrs and the passion of Christ. However, this relationship has often been obscured in more recent presentations. A collect in the Burial of the Dead asks:

> . . . that encouraged by [the saints'] examples, aided
> by their prayers, and strengthened by their fellowship,
> we also may be partakers of the inheritance of the saints
> in light. . . . (BCP: 504)

This excellent collect, taken from the Scottish Episcopal Prayer Book, draws out fully the implications of the
communion of saints for our common life: fellowship,
example, and prayer; but it does not speak of the continuation or manifestation of the Paschal victory of Christ.
One collect which appears to do so, however, is that for
St. Philip and St. James, which contains the petition
"Grant that we, being mindful of their victory of faith,
may glorify in life and death the Name of our Lord Jesus
Christ. . ." (BCP: 240). Nevertheless, the principal
focus of most of the collects for the festivals of saints is
an exhortation to imitate the saints' good example.

The collect for All Saints' Day speaks of the saints as
"knit together . . . in one communion and fellowship
in the mystical body of your Son" and prays that we may
have grace to follow them (BCP: 245). The final collect
in the Common of a Saint speaks of God as having
"made us one with your saints in heaven and on earth"
and asks that "in our earthly pilgrimage we may always
be supported by this fellowship of love and prayer, and
know ourselves to be surrounded by their witness to
your power and mercy" (BCP: 250).

Although these collects do not speak the language of the rubric we quoted from *Lesser Feasts and Fasts* about the saints' continuing and manifesting the Paschal Mystery, they do speak of the union of the Church on earth with the saints in heaven in a fellowship of love, prayer and witness.

Nowhere does the Prayer Book ask the prayers of the saints, but both in the above prayer from the Burial of the Dead and in the above collect the Prayer Book makes explicit that we do believe that the saints pray for us because of our union with them in the mystical body of Christ. No earlier version of the American Prayer Book speaks so explicitly about the prayers of the saints, although the collect we quoted from the burial service appeared in the Scottish Prayer Book of 1929. Finally, another significant collect, one which also appeared in the 1928 American Prayer Book, invokes the image from Hebrews 12 of the "cloud of witnesses" cheering us on as we run our earthly race (BCP: 198).

Overall, the festivals of the saints in the *Book of Common Prayer* speak to us of our union with the saints in fellowship and prayer within the mystical body of Christ. The saints are fellow participants in our worship; they pray for us; and they encourage us by their example and witness. The great number and variety of these commemorations in the Prayer Book calendar makes it plain that the communion of saints is large indeed, and restricted neither by time nor place. As we shall see, however, the sheer number of these commemorations is a liturgical problem.

The calendar gives first place to the "feasts of our Lord Jesus Christ" (BCP: 16), both the weekly Lord's Day and the annual festivals such as Christmas. The Nativity of St. John the Baptist, the Presentation, the Annunciation and the Visitation (all of which are also festivals of St. Mary the Virgin) are also considered to be feasts of our Lord. The other Major Feasts are generally those of the Apostles and other biblical figures, such as Stephen, Joseph, or Mary Magdalene. The feasts of non-biblical saints are described as Commemorations (BCP 17f).

The problem with the large number of these feasts—even of the Major Feasts—is that, for most of us, they are not proper festivals. They are mere "memorial days," as Pieper uses the term. It is very difficult to celebrate many of them festively, and they are frequently perceived as only pedagogical and as occasions for giving an historical lecture as a homily. The collects, particularly those in *Lesser Feasts and Fasts*, often heighten the sense of the instructional by pointing out precisely in what way the example of the particular saint being commemorated can be useful to us. At their best, these commemorations help us to realize the depth and breadth of the communion of saints and to make some of its members real to us. Nevertheless, the distinction between those major festivals which we truly "celebrate" and those which we simply "commemorate" remains and retains its validity.

It is worth noting that the Prayer Book does not require every congregation to celebrate every lesser feast. It recognizes that some feasts will be of significance to a particular congregation, while others will not. There is no reason to celebrate festivals which will be meaningless, but celebrating those that have meaning to a particular congregation can help to enrich its liturgical and devotional life. As Massey Shepherd's writes, "Each single feast renews the fulness of the Feast of feasts, our death and resurrection with Christ."[12] Such remains the basic theological reason for including saints' days in our calendar.

Chapter Three:
The Daily Office

As we have seen in Chapter One, Daily Morning and Evening Prayer are "regular services appointed for public worship in this Church" (BCP: 13). The Prayer Book gives no particular rationale either for the provision of Daily Offices or for the particular services it sets forth. They are simply assumed to be a part of the fabric of daily Christian living. The Daily Office Lectionary (BCP: 933-1001) provides three readings for every Sunday and weekday over a two-year cycle, and it seems to expect that the Office will be read either once or twice every day (BCP: 934). On the other hand, it is not at all clear that the contemporary Church either sees a need for the Daily Office or is willing to make a place for it in its liturgical life.

The consecration of the first and last hours of the day with prayer can be traced back to the apostolic Christian community and to traditional Jewish practice.[1] For the devout Jew, the obligation to pray daily rested upon the divine commandment. Deuteronomy 6:4-7 reads:

> Hear, O Israel: the Lord your God is one Lord; and you shall love the Lord your God with all your heart, and with all your soul, and with all your might. And these words which I command you this day shall be upon your heart; and you shall teach them diligently to your children, and shall talk of them when you sit in your house, and when you walk by the way, and when you lie down, and when you rise.

This was understood to require that one recite the
Shema (the verse, "Hear, O Israel. . . ," to which the
commandment to love was attached) when one rises in
the morning and retires at night. There is also the
tradition recorded in Daniel 6:11 that prayer be offered
to God three times a day. The morning and evening
prayers were apparently set at the hours at which the
daily sacrifices were offered in the Temple in Jerusalem. Indeed, Daniel 6 affirms that the windows of
Daniel's bedroom faced Jerusalem and that he opened
his windows and knelt facing the Holy City to pray. It is
generally believed that by the first century A.D., the
synagogue service was a threefold daily prayer, the
Shema being a part of the morning and evening services.
The practice of the present-day synagogue where a core
group (not necessarily including the rabbi) gather for
daily prayer, while the majority of the congregation join
them only on the Sabbath and the festivals, can be seen
as typical of normative Christian practice as well. Robert Taft, S.J., describes the early Christian experience
this way:

> Christians by faith had the supreme joy of knowing that
> they lived a new life in Christ, a life of love shared with
> all of the same faith. What could have been more nor-
> mal, then, than for those who were able to gather at
> daybreak and to turn the first thoughts of the day to this
> mystery of their salvation and to praise and glorify God
> for it? And at the close of the day they came together
> again to ask forgiveness for the failings of the day and to
> praise God once more for His mighty deeds. In this way
> the natural rhythm of time was turned into a hymn of
> praise to God and a proclamation before the world of
> faith in His salvation in Christ.[2]

The lesser Hours, represented in the *Book of Common
Prayer* by "An Order of Service for Noonday" (BCP:
103-7) and "An Order for Compline" (BCP: 127-35),
also have their roots in the Acts of the Apostles and in

Jewish practice. They were clearly occasions of private
and family prayer, and their development into corporate Offices is a distinct outgrowth of the rise of monas-
ticism. They are the family prayers of a Christian
household, prayers formalized and expanded by a
household devoted primarily to the work of prayer (i.e.,
by a monastery).

The Prayer Book, in addition to Daily Morning and
Evening Prayer in both Rite One and Rite Two versions, Noonday Prayer, and Compline, includes forms
intended as "Daily Devotions for Individuals and Families" (BCP: 136-40) to maintain the traditional link
between individual and corporate prayer. "These devotions follow the basic structure of the Daily Office of the
Church" (BCP: 136) and are intended to form a devotional framework for the lives of ordinary Christians,
relating them to the ongoing "prayer of the Church" in
the Daily Offices. Those who pray privately in this manner may consider themselves to be a part of a vast choir
of Christians throughout the world who join in the same
prayer at the focal points of the day. This thought has
powerfully refreshed many who felt themselves alone
and isolated from the support and communion of their
fellow Christians.

Cathedral and Monastic Office

The Prayer Book Offices of Morning and Evening
Prayer are heavily influenced by the traditions of the
monasteries in which the Offices developed and thrived
for centuries. By the time of the Reformation the differences between parochial, or "cathedral," and monastic offices were no longer understood, or even known.[3]
The "cathedral office," as the phrase is used here, does
not mean choral Evensong as it is celebrated in Anglican
cathedrals. Rather, it means the corporate Offices of

Lauds or Morning Praise (traditionally known as Mattins in England) and Vespers or Evensong as they were celebrated by the ecclesial community, usually in a cathedral or large parish church, rather than in a monastery. Like the eucharist, these Offices were "regular services appointed for public worship" (BCP: 13) in the Church, which monastics attended along with ordinary Christians. These services, as they came to be celebrated in the great churches of the ancient Christian world, have been described as "reasonably brief, colorful, ceremonious, odiferous, and full of movement . . . very churchy, somewhat vulgar, clergy-dominated, and impossibly simple to participate in."[4] By contrast, the classic monastic office was ascetic, nonceremonious, meditative, and did not involve the clergy.

All of the forms of the Office with which Cranmer was familiar were the result of the interaction of these two forms, so that monastic principles had heavily influenced parochial liturgy, and "cathedral" elements had taken their place in the monastic office. The Preface to the *First Book of Common Prayer* (BCP: 866) attributes solid monastic principles to "the ancient fathers" as "the first original and ground" of the "common prayers in the Church, commonly called Divine Service." The principles in question are the course recitation of the greater part of the Bible (i.e., its reading from beginning to end) and the integral recitation of the Psalter in numerical order. Cranmer took these to be primitive principles and made them central to his revision of the Office, although it is now clear that these are monastic principles which entered the "cathedral" office only in the Middle Ages when monastic prayer was seen as ideal for all Christians and was copied by clergy and laity alike. Parochial, or cathedral, Offices contained only certain psalms, chosen for their appropriateness to the time of day or the festival or season being celebrated, and either no biblical readings at all or short readings likewise chosen for the occasion, much like the readings at the eucharist. The "cathedral" Office was almost pure praise. It was not primarily concerned with edification or instruction, although these were major concerns for Thomas Cranmer and other 16th-century Reformers.

The 1549 Prayer Book, following what Cranmer believed to be primitive principles, provided for the course reading of the Bible according to the calendar year and the monthly reading of all 150 psalms in numerical order, with interruptions for only the greatest feasts. All subsequent revisions have moved away from Cranmer's rigid structure and provided proper psalms and lessons, at least for Sundays and Holy Days when the largest congregations are anticipated. The present Prayer Book, specifically, does not require the use of the entire Psalter but has chosen a cycle of psalms, normally over a seven-week period, with proper attention paid to the time of day and the day of the week when they will be used, and with proper psalms for Sundays and Holy Days. Proper lessons are provided for Sundays and Holy Days (BCP: 934-5). Even more significantly, the eucharistic Lectionary is used when the Office is the principal morning service, and one of the other years of the three-year Sunday cycle may be used for the Office "when the same congregation is present for Morning or Evening Prayer, in addition to the Eucharist" (BCP: 888). This is a major move in the direction of the "cathredral office" structure.

Nevertheless, the Offices of the *Book of Common Prayer*, like almost all other contemporary Offices, remain heavily monasticized. There is, however, provision for celebrating the Evening Office in a "cathedral" or non-monastic manner through the use of "An Order of Worship for the Evening." This Office begins with the *lucernarium* or lamp-lighting, includes selected psalms and readings, incense, ceremony and corporate litanies, and concludes with a blessing by the priest-officiant (BCP: 108-14).

Rite One and Rite Two

For Morning and Evening Prayer (although not for Noonday Prayer and Compline, which were not in earlier versions of the Prayer Book), the Prayer Book includes both the traditional language forms of Rite One, i.e., addressing God as "Thou," and the contemporary language forms of Rite Two, i.e., addressing God as "You." There is no theologically significant difference in content between the two versions of the Offices. As mentioned in Chapter One, the principal theological importance for including both versions is to establish the continuity of this rite with that of the earlier Prayer Books. The argument over whether God is more appropriately addressed as "Thou" or "You" is really one of taste and concerns the connotations of both pronouns to the person making the argument.⑤ Presumably God understands both 16th- and 20th-century English, as well as all other languages. The choice of language for the service depends not on God's ear, but on the makeup of the congregation. The collect commemorating *The First Book of Common Prayer* in *Lesser Feasts and Fasts* includes these words:

> Almighty and everliving God, whose servant Thomas Cranmer, with others, restored the language of the people in the prayers of your Church: Make us always thankful for this heritage; and help us to pray in the Spirit and with the understanding, that we may worthily magnify your holy Name. . . . (LFF: 231)

The preface to the 1549 Prayer Book speaks of all being "in such a language and order as is most easy and plain for the understanding, both of the readers and the

hearers." It also provides that "where men say Mattins
and Evensong privately, they may say the same in any
language that they themselves do understand" (BCP:
867). The current Prayer Book attempts to continue
Cranmer's tradition by providing worship "in the language of the people" in continuity with the *First Book of
Common Prayer.* For this reason, services have been provided in contemporary English; the entire book has
been translated into French and Spanish, and portions
of it into Korean and other languages so that all may
pray not only in the Spirit, but also with understanding.

Morning Prayer

One positive inheritance from the monastic tradition is
the recognition that lay persons may lead the Office. It
is appropriate worship for any group of Christians, clerical or lay, and as in family prayers, any member may be
asked to lead. Other persons are assigned to read the
lessons and to take other parts of the service, which
makes it clear that this is corporate worship by a body of
Christians, not simply the private prayers of the Officiant in which others are permitted to join. "The bishop,
when present, appropriately concludes the Office with a
blessing" (BCP: 74) as the "Father in God" of the
family.

The proper beginning of the Office is the prayer of
the Officiant, "Lord, open our lips," with its response,
"And our mouth shall proclaim your praise" (BCP: 80).
This verse from Psalm 51, the greatest of the penitential psalms, is an appropriate beginning for the day's
prayers. In the monastic tradition it marked the end of
the Great Silence which had lasted from the end of
Compline the previous night. It is no less appropriate in
a modern context, for it recognizes that only God can
enable us to pray. Beginning with a verse from the
Miserere, the traditional structure of Morning Prayer

starts with penitence and rises to unbounded praise. Since 1552 this opening dialogue has been preceded by a Confession of Sin and a priestly Absolution which serves to sound an even stronger penitential note at the beginning of the day's prayer. Since 1928 the Confession and Absolution have been optional at Morning Prayer, and in the 1979 Prayer Book they may always be omitted. Given the present provision, therefore, we shall discuss the theology of a General Confession later in the context of the eucharist.

The optional Opening Sentences (BCP: 75-8), although originally intended to form a penitential introduction to the Confession, are now intended to set a tone or theme for the entire service. They are highly seasonal in content and have become a "call to worship" inviting the congregation to join in the celebration.

The *Gloria Patri* and the festal shout "Alleluia" follow the opening dialogue. This traditional ascription of praise to the Triune God, originally set in this form to assert the equality of the divine Persons against Arians and other heretics, sounds a distinctly Christian note of praise at the beginning of a section of passages from the Hebrew Bible. Its use here and at the end of the psalms is a way of appropriating the Hebrew Scriptures to Christian liturgical use and asserting that the Old Testament is also Christian Scripture.

The Prayer Book gives two alternative Invitatory Psalms: Psalm 95, commonly called the *Venite* from its opening word (or *incipit*, in Latin) and Psalm 100, also called the *Jubilate*. Either is preceded and followed by antiphons which point the meaning of the psalm to the specific occasion. All such antiphons include the phrase "Come let us adore him" (BCP: 80-2), which underscores that coming to the Lord in worship and adoration is the meaning of Morning Prayer.

The *Venite* (BCP: 82), after praising God for his rule over creation, comes both structurally and theologically to this climax:

> Come, let us bow down, and bend the knee, and
>   kneel before the Lord our Maker.
> For he is our God,
> and we are the people of his pasture and the sheep of
>   his hand.
>   Oh, that today you would harken to his voice!

The notes of penitence, praise and eschatological urgency are clearly sounded. Unfortunately, the last line of this section was deleted from the *Venite* in the First American Prayer Book and Psalm 96:9, 13 was substituted. This practice has continued into Rite One of the present Prayer Book. Although the thoughts are similar, the expression is not as strong:

> O worship the Lord in the beauty of holiness;
>   let the whole earth stand in awe of him.
> For he cometh, for he cometh to judge the earth,
>   and with righteousness to judge the world
>   and the peoples with his truth. (BCP: 45)

Jubilate lacks the *Venite*'s note of judgment, and has coming to the Lord as its central theme:

> Enter his gates with thanksgiving;
> go into his courts with praise;
>   give thanks to him and call upon his Name.
>   (BCP: 83)

All of these are proper theological themes to introduce the day's worship, and both psalms have been traditionally used at the beginning of morning Offices. A third alternative is restricted to the Easter Season. *Pascha nostrum* was compiled by Cranmer for the 1549 Prayer Book to be used before Morning Prayer for a procession. It is a *cento* of New Testament verses about

the resurrection. It is filled with theologically significant material expressing the Church's central belief in
the resurrection of Christ. Its meaning is well summarized in its opening and concluding verses:

> Alleluia.
> Christ our Passover has been sacrificed for us;
>   therefore let us keep the feast . . .
> For as in Adam all die,
>   so also in Christ shall all be made alive. Alleluia.
>   (BCP: 83)

The reading, or more properly the singing of the
psalms, follows the Invitatory. The psalms are, of
course, hymns, and singing is the most natural way to
render them, but they are also superb poetry which can
stand without the music. To discuss their theological
content, whether their meaning to their Jewish authors
or the traditional meaning Christian liturgy has given to
them, would be a major study in its own right and well
beyond the scope of this work. We must note, however,
that the Lectionary has considered the content of the
psalms in assigning them to specific days and seasons.
Frequent use is made on Sundays of the Laudate psalms
(Psalms 148-50) and other psalms of praise. It was the
use of these psalms at Morning Prayer which gave the
Latin name Lauds to the Office.

From monastic usage comes the Anglican tradition of
reading the Scriptures at the Office, and lessons from
both the Old and New Testament are assigned by the
Lectionary. This extensive use of Scripture readings
makes Morning Prayer a possible alternative to the
eucharistic Ministry of the Word, and this is permitted
by the rubrics (BCP: 74). A sermon may be preached
after the readings (BCP: 142), so that the Word which
has been read may be broken open and expounded to
the congregation. This option reinforces the Office as
a Liturgy of the Word. A sermon is not an integral part
of the Office as it is of the eucharist, however, and no

previous Prayer Book has even made provision for one, although they were frequently preached.

The Canticles

Each reading is normally followed by the singing of a canticle, a psalmlike hymn usually taken from the Bible. The Prayer Book (BCP: 144-5) contains a table recommending different canticles for the days of the week. The table, like the provision of psalms and lessons for every day in the Lectionary, points up the expectation that the Office will be celebrated daily, although this is frequently not the case. When the Office is celebrated only occasionally, appropriate canticles which the congregation is able to sing are usually selected. The selection, however, is not supposed to be arbitrary.

Most of the canticles are hymns of praise and are intended to complete the movement of Morning Prayer from penitence to praise. Two of the canticles, 10, The Second Song of Isaiah *Quaerite Dominum*, and 14, A Song of Penitence *Kyrie Pantokrator*, are overtly penitential. The first is assigned to Friday, the weekly memorial of the crucifixion, and the second to Lent. They are intended to be used after the First Lesson, so that a hymn of praise may follow the final reading. *Kyrie Pantokrator* (BCP: 90-1), from the Apocryphal Prayer of Menassah, has always been considered a classic penitential prayer. It calls upon the merciful and compassionate God; acknowledges personal guilt: "I have sinned, and I know my wickedness only too well"; asks for forgiveness; and concludes with a song of praise:

> Unworthy as I am, you will save me,
> in accordance with your great mercy,
>> and I will praise you without ceasing all the days of
>> my life.
> For all the powers of heaven sing your praises,
>> and yours is the glory to ages of ages. Amen.

Quaerite Dominum (BCP: 86-7) is penitential, calls
upon the wicked to forsake their ways and the evil ones
their thoughts, and promises them God's pardon. Both
canticles proclaim the forgiveness of God to those who
repent, and both bring the theme back to the praise of
the God who forgives sinners.

Canticle 12, A Song of Creation (*Benedicite, omnia
opera Domini*), is sometimes considered a penitential canticle because earlier Prayer Books gave it as a lenten
substitute for the *Te Deum,* but there is nothing penitential about it. It is a hymn of praise to the Creator on
behalf of all creation, which calls upon men and women
to join in the hymn of the universe. The introduction to
The Taizé Office explains, "The prayer of the Daily
Office is a part of the praise of the whole creation
offered to its creator. . . . Man's first and ultimate
vocation is to give an intelligible form to this universal
praise."[6] The Benedicite gives clear voice to that theology. It therefore expresses the meaning of the Office
itself and the meaning of Christian life. It is suggested
for Saturday morning, the weekly memorial of the creation. Canticle 13, A Song of Praise (*Benedictus es,
Domine*), taken, like the *Benedicite,* from the Song of the
Three Young Men (an Apocryphal addition to Daniel
3), is a shorter hymn of cosmic praise (see BCP: 90).
However, it omits all mention of human participation in
the celestial chorus, and thus it is theologically less significant than the *Benedicite.*

Canticle 16, The Song of Zechariah (*Benedictus Domi-
nus Deus*), usually called just the *Benedictus,* and Canticle
21, You Are God (*Te Deum laudamus*), are the traditional Morning Prayer canticles. The *Benedictus* leads
up to the lines which have formed the climax of the
morning praise of Christians for centuries:

> In the tender compassion of our God
>   the dawn from on high shall break upon us,

To shine on those who dwell in darkness and the
    shadow of death,
  and to guide our feet into the way of peace.
    (BCP: 93)

The *Te Deum*, one of the few non-biblical canticles and
itself a great hymn of praise, concludes with the prayer:

Come then, Lord, and help your people,
bought with the price of your own blood,
and bring us with your saints
to glory everlasting. (BCP: 96)

Canticle 20, Glory to God (*Gloria in Excelsis*), commonly called the Gloria, is the other non-biblical canticle (BCP: 94-5). It is usually thought of as the festal
canticle at the eucharist, although the American Prayer
Book has always permitted its use in the Offices, and it is
traditional at Morning Prayer in the Eastern liturgies.
It is almost pure praise. God is adored as King and
Father. Jesus is addressed as "Lord" and "Christ" and
"only Son of the Father" (*monogenes*), the Lamb of God
who takes away sin. Jesus is asked to "receive our
prayer," and praise is offered to the Trinity.
    Canticle 8, The Song of Moses (*Cantemus Domino*), is
associated in the Book of Exodus with the crossing of
the Red Sea. It is a part of the celebration of the Christian Passover. Most of its content relates to the historical circumstances of the Exodus, but its great message is

The Lord is my strength and my refuge;
  the Lord has become my Savior.
This is my God and I will praise him,
  the God of my people and I will exalt him.
    (BCP: 85)

Canticles 9, The First Song of Isaiah (*Ecce, Deus*), and
11, The Third Song of Isaiah (*Surge, illuminare*), are the
two remaining Old Testament canticles (BCP: 86-8).
Either is intended to be used after the First Lesson when

more than one lesson is read. *Ecce, Deus* is a call to make known the saving deeds of the Lord, "for the great one in the midst of you is the Holy One of Israel," while *Surge, illuminare*, taken from Isaiah 60—the first reading at the eucharist for Epiphany—provides another thoroughly festal song praising the Lord as "everlasting light" and "glory."

Canticles 15, The Song of Mary (*Magnificat*), and 17, The Song of Simeon (*Nunc dimittis*), are traditional Evening Prayer canticles (BCP: 91-3), although their use at Morning Prayer is permitted. Like the *Benedictus*, they are from the Gospel according to St. Luke. The daily use of the *Magnificat* at Evening Prayer has often been cited by Anglican writers as evidence for Anglican devotion to the Blessed Virgin Mary. The hymn itself cannot be separated from its context in the gospel narrative, and the verse "From this day all generations will call me blessed" refers to the "great things" the Almighty has done for Mary in the Annunciation story. The remainder of the canticle gives praise to God for raising up the lowly and casting down the proud in fulfillment of God's promises to God's people. The *Nunc dimittis* seems admirably suited for Evening Prayer or Compline, and it is difficult to imagine using it in the morning. It has especially been associated by Anglicans with Evensong and seen as a prayer to be recited before retiring for the night. The prayer's message is Simeon's, a message of freedom and rest because "these eyes of mine have seen the Savior, . . . A Light to enlighten the nations, and the glory of your people Israel."

Canticles 18, A Song to the Lamb (*Dignus es*), and 19, The Song of the Redeemed (*Magna et mirabilia*), are hymns from the Book of Revelation used as canticles at the Offices (BCP: 93-4). They are among the earliest Christian hymns. *Dignus es* praises the "Lamb that was slain" for redeeming us and calling us "from every family, language, people, and nation" to be "a kingdom of priests to serve our God." This same language is found in 1 Peter 2:9-10 to describe the Christian community, and speaks of our vocation to serve and to worship God. *Magna et mirabilia* is probably best known in the metrical version "How wondrous and great Thy works, God of praise!" It is again an appropriate hymn of praise with which to conclude the readings at the Office.[7]

Common Prayer

With the singing of the canticle after the final reading and the recitation of the Apostles' Creed, Morning Prayer moves from praise to "common prayer." The Apostles' Creed is actually the old Roman baptismal creed. Its use in the Office is a renewal of the baptismal covenant by the Christians assembled to pray together. It reminds us of our common baptism as the ground of our common prayer.

The Lord's Prayer stands first among the common prayers of the Daily Offices. Its corporate recitation is based upon a traditional Christian understanding of our Lord's command in Matthew 6 and Luke 11 that the Lord's Prayer should take first place in their prayers. All other prayer flows from it.

The suffrages follow the Lord's Prayer and precede the collects. The Prayer Book gives alternative sets. The suffrages are a means of involving the people in the common prayers. Set A prays for the ministry, peace, justice, the nation, the world, the poor and needy, and spiritual renewal. This set is also in Evening Prayer. Set B is specific to the morning. It asks for God's blessing and preservation from sin throughout the day, and it speaks of the daily praise of God's name. Both are traditional and appropriate themes for our morning prayers, whether individual or corporate.

The dialogue of the suffrages introduces the collects. The Collect of the Day may be included, but seven

Morning Prayer collects are also given. Three are specifically designated for Sundays, Fridays, and Saturdays
respectively, and it is difficult to avoid the inference that
the other four are for Mondays, Tuesdays, Wednesdays,
and Thursdays. The collects assigned to specific days,
as we have mentioned in Chapter Two, link those days
to the events of which they are the weekly memorials:
Friday to the crucifixion, Saturday to God's sabbath rest
after creation and preparation for Sunday worship, and
Sunday to the resurrection. The remaining collects are
proper to the morning hour; they ask God to preserve
and help us during the day. The prayer for mission is
intended to assure that the universal and evangelistic
concerns of the Church are not neglected in common
prayer.

The Prayer Book states that "authorized intercessions and thanksgivings may follow" (BCP: 101). It is
here that the various concerns of the particular congregation offering common prayer may be expressed.
Although this appears to be simply an optional addition
to the service, it is omitted by the Officiant at peril.
Praying for our own needs, for those of others, and
giving thanks are central to the Daily Office as *common*
prayer.

A hymn or anthem may be sung after the prayer for
mission and prior to the intercessions (BCP: 101). This
is not simply a musical interlude but an opportunity to
include choral prayer by the choir in the common
prayer.

Two traditional fixed prayers may be included before
the close of the Office (BCP: 101): the General
Thanksgiving, and A Prayer of St. Chrysostom. Both
have a firm place in the affections of those who pray the
Office regularly. The General Thanksgiving, a 17th-
century composition, is just what its name suggests. It
gives thanks "above all for your immeasurable love in
the redemption of the world by our Lord Jesus Christ;

for the means of grace, and for the hope of glory" (BCP: 101). There is little doubt that this love is the chief cause for Christian thanksgiving. Equally significant is its conclusion that thankfulness should be manifested "not only with our lips, but in our lives" by dedicating them to God's service. The Prayer of St. Chrysostom, which was taken by Cranmer from a Latin translation of the Liturgy of St. John Chrysostom and is not actually by the 4th-century bishop, expresses well the theology of common prayer. God has promised that "when two or three are gathered together in [Christ's] name, [he] will be in the midst of them." The presence of the Lord in the *synaxis*, the coming together of the people no matter how small the assembly, is the specific promise attached to common prayer. The Prayer of St. Chrysostom asks that our petitions may be fulfilled "as may be best for us; granting us in this world knowledge of [God's] truth, and in the age to come life everlasting." There is no assurance that we will receive what we ask, unless *it is best for us*, but knowledge and eternal life are explicitly requested as appropriate gifts.

The Office may conclude with a dismissal and an ascription of praise from the Scripture. Although both are optional, they form an appropriate conclusion. Begun in penitence, moving to praise, and concluding with common prayers and thanksgiving, Morning Prayer is largely from the Psalter and other parts of the Bible.

Evening Prayer

The structure of Morning and Evening Prayer are identical, but their content is different. Most of what we have said about Morning Prayer will apply also to Evening Prayer. The movement of Morning Prayer is rising, from "Lord, open our lips," to praise, petition, and intercession for the coming day. The movement of Evening Prayer, however, is descending, with its dominant themes of thanksgiving for the day and prayer for forgiveness for our sins and failures.

The opening greeting of Evening Prayer, "O God, make speed to save us," and the response, "O Lord, make haste to help us," (BCP: 117) acknowledge that it is only by God's saving help that we are able to do anything, including to pray. The Invitatory in the evening is "O Gracious Light," or *Phos hilaron* (BCP: 118), a hymn already considered to be ancient and traditional by St. Basil the Great in the 4th-century. There are several well-known metrical versions. The hymn is traditionally associated with the lighting of the evening lamps, a practical necessity before the invention of electric lights if an evening service was to be held. The "vesper light" is symbolically identified with Jesus Christ, "pure brightness of the everliving Father in heaven," to whom praise is given by the happy voices of the worshipers. Evening Prayer thus begins with a song of praise which leads to the singing of the evening psalms. Although the Prayer Book anticipates the use of a single lesson at Evening Prayer, followed by the singing of either the *Magnificat* or *Nunc dimittis*, it permits the use of two or even three readings, followed by any of the canticles (BCP: 934, 118-9). Both the *Magnificat* and the *Nunc dimittis* speak of a sense of completion and fulfillment which culminates the movement from the praise of the *Phos hilaron* to thanksgiving for God's activity in all of creation and in our lives during the past day.

Suffrages A (BCP: 121-2) are identical to those at Morning Prayer, but Suffrages B are based on a Byzantine evening litany and sound the major Evening Prayer themes:

That this evening may be holy, good and peaceful . . .

> That your holy angels may lead us in paths of peace and
>   goodwill . . .
> That we may be pardoned and forgiven for our sins and
>   offenses . . .
> That there may be peace to your Church and to the
>   whole world . . .
> That we may depart this life in your faith and fear, and
>   not be condemned before the great judgment seat of
>   Christ . . .
> That we may be bound together by your Holy Spirit in
>   the communion of [_____ and] all your saints,
>   entrusting one another and all our life to Christ,
> *We entreat you, O Lord.* (BCP: 122)

Pardon, peace, protection during the coming night,
eternal salvation, and unity with Christ in the communion of saints are not only the traditional Evening
Prayer themes; it would be difficult to think of others
more appropriate for the evening Office. We find these
same themes in the evening collects, of which there are
seven (BCP: 123-124), as there are at Morning Prayer.
The Collect for Sundays speaks of the triumph of
Christ "over the powers of death" and asks that we
"who have this day given thanks for his resurrection,
may praise you in that City of which he is the
light. . . ." It thus combines three themes. Christ as
the true Light; the recognition of Sunday as the memorial of the resurrection; and a prayer for our membership in the heavenly Jerusalem, the communion of
saints. The collect for Fridays prays that we may follow
Christ into the grave, where he has led the way, and
petitions that we may "fall asleep peacefully" in Christ
"and wake up in [his] likeness." It thus combines the
crucifixion theme with the themes of sleep, rest and
eternal life. The Saturday collect asks that God, "the
source of eternal light," give us unending day "that our
lips may praise you, our lives may bless you, and our
worship on the morrow give you glory." There is no

mention of sabbath. The theme is of light and preparation for Sunday worship. The other collects all express variants on the themes we have seen in the suffrages, except the last, "A Collect for the Presence of Christ." This is based upon the Emmaus story (Luke 24:13-35) and asks for the presence of Christ when "evening is at hand" to kindle our hearts, awaken our hope, and make himself known "in Scripture and the breaking of bread."

Hinges of Daily Prayer

The two Offices of Morning and Evening Prayer as "regular services appointed for public worship in this Church" (BCP: 13) have a different status from Noonday Prayer and Compline, not only historically, but in the formularies and practice of the contemporary Church. This same understanding was expressed by Vatican Council II in paragraph 89 of the *Constitution on the Sacred Liturgy*:

> By the venerable tradition of the universal Church, Lauds as morning prayer, and Vespers as evening prayer are the two hinges on which the daily office turns. They must be considered as the chief hours and are to be celebrated as such.[8]

Robert Taft, S.J., concludes an article on the theology of Vespers entitled "Thanksgiving for the Light" with a statement which summarizes well what we have found in our examination of these Offices:

> The Offices at the beginning and end of the day are just ritual moments symbolic of the whole of time. As such they are a proclamation of faith to the world and partake of our mission of witness to Christ and His salvation. They are also a praise and thanksgiving for this gift of salvation in Christ. Lastly they are our priestly prayer as God's priestly people for our needs and those

of the entire world. That is what Liturgy means. That is what Vespers means.

As a matter of fact, that is what life means.[9]

The Taizé community explains the theology of the Office this way:

> Christ, the Son of God, by his coming into the world, and by his sacrifice and his resurrection, restored to man free access to God. . . . On the day of his ascension, he became our High Priest, presenting the praise and intercession of the Church with the memorial of his sacrifice. In the communion of saints, all Christians pray with Christ and in him. The liturgy of the Church, the Daily Office, is part of the heavenly liturgy, of the office of Christ and the angels, presenting before the throne of the Father the prayers of the saints, together with their own praise and intercession.[10]

An Order for Evening

This theology of the Office is also clearly expressed in An Order of Worship for the Evening (BCP: 108-114), a flexible order for a non-monastic or "cathedral" celebration of Evensong. The congregation assembles for Evensong in the unlighted church. A lighted candle or lamp is borne into the midst of the assembly, and they are greeted with "Light and peace in Jesus Christ our Lord." The theme of Jesus Christ as the light of the world (John 1:4-5, 8-9) is not only expressed in the words of the greeting; it is ritualized by the bringing of a light into the dark building. The theme is then further expounded in an optional short Scripture reading in praise of the Light and in the Prayer for Light said by the Officiant. There are several alternative prayers, including proper prayers for seasons and festivals. The first, which is representative, thanks God for surrounding us with the brightness of the vesper light as daylight

fades, and asks that "as you enfold us with the radiance
of this light, so you would shine into our hearts the
brightness of your Holy Spirit" (BCP: 110). The altar
candles are then lighted and the church is bathed in
light. The vivid ritual symbolism not only presses home
the theological point but also make the service "popular," less instructional and more worshipful. The lamp
lighting, or *lucernarium,* is the distinctive ceremonial
action of "Cathedral" Evensong and is found in almost
all classic vesper rites except the Roman and its related
uses, such as Sarum. The Reformers were unfamiliar
with it, and it has not been a part of most living Western
liturgies, except the Ambrosian Rite, until the present
liturgical renewal.

The Prayer Book permits the singing of an appropriate anthem or psalm during the candle-lighting (BCP:
112), and *The Book of Occasional Services* suggests several
such anthems, also called *Lucernaria* (BOS: 8-14). The
climax of the *lucernarium* is the singing of the *Phos
hilaron,* or some other appropriate evening hymn which
has the theme of light central to it. Good examples of
alternative hymns are the Advent hymns "Creator of
the Stars of Night" and "O Christ, you are both light
and day."[11] During the singing of the hymn, incense
may be used (BCP: 143). The use of incense in this
context not only adds dignity to the lamp-lighting to
emphasize its theological symbolism of Christ as Light
but is particularly associated with Psalm 141:2: "Let my
prayer be set forth in your sight as incense, the lifting up
of my hands as the evening sacrifice." Psalm 141 is a
traditional evening psalm and could be sung during the
actual lighting of the candles. This verse is the first of
the Opening Sentences for Evening Prayer (BCP: 115)
and is more familiar to most congregations than the rest
of the psalm. It identifies incense particularly with evening prayer and makes the offering of incense during

the *lucernarium* a symbol of the rising of our prayers to
the heavenly Father through Jesus Christ.

This lamp-lighting, or candle-lighting ceremony,
symbolizing the theological core of Evening Prayer,
may precede any evening assembly of the faithful,
including Evening Prayer and the eucharist, or it may
be used as a complete "cathedral" Evensong, continuing with a selection from the Psalter (BCP: 113). Traditional evening psalms are recommended (BCP: 143),
and the psalmody may be followed by silence and a
suitable collect. The Psalter collect is intended to give
the assembly a Christian focus for their praying of the
Psalter. No prayers called Psalter collects are in the
Prayer Book, although the Minister's Edition of the
Lutheran Book of Worship contains both the Prayer Book
version of the Psalter and Psalter collects for all 150
psalms. This is the Psalter collect for Psalm 141:

> Lord, from the rising of the sun to its setting your name
> is worthy of all praise. Let our prayers rise as incense
> before you, and may the lifting up of our hands be an
> evening sacrifice, acceptable to you, through your Son
> Jesus Christ our Lord.[12]

The Prayer Book itself has appropriate collects for
the above purpose. The collect for the Fourth Sunday
of Easter, for example, might be used with Psalm 23.
Collects are also used in this way following the respon-
sorial psalms after the readings at the Great Vigil of
Easter (BCP: 288-91).

The Office continues with a Bible reading, which
may be followed by silence, a sermon or homily, or a
reading from Christian literature. The latter might be a
part of a classic sermon on the Scripture passage read.
The *Magnificat,* or another canticle or hymn of praise,
follows the reading.

The common prayers always include the Lord's
Prayer, and the Prayer Book also recommends the use

of a litany form, such as Suffrages B from Evening Prayer, one of the eucharistic intercessions, the Great Litany, or some other suitable form, in order to include the entire congregation actively in the common prayer. Although proper or seasonal collects, or prayers from Evening Prayer or Compline, may also be used, two prayers are given for use at the conclusion of the common prayers. Both prayers summarize well the theology of the Office. The first praises God as "creator of the changes of day and night" who gives rest and renewal and "occasions of song in the evening." It asks God to extend the protection we have received during the past day throughout the coming night, to preserve us from sin, evil and fear: "for you [God] are our light and salvation, and the strength of our life" (BCP: 113). The second prayer, beginning with a reference to Psalm 141:2, the thematic verse for the evening Office, asks for grace to recognize the presence of God not only in Word and Sacrament but "in the lives of those around us." It concludes:

> Stir up in us the flame of that love which burned in the heart of your Son as he bore his passion, and let it burn in us to eternal life and to the ages of ages. (BCP: 113)

The prayer identifies light with the "flame of love" with which Christ loves us, and we ask that we may burn with that same love forever.

The Office concludes with a blessing or dismissal and the exchange of the Peace. Since the Office is a true liturgical assembly of the Church, it is appropriate that the pastor conclude it with a blessing. The Prayer Book supplies the Aaronic blessing, presumably suggesting its use (BCP: 114). The clerical presidency of the "cathedral" Office is one of its distinguishing characteristics, and the Order for Evening is intended as a choral celebration of the Church, not as private prayer. Thus, if there is no bishop or priest present to give the blessing, the lay Officiant dismisses the congregation. The Peace concludes the Office. As it does at the eucharist, the Peace follows the prayers of the people, giving visible expression to the unity in Christ for which they have prayed.

The Order for Evening is a good contemporary example of a parochial or "cathedral" Office. It is particularly useful for the congregation which does not gather regularly for Evening Prayer but wishes to sing Evensong with some dignity and ceremony on a particular occasion. The psalm and lesson are not part of a course reading but are chosen particularly for the occasion; the prayers should be directed toward the particular occasion and congregation. It is difficult to verbalize the theological significance of music, and we often assume it has none. But music is an integral part of this Office, and the Office is seriously impoverished if music is not used. If you imagine the effect of reciting rather than singing "Happy Birthday to You" at the cutting of a birthday cake or "The Star-Spangled Banner" at the beginning of a football game, you will easily see the integral place music has in celebrations. Even if we are unable to explain how, music's omission radically changes what is communicated.

Noonday Prayer and Compline

Noonday Prayer (BCP: 103-107) and Compline (BCP: 127-135) are not "regular services appointed for public worship" but lesser Hours which have their origin in the widely documented early Christian custom of praying at the third, sixth and ninth hours, and at bedtime. Originally they were services of private or family prayer. Prayer at the third, sixth and ninth hours, the breakpoints of the normal Roman work day, became formalized in the monasteries as the Hours of Terce, Sext and None. Modern schedules do not generally

favor such frequent pauses for prayer, and even religious orders today tend not to celebrate more than one
mid-day Hour. If it is desired to celebrate them all, the
first lesson and collect are traditional themes of Terce,
the second of Sext, and the third of None.

"An Order of Service for Noonday," however, is
intended to be more than a format for the prayers of
religious communities. It is a noon Office available for
those occasions when a pause for corporate prayer is
deemed appropriate, such as at conferences, on quiet
days, at diocesan conventions, or at the end of morning
meetings. It also provides a model for personal prayer
at noon.

The Office (BCP: 103-7) begins with the greeting also
used at Evening Prayer and the accompanying Gloria
and Alleluia. A "suitable hymn" precedes the psalmody, although no specific hymn is mentioned. A
number of suitable Office hymns may be found in *The
Hymnal 1982.* Selections from Psalm 119, the acrostic
psalm in praise of the Torah, or from the Gradual
Psalms (Songs of Ascent), Psalms 120-133, are recommended. These are the traditional psalms for the
Lesser Hours. A short lesson from Scripture follows.
The Prayer Book provides three choices, but any suitable passage may be used, and a core quotation from the
eucharistic readings for the day or season might well be
appropriate.

The common prayers include the Lord's Prayer and
free intercessions. The Lord's Prayer is the model
Christian prayer, and its use at each of the Hours places
those Hours in the context of the command "When you
pray, say 'Our Father. . .'" (Matthew 6:9; Luke 11:2).
The free intercessions provide the praying group the
opportunity to devote themselves to prayer for their
particular concerns, both corporate and individual. A
collect separates the Lord's Prayer from the free intercessions. If the day has its own collect, that prayer may

be offered. However, the three collects given are those we have mentioned as expressing the traditional theme of the Lesser Hours.

The first collect asks God to send the Holy Spirit into our hearts to direct and rule us, comfort and defend us. This collect logically accompanies the first lesson, Romans 5:5. The outpouring of the Spirit upon the Apostles at the third hour is the traditional theme of Terce. Although the combination of the collect and lesson could be used well at a lunch break, it is more suitable for a mid-morning Office.

The second collect is addressed to Christ hanging upon the cross at noon. It asks for the salvation of all the peoples of the earth through Christ. The accompanying lesson is 2 Corinthians 5:17-18, the new creation and reconciliation in Christ. This combination is obviously suitable anytime during the three hours from noon to three o'clock.

The third collect, commemorating St. Paul's conversion at noonday, asks also for the conversion of the nations and is an obvious alternative to the second collect. Either the second or third lesson goes well with it. Both remind us of the Christian missionary imperative. By asking God to accomplish the work directly and not requesting that we take any action to bring it about, they recognize that we cannot do anything by our own efforts, but only by God's grace going before us.

The final collect does not have a temporal reference, but prays for peace and unity on the basis of Christ's gift of peace to his Apostles (John 14:27). Accompanied by the third lesson, Malachi 1:11, the third collect is suitable not only for a mid-afternoon Office but also for one at noon. Since sub-apostolic times, Malachi 1:11 has been taken to refer to the missionary outreach of the Christian Church. The "pure offering" has sometimes been identified with the eucharist, but it should probably, like Psalm 141:2, be taken to refer to the offering of prayer throughout the world as a "pure" substitute for the sacrifices of the Jerusalem Temple.

The simple dismissal "Let us bless the Lord" concludes the Noonday Office. The Prayer Book neither requires nor expects this Office to be regularly used by most congregations but makes it available for those occasions when it is desired to follow the traditional Jewish and early Christian practice of praying at noon. The references to the time of day in the collects are a part of the offering of all times and seasons to the Lord by remembering God's mighty acts at this or that particular hour as a reason for marking the time with prayer.

Compline, or Night Prayer (BCP: 127-135), has been a popular Office among many people even though it was not in the *Book of Common Prayer* prior to the present revision. It originated in the dormitory prayers of religious orders and is a formalized corporate form of family bedtime prayer. Part of its appeal is the absence of variation, which makes it easy to follow in poor light or when tired.

The Office begins with a blessing, "The Lord Almighty grant us a peaceful night and a perfect end." These are the themes of night prayer: rest and sleeping with Christ in death.

The help of God is invoked, and all confess their sins of the past day. A prayer that God "may grant us forgiveness" follows the confession. Since this is not an ecclesial Office, there is no priestly absolution, for the Prayer Book does not expect that there will be a priest present to pronounce it. The Officiant offers a prayer for pardon, just as a lay Officiant does at Morning and Evening Prayer in the absence of a priest. A small group of nighttime psalms are used: Psalms 4, 31, 91, and 134. All have specific references to night or to sleep. Psalm 134 probably best epitomizes the spirit of Compline:

Behold now, bless the Lord, all you servants of the
    Lord,
  you that stand by night in the house of the Lord.

Lift up your hands in the holy place and bless the
    Lord;
  the Lord who made heaven and earth bless you
      out of Zion. (BCP: 131)

A short lesson, either from the alternatives given or
some other passage, follows the psalms. A "hymn suitable for the evening" is permitted, but no specific hymn
is suggested. The traditional Compline hymns are "To
you before the close of day" (*The Hymnal 1982*: 44) and
"O Christ, you are both light and day" (*The Hymnal
1982*: 41), but many other hymns are suitable, including
Thomas Ken's great "All praise to thee, my God, this
night" (*The Hymnal 1982*: 43). In selecting hymns and
prayers for Compline and for Evening Prayer it is
important to remember the difference between night
and evening. Those which speak as if we were going
immediately to bed are certainly proper for Compline.
However, such hymns lend a note of unreality to a five-
o'clock Evensong when most people are about to begin
what for them is the most enjoyable part of the day's
activities.

The Compline verse "Into your hands, O Lord, I
commend my spirit," with its response, "For you have
redeemed me, O Lord, O God of truth," from Psalm
31, and a second versicle, from Psalm 17:8, introduce
the prayers: the Kyrie, the Lord's Prayer, the Compline
collect, and optional additional prayers. There are several choices for the Compline collect. "Be our light in
the darkness" is probably the best known and well
expresses the central theme of the Office: "defend us
from all perils and dangers of this night." The alternatives bear much the same message. The third uses the
image of light and asks God, "illumine this night with

your celestial brightness" so that praise may continue by night as day. The fourth collect is from the Roman monastic tradition and assumes that the prayers are being offered in the place where the people live. It asks God to "visit this place" to keep away the enemy," let the angels dwell with us and keep us in peace. The imagery is that of a conflict between God and "the enemy" in which the assistance of the holy angels will grant us protection. The idea is traditional, and the image of a great supernatural conflict such as that described in Revelation 12:7 is powerful, but many contemporary Christians will wonder how literally these particular images are to be taken, and no guidance is given in the Prayer Book for answering that question.

The ministry of the angels is mentioned specifically in the collect and readings for the feast of St. Michael and All Angels (BCP: 244) and the Annunciation (BCP: 240), and their presence is embedded not only in the Old Testament narratives but in the Gospels and the Acts of the Apostles. It would be difficult to omit them from the Gospel and keep either the nativity or resurrection stories. We must therefore find some place for angels in our theology. The Prayer Book does not, of course, tie us into medieval angelology, but only into recognizing the existence of spiritual beings other than ourselves who serve God. In a universe as vast as we are coming to know this one to be, such recognition is probably a necessity.

The collect for Saturdays looks forward to the Sunday celebration of the Paschal Mystery and gives thanks for "revealing your Son Jesus Christ to us by the light of his resurrection."

Two additional prayers are included as possible intercessions. One is also a Prayer for Mission at Evening Prayer. It asks God to "watch with those who work, or watch, or weep this night" and to give the angels charge of those who sleep. It is a nighttime general intercession

and is probably more appropriate for Compline than for
Evening Prayer, unless Evening Prayer is celebrated
late in the evening. The other prayer prays specifically
for those "who work while others sleep" and asks "that
we may never forget that our common life depends
upon each other's toil." This expression of our mutual
interdependence in the Body of Christ, while not a
traditional Compline theme, is appropriate at any time,
and the recognition of the contribution to our common
life of those who work at night is a good contemporary
prayer.

The final act of the Office is the singing of the Song
of Simeon (*Nunc dimittis*), with its message of release and
rest. It is accompanied by an antiphon which applies its
meaning specifically to night prayers: "Guide us wak-
ing, O Lord, and guard us sleeping; that awake we may
watch with Christ, and asleep we may rest in peace."
The *Nunc dimittis* is the traditional Christian bedtime
canticle and forms a fitting conclusion to the Office,
which ends with a dismissal and with the Officiant giving a simple, familial, nonsacerdotal blessing which asks
God to bless us and keep us throughout the night.

Silence

In several places throughout the Office silence is permitted: before the confession, after the readings, after
the psalm in An Order for Evening, and after the collect
at Compline. Being still before the presence of God
reminds us that we really do have nothing to say. We
need to listen to the voice of God, who will pray in us.

Contemporary congregations are often afraid of
silence and tend to fill it with organ music, but silence is
an integral and necessary part of Christian worship.

The Great Litany

The Great Litany (BCP: 148-53), published initially in 1544 as the first liturgical service in the English language and a part of every edition of the Prayer Book, is not really a part of the Daily Office, although it is frequently used after the Collects of Morning or Evening Prayer. It is a general intercession written to be used in procession before the eucharist. It provides a good overview of the concerns for which this portion of the Church has publicly prayed during the last four centuries, and it is an Anglican classic.

It begins with the invocation of the Trinity as Creator, Redeemer and Sanctifier, applying these attributes to the three persons. It then asks the Lord Christ, in spite of our sins, to spare us from a variety of evils, to do this by virtue of his Incarnation, Nativity, submission to the Law, Baptism, Fasting, Temptation, Agony, Passion, Death, Resurrection, Ascension, the Coming of the Holy Ghost, and the Mighty Acts which he has accomplished for our salvation. It asks Christ to do this, now, in our times of need, and "in the hour of death and in the day of judgment."

The intercessions then begin: for the Church universal, its ministers and people, for those who have wandered away, for the civil authorites, for peace, and for all in need. Finally we ask for repentance and forgiveness for ourselves and for our enemies, for justice and for the eschatological triumph over evil, and for eternal life and peace for the dead, "that, in the fellowship of [_____ and] all the saints, we may attain to thy heavenly kingdom." Cranmer had included petitions for the prayers of the saints in his 1544 litany immediately after the invocation of the Trinity. This revised version introduces them here as part of the final consummation.

The Litany ends with traditional devotions, the *Agnus Dei, Kyrie,* Lord's Prayer, and a collect asking that we may obtain what we have prayed for. The Supplication (BCP: 154-5) is an addition to the prayers intended for use in time of war or similar emergency, asking for defense from our enemies. Its concluding collect does not conceal the likelihood that we ourselves are responsible for our difficulties and prays, "Turn from us all those evils that we most justly have deserved. . . ."

Chapter Four:
The Great Vigil
of Easter

At the introduction to the renewal of baptismal vows in the Great Vigil, the celebrant says:

> Through the Paschal mystery, dear friends, we are buried with Christ by Baptism into his death, and raised with him to newness of life. (BCP: 292)

This participation in the dying and rising again of Jesus is the center of Christian faith and life. It was this resurrection which the Apostles proclaimed to the world, and it is our sharing in it which makes us one with Christ. We have already seen (in Chapter Two) that the Paschal Mystery stands at the heart of the liturgical year. It underlies our weekly celebration of Sunday and our annual celebration of Good Friday and Easter. The Great Vigil is the fullest proclamation of that saving mystery. Central to it are the celebration of baptism, the sacrament of our entry into the Paschal Mystery, and the eucharist, the sacrament of our participation in it.

The Great Vigil is celebrated "between sunset on Holy Saturday and sunrise on Easter Morning" (BCP: 284). At its very beginning, the celebrant proclaims:

> Dear friends in Christ: On this most holy night, in which our Lord Jesus passed over from death to life, the Church invites her members, dispersed throughout the world, to gather in vigil and prayer. For this is the Passover of the Lord, in which, by hearing his Word and

celebrating his Sacraments, we share in his victory over death. (BCP: 285)

The Paschal Mystery

The Vigil marks not only the passage from Lent to Easter but Christ's Passover from death to life in the resurrection, and our participation in it. It is by hearing the "Word" and participating in the "Sacraments" that the congregation come to share in the Paschal Mystery. Underlying this statement is the "mystery theology" of Odo Casel and his definition of "mystery" in the ritual sense:

> The mystery is a sacred ritual action in which a saving deed is made present through the rite; the congregation, by performing the rite, take part in the saving act, and thereby win salvation.[1]

Dom Odo Casel, monk of Maria Laach and a leading theologian of the 20th-century Liturgical Movement, brought the name and concept of the Paschal Mystery to the forefront of the consciousness of contemporary liturgists. The Prayer Book certainly does not commit us to accepting Casel's theology of "mystery,"[2] but we should be aware that it was in the minds of those who edited the 1979 Prayer Book, as it was in the minds of those who drafted the *Constitution on the Sacred Liturgy* of Vatican Council II. It is significant that, while the *lex orandi* is normally what establishes the *lex credendi*, there are occasions, of which this is one, when a very specific secondary theology underlies a statement which is included in the liturgy precisely to express that theology. The liturgies of the Reformation provide classic examples, as does the hymn *Lauda, Sion,* written by Thomas Aquinas to express his theology of transubstantiation.[3] The Church is not committed to the secondary

theology of the compilers of the liturgy, however, but to
the theology which the liturgy itself expresses.

In the case of the Easter Vigil that theology includes
the recognition that we who participate in the rite, hearing the Word and celebrating the Sacraments, are
thereby partakers in Christ's resurrection. It is not, of
course, the Vigil rite, but the Paschal Mystery itself
which incorporates us into Christ's saving acts. We have
already found a similar idea in the second lenten preface, which asks that we may be "renewed by your Word
and Sacraments" and thereby "come to the grace which
you have prepared for those who love you" (BCP: 379).
The Vigil itself expresses this with dramatic simplicity.
A great light, the Paschal Candle, is kindled, and by its
light the Bible is read, prayer and praise offered, and
the Easter sacraments of baptism and eucharist celebrated. It is a celebration of the entire congregation,
with the bishop (if he is present), priests, deacons, and
lay persons taking active parts (BCP: 284).

The Lighting
of the Paschal Candle

The lighting of a candle at the beginning of a nighttime
service is a simple utilitarian act, but even this simple act
identifies the lighted candle with "The Light of
Christ," and the celebrant prays "that in this Paschal
feast we may so burn with heavenly desires, that with
pure minds we may attain to the festival of everlasting
light" (BCP: 285). That festival is the Pascha, the celebration of the victory of Christ over death and of our
participation in that victory.

The lighting of a *new* fire is itself a deeply symbolic
act. Before the invention of matches the kindling of a
fire was a serious matter, and the ritual extinguishing of
the old fire and the kindling of a new one was an obvious
act of renewal. It characterized the beginnings of new

things,[4] and the kindling of a fire in the darkness at the beginning of the Great Vigil is a symbol of the new life in Christ which the resurrection proclaims and ushers in.

The lighting of the Paschal Candle is a solemn *lucernarium*, and what has been said about that ceremony in the context of An Order for Evening in Chapter Three applies here also. "The Light of Christ" dispels the darkness as the deacon carries the lighted candle into the dark church. "Other candles and lamps," including candles held by individual worshipers, are lighted from the candle, and the new light, "the true light that enlightens every man" (John 1:9), is seen as spreading his light over the whole body of the faithful (BCP: 286). The new light of Christ has broken into the world of sin and death.

By the light of the Paschal Candle, "this marvelous and holy flame," the deacon sings the Exsultet, the poetic prayer for light which celebrates "the victory of our mighty King" (BCP: 286) who has vanquished darkness, and prays:

> Holy Father, accept our evening sacrifice, the offering of this candle in your honor. May it shine continually to drive away all darkness. May Christ, the Morning Star who knows no setting, find it ever burning—he who gives light to all creation, and who lives and reigns for ever and ever. (BCP: 287)

The real focus of the Exsultet, however, is not the symbolism of light, but the Paschal Mystery, Jesus Christ, "the true Paschal Lamb, who at the feast of Passover paid for us the debt of Adam's sin, and by his blood delivered your [God's] faithful people" (BCP: 287).

The opposition of Christ, the new *anthropos*, and Adam, the prototype, is a commonplace of Christian theology, rooted in such biblical passages as 1 Corinthians 15:20-21, 45-46. We who by our birth bear the image of Adam, the archetypal human being, are also to bear the image of the new humanity in Christ, with whom we are united in the Paschal Mystery. As human beings we are sinners bound for death, but as members of Christ we are united with him who has overcome sin and death, and we share in his risen life. The language of the Exsultet commits us neither to belief in the existence of Adam as an historical person nor to any of the particular varieties of medieval theology which viewed salvation as basically a bookkeeping transaction in which God in Christ paid off the debts we owed the Father as a result of sin, both that of Adam and our own. What it does proclaim is that by the blood of Christ we are saved from sin and death.

> How wonderful and beyond our knowing, O God, is your mercy and loving-kindness to us, that to redeem a slave, you gave a Son. (BCP: 287)

As we noted in Chapter Two, the Exsultet identifies "this night" with the Pascha.

> This is the night, when you brought our fathers, the children of Israel, out of bondage in Egypt, and led them through the Red Sea on dry land.

> This is the night, when all who believe in Christ are delivered from the gloom of sin, and are restored to grace and holiness of life.

> This is the night, when Christ broke the bonds of death and hell, and rose victorious from the grave. . . .

> How holy is this night, when wickedness is put to flight, and sin is washed away. It restores innocence to the fallen, and joy to those who mourn. It casts out pride and hatred, and brings peace and concord.

> How blessed is this night, when earth and heaven are joined and man is reconciled to God. (BCP: 287)

The Exsultet is poetry, but it is the poetic language of worship which has often expressed the piety which theologians have sought and fought to state dogmatically.[5] In the Paschal Mystery we celebrate the Exodus from Egypt, the central saving act of God in the Old Testament, and the resurrection of Christ, the central saving act of God in the New Testament. But it is also the night of *our* salvation, in which "all who believe in Christ" are saved from sin and death. In the baptismal waters sin is washed away and grace given—a grace which establishes, through Christ, a new relationship between God and the race of Adam.

The Liturgy of the Word

The Paschal themes, the Good News of Easter, are expounded in the Exsultet at the beginning of the Vigil. They are amplified in the readings, psalms, and collects which follow in the Liturgy of the Word. The readings catch up the great themes; the psalms reflect on them meditatively; and the collects apply them to the Easter baptismal celebration. Not all of the readings are usually used at the celebration of the Great Vigil, but all provide insights into different aspects of the mystery, and all must be considered in any discussion of the Vigil's meaning. They are introduced by the celebrant as "the record of God's saving deeds in history," with the prayer that "God will bring each of us to the fullness of redemption" (BCP: 288).

The Story of Creation (Genesis 1:1—2:2) provides the context for the proclamation of salvation by telling again the cosmogenic myth: "In the beginning God created the heavens and the earth" (Genesis 1:1). It is the beginning of the story of the people of God. Psalm 33 makes the creation its reason for rejoicing and praising the Lord:

By the word of the Lord were the heavens made,
  by the breath of his mouth all the heavenly
    hosts. . . .

Let all the earth fear the Lord;
  let all who dwell in the world stand in awe of him.

For he spoke, and it came to pass;
  he commanded, and it stood fast. (BCP: 626)

The "word of the Lord" by which (or whom) God created the heavens is identified in the prologue of the Fourth Gospel as Christ, the Logos, while "the breath of his mouth" has been identified with the Holy Spirit. These are certainly not the meanings which the original author of the psalm had in mind, but they cannot help but leap to the mind of Christians, and they are part of the reason for using this psalm to reflect on the creation story. Identifications of this sort are traditional among Christians, who have made the Psalter a Christian liturgical book, reading it in the light of the Gospel and of our own tradition. The alternative psalm (Psalm 36:5-10) speaks of the love and faithfulness of God and includes the verse "in your light we see light" (BCP: 632), invoking God as the source of light and life. The collect prays "that we may share the divine life of him who humbled himself to share our humanity" (BCP: 288). Creation is taken as the type of the new creation, and the God who made us is asked to save us through Jesus Christ our Lord.

The Flood Narrative (Genesis 7:1-5, 11-18; 8:6-18; 9:8-13) leads to the prayer "that we, who are saved through water and the Spirit, may worthily offer to you our sacrifice of thanksgiving" (BCP: 289). Noah becomes the sign of our salvation through the waters of baptism.[6] As the rainbow was the sign of God's covenant with Noah, so the Christian sacraments, the baptismal water and the eucharistic sacrifice, are the signs of the New Covenant.

THE GREAT VIGIL OF EASTER

Genesis 22:1-18, Abraham's Sacrifice of Isaac, or more properly the Binding of Isaac—since the story makes the point that Abraham did not sacrifice Isaac though he was willing to—has been prominent in both Jewish and Christian devotion. Abraham, who did not refuse to give up his only son, has been seen by Christians both as an example of one who was willing to give up everything of value in order to follow the command of God and also as a symbol of God's sacrifice of his only Son for us. Christian tradition has identified the ram which God provided as a sacrifice in place of Isaac with Jesus, the Paschal Lamb. As Isaac was saved by the sacrifice of the ram, so we are saved by the sacrifice of Christ, the Lamb of God.

The psalm emphasizes God's deliverance from death. Psalm 33:12-22 speaks of the "eye of the Lord" being upon those who fear him, "to pluck their lives from death" (BCP: 627). Psalm 16 affirms the psalmist's loyalty to the Lord:

> For you will not abandon me to the grave,
>   nor let your holy one see the Pit.

> You will show me the path of life;
>   in your presence there is fullness of joy,
>   and in your right hand are pleasures for evermore.
>   (BCP: 600)

The collect asks that "the Paschal sacrament" of baptism may increase the number of God's children, "that your [God's] Church may rejoice to see fulfilled your promise to our father Abraham," (BCP: 289). In Galatians 4:28 and 3:27-30, St. Paul reminds us that we, like Isaac, are heirs of the promises to Abraham because of our baptism. The collect combines the two insights into a prayer not only for those to be baptized but for all the faithful, that we may all receive the promises of God. The Scripture, psalm and collect combine to say, in effect, that the promise made to Abraham and the rescue afforded Isaac have been fulfilled in the death and resurrection of Christ and are, this night, *ours* through Word and Sacrament.

The account of Israel's Deliverance at the Red Sea (Exodus 14:10—15:1) is always read (BCP: 289). The Exodus is a part of the Paschal celebration, and the reading of the Exodus story is central to the proclamation of the celebration's meaning. The reading concludes with The Song of Moses, a hymn of praise for the mighty act of God in saving the people of Israel. The collect then petitions God that as "you once delivered by the power of your mighty arm your chosen people from slavery under Pharaoh, . . . be a sign for us of the salvation of all nations by the water of Baptism," so that "all the peoples of the earth may be numbered among the offspring of Abraham, and rejoice in the inheritance of Israel" (BCP: 289). In this, as in the previous reading, we Christians are claiming our Old Testament heritage, applying to ourselves the promises of God to the people of Israel and accepting, as a part of that heritage, God's judgment against us for our sins. The particular focus of this collect is the universality of God's promise of salvation. Not one people only, but all the peoples of the earth (i.e., the Gentiles) are to be numbered among the children of Abraham. The catholicity of the Gospel and of the Church gives a new dimension to the Exodus story.[7]

The fifth reading (Isaiah 4:2-6) is a prophecy of God's Presence in a Renewed Israel. The reading symbolizes God's presence by the pillar of cloud and fire (Isaiah 4:5) which marked the presence of the Lord in the Exodus. The collect uses these symbols and the others in Isaiah's vision to speak of the hope of glory which God holds out to us. It prays that we "may come to the joy of that heavenly Jerusalem, where all tears are wiped away and where your saints for ever sing your praise" (BCP: 290).

Isaiah 55:1-11, characterized by the Prayer Book as Salvation Offered Freely to All, is not only one of the great messianic passages from Second Isaiah, but it also speaks of God's new covenant and the universality of God's reign. The First Song of Isaiah, the canticle recommended as a response, sings of drawing water with rejoicing from the springs of salvation (BCP: 86). The alternate psalm, Psalm 42, picks up the opening theme of the reading ["Lo, every one who thirsts, come to the waters . . . " (Isaiah 55:1)] in its second verse: "My soul is athirst for God, athirst for the living God. . ." (BCP: 643). Both responses are songs of praise for what God has done for us. Clearly referring to baptism, the collect asks that those who thirst may be given the water of life "that they may bring forth abundant fruit in your glorious kingdom" (BCP: 290). The entire passage calls us to the baptismal water, where we receive forgiveness of sins and become participants in God's reign. In this liturgical context the prophet proclaims Christ as the saving Word which has gone forth from God's mouth and accomplished God's purpose (Isaiah 55:11) and which in our Paschal celebration of baptism will "bring forth abundant fruit" through water and the Holy Spirit and not return to God empty, but prosper in that for which God sent it.

The seventh reading, A New Heart and a New Spirit (Ezekiel 36:24-28), seems to Christians to be speaking directly about baptism:

> I will sprinkle clean water upon you, and you shall be clean from all your uncleannesses. . . . A new heart I will give you, and a new spirit I will put within you. . . . And I will put my spirit within you, and cause you to walk in my statutes. . . ." (Ezekiel 36:25-27)

The collect makes the connection between the reading and baptism plain: it speaks of "the new covenant of
reconciliation" and prays that "all who are reborn into
the fellowship of Christ's Body may show forth in their
lives what they profess by their faith" (BCP: 290f). Baptismal regeneration, the forgiveness of sins, and the
need for the lives of Christians to conform to the faith
they profess are primary topics for baptismal catechesis;
that is, they are traditionally part of the basic teaching
given to those who are becoming Christians. Baptismal
regeneration became a hotly debated concept in the
19th century.[8] As used here, and elsewhere in the liturgy, baptismal regeneration is solidly based on the biblical teaching of John 3:3-8 and Titus 3:5-6. The
Johannine concept of baptism as rebirth is clearly similar to the Pauline view of baptism as resurrection. The
liturgy, both here and in the baptismal rite itself, affirms
that the newness of the life in Christ becomes ours
through baptism and that reconciliation with God and
the forgiveness of sins are signs of that new life.

These scriptural passages and their Christian interpretations in the collects are intended to be a part of the
passing on of the Church's tradition concerning the
risen life in Christ to a new generation of Christians. A
sermon on each of the readings at the Great Vigil would
be a short course in basic Christian doctrine for those
about to be baptized. Reading the passages, singing
their accompanying psalms or canticles, and praying the
collects provide those who have already received such
basic instruction with a prayerful review and bring the
central truths of the Christian faith to consciousness as
we move to the celebration of the Easter Sacraments.

The process continues with the reading of the vision
of The valley of dry bones (Ezekiel 37:1-14). Here the
resurrection is the Christian theme which Ezekiel's
vision presents:

Thus says the Lord God: Behold, I will open your graves, and raise you from your graves, O my people. . . . And I will put my spirit within you and you shall live. . . . (Ezekiel 37:12, 14)

Psalm 30 gives God thanks because, "You brought me up, O Lord, from the dead; you restored my life as I was going down into the grave," and it contains lines certainly appropriate for a vigil:

Weeping may spend the night,
    but joy comes in the morning. (BCP: 621)

The alternate psalm, Psalm 143, moves from near despair to the fervent prayer "Let me hear of your loving-kindness in the morning, for I put my trust in you" (BCP: 799). Then it asks God both to teach us what God wants us to do and to lead us with "your good Spirit." The collect collects these thoughts well and focuses them:

Almighty God, by the Passover of your Son you have brought us out of sin into righteousness and out of death into life: Grant to those who are sealed by your Holy Spirit the will and power to proclaim you to all the world. (BCP: 291)

The catechism says that "union with Christ in his death and resurrection, birth into God's family the Church, forgiveness of sins, and new life in the Holy Spirit" is the inward and spiritual grace in baptism (BCP: 858). The collect focuses upon these gifts, as step by step the liturgy sets the sacrament of Holy Baptism in a context in which its meaning will be manifested through Scripture, psalm and prayer, as well as through the opportunity for direct instruction through the preaching of a homily after any of the lessons (BCP: 292).

The final reading, The Gathering of God's People (Zephaniah 3:12-20), is a great shout of praise for the

Lord's victory and God's promise. "I will bring you home" (Zephaniah 3:20). The reading exhorts us not to fear, for "The Lord, your God, is in your midst" (3:17). The collect is an ancient prayer for the Church, used also in the Prayer Book on Good Friday and at ordinations. It asks that God bring to completion and perfection the mighty works which God has begun for our salvation. In this position in the liturgy, the collect serves to introduce the celebration of Holy Baptism.

The Preparation of Catechumens

As mentioned above, the Paschal and baptismal themes in the readings of the Great Vigil are a summary course of preparation for baptism. *The Book of Occasional Services*[9] provides directions and liturgical rites for a traditional adult catechumenate (BOS: 112-125): "The enrollment of candidates for Baptism at the Great Vigil of Easter normally takes place on the First Sunday in Lent" (BOS: 120). At that time they write their names in the parish register, adding them to the parish roll (BOS: 121). On the Third, Fourth and Fifth Sundays in Lent public prayer is offered for them at the eucharist (BOS: 124f). In the early Church, the Gospels for these Sundays (today used during year A) were used to instruct the candidates, who would be present in the church for the Ministry of the Word. The lenten Sunday Gospels for Year A in the Prayer Book introduce many of the themes we have found in the readings for the Great Vigil.

On the Second Sunday in Lent, the ringing proclamation from the story of Nicodemus (John 3:1-17) is read: "Unless one is born of water and the Spirit, he cannot enter the kingdom of God." The reading concludes with the well-known passage "God so loved the world. . . ." Thus, the Scripture invites the preacher to speak of salvation through Christ, with baptism as its sacramental sign, and to place the reading within the baptismal context as part of the preparation of baptismal candidates.

The Gospel appointed for the Third Sunday in Lent is the story of Jesus and the woman at the well of Samaria (John 4:5-42). It introduces the theme of water: "Whoever drinks the water that I shall give him will never thirst; the water that I shall give him will become in him a spring of water welling up to eternal life." The discourse then moves to worship in spirit and truth as a requirement for those who will worship validly. The woman herself can be compared to the catechumens. She responds to the call of Jesus, asks him questions, makes the request "Sir, give me this water," receives instruction in ethics and true worship, accepts Jesus as Messiah, and finally brings others to him. Again, the gospel reading introduces the very themes necessary for the instruction of candidates for baptism, especially Jesus as Messiah, the baptismal water and the elements of true worship.

The Gospel of the Fourth Sunday in Lent presents the story of Jesus healing the man born blind. In the reading's most powerful passage Jesus says, "I am the light of the world" and sends the man to wash in the pool of Siloam, where he regains his sight. We, too, are sent to wash. We wash in the pool of baptism to regain our lost sight and see Jesus, the light of the world, who restores us.

The Gospel of the Fifth Sunday in Lent climaxes the series of baptismal catecheses. It presents the raising of Lazarus (John 11); its central text is "I am the resurrection and the life" (John 11:25). The Gospel helps us recognize that we participate in the resurrection of Jesus through the baptismal experience. That recognition ties the preparatory lenten Gospels together and completes a sounding of central baptismal themes. It also leads naturally into the Passion narrative on the

following Sunday (Passion/Palm Sunday) and into the
Holy Week celebration.

These gospel themes were intended to prepare candidates for baptism to hear the Old Testament readings of
the Great Vigil and to understand them in the light of
the Gospel. They are, as we have suggested, much more
texts for preaching than presentations of doctrine.
These lenten Gospels and the Vigil's lessons tell the
central stories of the Church to its members and to the
candidates for membership. Together, these Scripture
readings provide the context for the celebration of the
sacraments and the proclamation of the Easter Gospel.

The Renewal of Baptismal Vows

The celebration of Holy Baptism, which will be treated
in Chapter Five, takes place after the reading of the
lessons or after the Easter Gospel has been proclaimed
(BCP: 292). Baptism is both structurally and theologically the climax of the Great Vigil, which is seriously
impoverished if Holy Baptism is omitted. As we celebrate the resurrection of the Lord and our own participation in that resurrection through baptism, we add
new members to the Body of Christ. As they pass
through the waters of the font, they also pass with
Christ through the grave and gate of death to be united
with him in his resurrection.

The Great Vigil is also the opportunity for every
member of the Church to renew his or her own baptismal vows. This renewal recommits us to living the new
life in Christ into which we entered at our baptism.
Even if there are no candidates for baptism, the renewal
of vows takes place, although it is best celebrated in the
context of new baptisms.

The resurrection makes all things new. The Church
is doubly renewed: by the addition of new members, and

by a reappropriation of its own participation in the Paschal Mystery. In a significant theological sense, this renewal happens in the celebration of the Easter eucharist and the congregation's joining in the reception of communion. However, the renewal of baptismal vows makes explicit what is implicit in the eucharistic celebration.

The Easter Eucharist

The Great Vigil culminates in the celebration of the Easter eucharist. The celebration completes the passage from Lent to Easter and our passage with Christ from death to life. The altar candles are lighted, the shout of "Alleluia. Christ is risen," is heard, and a festal canticle is sung (BCP: 294). All symbolize the end of Lent and the beginning of the Easter celebration. The use of the Easter acclamation at the Vigil is actually optional. Some places prefer to mark the passage from Lent to Easter non-verbally with the use of bells, organ and other sounds of festivity, saving the use of words for the festal canticle of praise.

The second of the alternative collects restates the themes we have examined in the Vigil: God has "made this most holy night to shine with the glory of the Lord's resurrection" (BCP: 295). The Paschal Candle shining in the darkness and the lighting of the altar candles as the eucharist begins have already sounded this note. The principal petition of the collect, "Stir up in your Church that Spirit of adoption which is given to us in Baptism," ties baptism, eucharist, and the gift of the Spirit to the resurrection light. We pray for renewal in body and mind—a principal theme in the Vigil's lessons and collects and the core of the sacramental experience of the Great Vigil—so "that we may worship you in sincerity and truth." All is done to the greater glory of God (BCP: 295). The collect itself is from the early

Latin sacramentaries, our earliest sources for collects.
Its ancient source demonstrates the continuity not only
of actual texts but of theological content in the Easter
Vigil from the earliest days.[10]

The first collect, which initially appears as a collect
for Wednesday in Holy Week in the Gregorian Sacramentary but was appointed for a first Easter celebration
in the 1928 Prayer Book, speaks of redemption by the
cross and deliverance by the resurrection from "the
power of our enemy," the evil one or the devil. It prays
that we may die daily to sin and live forever with Christ
"in the joy of his resurrection" (BCP: 295). The collect
reflects Christ's breaking of the bonds of hell and death
—already mentioned in the Exsultet—and sets the
entire drama of the crucifixion and resurrection on a
cosmic scale. Thus, it expresses what Gustav Aulén calls
a *Christus victor* theology of the atonement,[11] a theology
well expressed in the third stanza of the 11th-century
Easter hymn "Christians to the Paschal victim":

Death and life have contended
in that combat stupendous:
the Prince of life, who died, reigns immortal.
(*The Hymnal 1982*: 183)

On the cross Christ triumphed over the forces of evil,
thereby winning salvation for the human race and
redeeming us from the power of sin and death. Marion
Hatchett says of this collect, "Its content, and its original association with Holy Week, makes it a fitting transition from the time of meditation upon the passion to the
celebration of the resurrection."[12] Its content certainly
makes it appropriate for Easter, although the idea of
dying daily to sin seems more suitable to Holy Week.
Living the resurrection life daily in the power of
Christ's victory over sin, however, is not only a traditional topic to present to the newly baptized; it is an
important undertaking for all Christians. Thus, the

theme may also be found in the Epistle for Easter Day (Colossians 3:1-4), and it is also one of the themes in the Epistle at the Vigil itself.

The Vigil's Epistle (Romans 6:3-11) is the classic passage on the meaning of baptism: "Do you not know that all of us who have been baptized into Christ Jesus were baptized into his death?" Christ has been raised from the dead, and we who have been united with him in baptism "shall certainly be united with him in a resurrection like his." We are no longer enslaved by sin, but "alive to God in Christ Jesus." The passage is the perfect conclusion to the Vigil's Old Testament readings. The meaning of baptism as participation in the resurrection, and its ethical implications for the life which Christians must now live, are presented to the assembled Church which has just celebrated, or is about to celebrate Holy Baptism and the renewal of baptismal vows. The resurrection is not something external to those participating in the Vigil. "All of us who have been baptized into Christ Jesus" are intimately and personally concerned, for "if we have died with Christ, we believe that we shall also live with him."

The Easter shout of "Alleluia" and the great Passover psalm (Psalm 114), "When Israel came out of Egypt . . .," may be sung. Both tie the Christian *Pascha* to the Jewish and affirm the unity of the Old and New Testaments in praising the God who saves and redeems his people.

The Gospel (Matthew 28:1-10) is the resurrection narrative. The Matthean version begins, "After the sabbath, toward the dawn of the first day of the week. . . ." The reference to the dawn of the new day makes it an obvious choice for the close of a Vigil.[13] The core of its proclamation is the angel's words, "I know that you seek Jesus who was crucified. He is not here; for he has risen, as he said," and the meeting of the women with Jesus himself. Twice we hear the command

"Go and tell. . . ." To proclaim the resurrection is the mission of the Church.

The celebration of baptism may follow the Gospel and the homily, or it may precede the eucharistic lections. The choice will influence the direction the preacher will take in the homily. In either case, the liturgy proceeds to the Prayers of the People, the Peace, and the celebration of the Easter eucharist, at which, ideally, all of the faithful (i.e., all baptized members of the Church in good standing), receive communion and welcome for the first time the newly baptized. The reception of communion is the great rite of incorporation and renewal which identifies those who receive as the community of the risen Christ and binds them in union and communion with Christ and with one another. To exclude Christians from Easter communion is to excommunicate them, to separate them from the Church, to declare that they are "not in good standing." For Christians to exclude themselves is to do the same thing.

Since it is in the Great Vigil of Easter that the Church is renewed by the power of the risen Christ, Easter communion has always been considered most important, because it includes the individual Church member in that renewal. We can view this inclusion as many contemporary people do, as primarily a benefit to the individual, but there is good reason to view it, as Christians of the patristic age did, as primarily for the building up of the Church. The Church is weakened by the absence of any member and is strongest and most completely renewed when all members participate. Recognizing that not every Christian can be present at the Great Vigil, the Church provides other opportunities throughout the Easter season for all—including the sick and shut-ins—to receive communion. For the same reason, the renewal of baptismal vows is often included in the other services of Easter Day, and a second baptismal celebration is held at the close of the Great Fifty Days on the Day of Pentecost.

Our treatment of the Great Vigil would necessarily be incomplete without a thorough discussion of the Gospel Sacraments (baptism and eucharist) and their inter-relationship. This discussion follows in the next two chapters. The Vigil provides the context for that discussion. The Vigil also presents most fully the Church's resurrection faith. Many of the Paschal themes of the Great Vigil, which are the core of this faith, are continually proclaimed throughout the Easter Season in the Easter preface:

> But chiefly are we bound to praise you for the glorious resurrection of your Son Jesus Christ our Lord; for he is the true Paschal Lamb, who was sacrificed for us, and has taken away the sin of the world. By his death he has destroyed death, and by his rising to life again he has won for us everlasting life. (BCP: 379)

Chapter Five:
Christian Initiation

The opening rubric of the baptismal liturgy reads, "Holy Baptism is full initiation by water and the Holy Spirit into Christ's Body the Church. The bond which God establishes in baptism is indissoluble" (BCP: 298). "Initiation" is defined by the historian of religions Mircea Eliade as "a body of rites and oral teachings whose purpose is to produce a decisive alteration in the religious and social status of the person to be initiated."[1] For us Christians, this "decisive change" occurs in the waters of baptism. It is described by the Prayer Book Catechism as "union with Christ in his death and resurrection, birth into God's family the Church, forgiveness of sins, and new life in the Holy Spirit" (BCP: 858). These constitute the indissoluble bond established by God in baptism. Eliade describes as existential the change effected by initiation.[2] St. Paul describes his initiation experience in the words "It is no longer I who live, but Christ who lives in me" (Galatians 2:20). We might summarize the teaching of the Prayer Book in New Testament terms the same way. We who were many have become one Body in Christ. We who were not a people have become God's people. We who have been buried with Christ in his death have been made partakers of his risen life, and in him we are made kings and priests. We who have died to sin have been raised to new life in the Holy Spirit.[3] By uniting us to himself, the Great High Priest and King of kings ordains us to the royal priesthood of all believers and fills us with his Holy Spirit, forgives our sins, gives us a share in his new life in the communion of saints (the one, holy, catholic and apostolic Church), and looks foward to "the day of redemption."

The Context of Holy Baptism

We have already placed this sacrament in the context of the Great Vigil of Easter, and it is there that its theology is most fully expressed and proclaimed. But even when baptism is not celebrated within the Easter Vigil, it is by its nature a sacrament of the resurrection. The Prayer Book expects that baptism will be celebrated in the context of "the Eucharist as the chief service on a Sunday or other feast" (BCP: 298) and recommends that it be reserved to specific occasions: the Easter Vigil, Pentecost, All Saints, the Feast of the Baptism of our Lord, and the bishop's visitation (BCP: 312). The placing of baptism in the context of the weekly celebration of the resurrection (the principal parish eucharist) provides a setting for the sacrament which makes clear its close relationship to the eucharist, the other Gospel sacrament of the dying and rising of Christ; it also involves the entire congregation in the celebration. When we discuss the theology of baptism, we need to remember that the Scripture readings of the ministry of the Word and the actions of the eucharist proper are intended to be a part of the celebration. In fact, the participation of the newly baptized in the eucharist is really the final, climactic act of the baptism. The theological and pastoral context of the sacrament is further enhanced when baptism is celebrated on the recommended baptismal days as major festivals of the congregation.

The celebration of baptism on the Day of Pentecost, the fiftieth and final day of the Easter season, not only maintains the Paschal setting of baptism but also provides an additional focus on the baptismal gift of the Holy Spirit. All Saints' Day (or the Sunday following) is

a convenient occasion for autumn baptism, for it there emphasizes the union of all who have been baptized with Christ and with one another in the communion of saints. As we saw in Chapter Two, it also demonstrates that "the triumphs of the saints are a continuation and manifestation of the Paschal victory of Christ" (LLF: 56). All Saints' Day itself is therefore a Paschal feast. The Feast of the Baptism of our Lord (the Sunday after Epiphany) is also an obviously appropriate occasion. The account of the baptism of Christ forms a background for our baptismal celebration, and the Epiphany
∨ image of light is a major baptismal image. Finally, the occasion of the bishop's visitation provides an excellent opportunity for him to preside at baptism, especially the baptism of adults, and for the local Church to gather under the leadership of its chief priest and pastor for its most solemn rites: the celebration of the Gospel sacraments and the preaching of the Word of God.

In most parishes these occasions will provide sufficient opportunities for the celebration of baptism. If the parish has more baptisms than can be conveniently administered on these five occasions, the principal eucharist on another Sunday may be selected for an additional celebration. If there are no candidates for baptism on one of the above baptismal feasts, the Renewal of Baptismal Vows from the Easter Vigil may be used at the eucharist in place of the Nicene Creed (BCP: 312). It can be used most effectively as the conclusion of a sermon on whichever particular aspect of our baptismal life in the Body of Christ the festival celebrates.

Preparation for Baptism

The Prayer Book does not expect baptism to stand alone without preparation or follow-up. In the case of the baptism of children, the Prayer Book requires that their parents and godparents be instructed "in the meaning of Baptism, in their duties to help the new Christians grow in the knowledge and love of God, and in their responsibilities as members of his Church" (BCP: 298). Obviously this instruction is pre-baptismal. To fulfill their duties, the parents, godparents, and the entire parish must commit themselves to considerable follow-up. In the baptismal service the parents and god-parents promise to see that the children they present are brought up in "the Christian faith and life." Like-wise, the entire congregation undertakes to support them by prayers and witness. The fulfillment of this promise would seem to require not only Christian edu-cation in the academic sense, but spiritual formation— the provision of an environment in which new Chris-tians can experience the living of the Christian life and can learn to live it themselves. This support is necessa-rily a major activity of the local congregation, but it is one which is often sadly neglected.

In the case of adult candidates, the Prayer Book asks them the single question, "Do you desire to be bap-tized?" (BCP: 301). If they are to respond, "I do," some form of preparatory instruction is obviously necessary. Their sponsors, by presenting them for baptism, "sig-nify their endorsement of the candidates and their intention to support them by prayer and example in their Christian life" (BCP: 298).

The Book of Occasional Services contains an entire sec-tion entitled "Preparation of Adults for Holy Baptism," which provides a framework for a traditional cat-echumenate in preparation for baptism (BOS: 112-25). Two significant statements stand at the beginning of this section:

> The systematic instruction and formation of its catechu-mens is a solemn responsibility of the Christian commu-nity. Traditionally, the preparation of catechumens is a responsibility of the bishop, which is shared with the

presbyters, deacons, and appointed lay catechists of the diocese.

The catechumenate is a period of training and instruction in Christian understandings about God, human relationships, and the meaning of life, which culminates in the reception of the Sacraments of Christian Initiation. (BOS: 112)

Eliade's definition of initiation quoted at the beginning of this chapter speaks of it as "a body of rites and oral teachings," and here we begin to see that Christian initiation is more than simply a single event. Rather, it is a process which includes both liturgical rites and oral instruction of which the celebration of the sacraments is the focus and climax. Since the provision for instruction, preparation and follow-up is included in the opening rubrics of the rite of baptism, we need not hesitate to include the material concerning the catechumenate from *The Book of Occasional Services* in our discussion of Christian initiation. In calling baptism "full initiation" (BCP: 298), the Prayer Book does not mean to remove the necessary preparation from the process of Christian initiation, but rather to insist on the sufficiency of the sacramental actions of the rite itself. No additional rite is necessary to complete Christian initiation, neither confirmation nor charismatic "baptism in the spirit." The one who is baptized is fully a member. The rites associated with the catechumenate are also unnecessary to the completeness of the sacrament. They are simply a liturgical framework and ritualization of the necessary instruction and spiritual preparation of the candidates which the Prayer Book requires in a single rubric.

The preparation of adults for baptism falls naturally into four stages, which are outlined in the section "Concerning the Catechumenate" (BOS 112-13).[4] The first is The Pre-Catechumenal Period. This is the period of evangelization during which the Christian Gospel makes its impact on the life of the non-Christian. He or she really hears the Good News of Jesus Christ for the first time in a way that elicits a response and turns the candidate toward Christ and the acceptance of new life in him. It is as a result of this process of evangelization that people approach the Church and inquire about the Christian faith.

> To this stage belong inquirers' classes with sufficient preparation to enable persons to determine that they wish to become Christians. (BOS: 112)

When candidates reach the point of deciding that they do wish to become Christians, they are formally admitted as catechumens. Admission as a catechumen marks the beginning of the second stage (Catechumenate Period). This is a serious step, but it is more like engagement than marriage. As a catechumen the inquirer begins "to pursue a disciplined exploration of the implications of Christian living" (BOS: 112).

The Admission of Catechumens is a public liturgical act involving the entire congregation. The inquirers stand before the congregation at a principal Sunday liturgy and are asked to accept the summary of the divine law as a standard of life, to open heart and mind to receive the Lord Jesus and to be regular in attending worship and instruction. The congregation is asked to help them by prayer and example. Finally, the celebrant and sponsors mark the candidates' foreheads with the cross as a sign of their admission as catechumens (BOS: 115-7).

The catechumenate might be described as a period of acculturation. It provides not only a time of instruction but a time of support and assimilation for the catechumens. The catechumens are now formally associated with the Church and have an opportunity both to participate regularly in worship and to try to live the Christian life. Their formal instruction includes prayer,

Scripture study, and Christian living. "From the time of admission, a catechumen is regarded as a part of the Christian community" (BOS: 113).

> *During this period . . . formal instruction is given to the catechumens. At the conclusion of each session, a period of silence is observed, during which the catechumens pray for themselves and one another. Sponsors and other baptized persons present offer their prayers for the catechumens. The instructor then says one or two . . . suitable prayers, and concludes by laying a hand individually on the head of each catechumen in silence. It is traditional that this act be performed by the instructor, whether bishop, priest, deacon, or lay catechist.* (BOS: 117)

Admission to the catechumenate really is the point at which the inquirer becomes a Christian, although not yet in a full sense. Nevertheless, catechumens are participants in the liturgical action. They are the object of the prayers of the congregation and the recipients of the special blessing described above. For all this, the catechumenate is fairly low key. Its length depends on how new and different Christianity is to the individual catechumen. For some people, the catechumenate may be quite brief; for others with no prior knowledge of the Gospel, it might take some time. The early Church felt three years was a good standard for converts from paganism.

The pivotal point in the catechumenate comes when the catechumen is enrolled as a candidate for baptism. This is normally done on the First Sunday in Lent, with baptism to take place at the Great Vigil of Easter. For those preparing for baptism on the Feast of the Baptism of our Lord, the enrollment takes place on the First Sunday of Advent (see BOS: 120). Enrollment marks the beginning of a period of intensive preparation for baptism. It involves public acts at the Sunday eucharists, and, for the individual, fasting, examination of conscience, and prayer, so that each candidate may be spiritually and emotionally ready for baptism (BOS: 113).

The enrollment of the candidates takes place after the Creed at the eucharist. The sponsors are asked if the catechumens have been regular in attending worship and instruction and if they are seeking to live in accordance with the Gospel. Then the entire congregation is asked:

> As God is your witness, do you approve the enrolling of *these catechumens* as *candidates* for Holy Baptism? (BOS: 121)

The congregation's response provides the entire Church a part in the preparation of the candidates. Then the celebrant asks the sponsors to testify that those whom they present are ready to move toward the reception of baptism. Afterwards the candidates write their names in a large book, literally *enrolling* in the local congregation of the Christian Church. The celebrant says:

> In the Name of God, and with the consent of this congregation, I accept you as *candidates* for Holy Baptism, and direct that your *names* be written in this book. God grant that *they* may also be written in the Book of Life. (BOS: 121)

The words of the priest make clear that the symbolism underlying the ceremony of enrollment is the biblical image of the names of the elect written in the Book of Life (Philippians 4:3). A special litany for the candidates follows their enrollment (BOS: 122f).

On three consecutive Sundays before their baptism, the candidates may traditionally be called forward to kneel for the prayers and blessings of the Church. And both they and their sponsors are prayed for by name in the Prayers of the People (BOS: 124f).

This third stage culminates in the celebration of baptism and eucharist, which marks the movement to a fourth period in which the Church, through the members of the local congregation, assists the new Christians "to experience the fullness of the corporate life of the Church and to gain a deeper understanding of the sacraments" which they have received. For those baptized at the Easter Vigil, the fourth period corresponds to the Fifty Days of Easter (BOS: 113).

Baptism, then, stands as the climax of a process, whether the candidates are children or adults. It is a process which involves not only the clergy, candidates, and their friends, but the entire congregation. It is set in significant parochial liturgies.

The Baptismal Liturgy

The Prayer Book not only expects the baptismal liturgy to involve the entire congregation at a principal Sunday liturgy; it expects that the entire body of clergy will participate as well. The bishop is described as the normal celebrant, who is to preach the Word and preside at both baptism and eucharist (BCP: 298). If the bishop is not present, a priest presides. Deacons do not normally preside at baptism, but they may read the Gospel, fulfill their usual ministries in the baptismal eucharist and assist in the administration of the water (BCP: 307). Lay persons read the lessons. The Prayer Book suggests that baptismal sponsors read the lessons and lead the prayers for the candidates (BCP: 312).

Entering the Baptismal Covenant

After the sponsors present the candidates, the celebrant asks them two sets of three questions. The first set asks the candidates to renounce evil, the second to promise adherence to Christ. The renunciations are as follows:

> Do you renounce Satan and all spiritual forces of wick-
> edness that rebel against God?
>
> Do you renounce the evil powers of this world which
> corrupt and destroy the creatures of God?
>
> Do you renounce all sinful desires that draw you from
> the love of God? (BCP: 302)

To all three questions the candidates (or, if they cannot
speak for themselves, their parents and godparents)
respond, "I renounce them."

These three questions are the traditional renunciations of "the world, the flesh, and the devil," terms that
could be greatly misleading in contemporary English.
First, the candidates renounce cooperation with the cosmic forces of spiritual wickedness which place themselves in rebellion against God. Satan, a Hebrew word
for Adversary, is the biblical and traditional personifica-
tion of these forces. Many people today would rebel at
the idea of belief in a personal devil, but the biblical
images are the best and strongest way to present the
challenge of evil. The notion of a personal Satan is
found in the Book of Job as the Adversary who tempts
Job. Although we also find "Satan" in the New Testament in St. Mark's Gospel (2:12-13) described as the
tempter of Jesus in the wilderness, we are led almost
inevitably to the figure of the "devil" tempting Christ in
the fuller (parallel) accounts of the temptation: in Matthew, Jesus calls the devil Satan (Matthew 4:1-11); in
Luke, the name Satan does not occur (Luke 4:1-13).
The traditional picture of Satan as the leader of a band
of rebel angels in a cosmic conflict is graphically
described in Revelation 12:7-9:

> Now war arose in heaven, Michael and his angels fight-
> ing against the dragon; and the dragon and his angels
> fought, but they were defeated, and there was no longer
> any place for them in heaven. And the great dragon was
> thrown down, that ancient serpent who is called the

Devil and Satan, the deceiver of the whole world—he
was thrown down to the earth, and his angels were
thrown down with him.

This is clearly apocalyptic imagery and we are not
intended to take the details of the story literally, but it
does remind us that the conflict between good and evil
is not waged simply within our own psyches; rather, it is
a cosmic conflict involving the redemption of the world
"by the blood of the Lamb" (Revelation 12:11). What
the candidates for baptism are asked to renounce is
cooperation with all of those "spiritual forces of wickedness" in this world for which we are not responsible but
in which we are caught up. We recognize them as dia-
bolical and stand with Christ against them.

The second question narrows our canvas to "this
world." Those who are baptized are asked to stand
against the forces of corruption and destruction,
whether their victims be our fellow human beings or
other "creatures of God." Christians are not asked to
renounce "the world" in its totality, but only the cor-
rupting and destructive forces in it. The third question
returns us to the interior battleground of ourselves and
our "sinful desires." The older term, "the flesh,"
might lead us to suppose that all of these desires are
carnal, if not sexual, but that is too narrow. Greed and
the thirst for power have probably drawn at least as
many people "away from the love of God" as have glut-
tony and lust.

The second set of questions, balancing the three
renunciations, asks the candidates to "turn to Jesus
Christ and accept him as your Savior, . . . put your
whole trust in his grace and love . . . [and] promise to
follow and obey him as your Lord" (BCP: 203f). The
English expression "turn to" translates the Latin "con-
vertere," from which we derive the word "convert."
Turning to Jesus Christ is an activity of heart, soul and

mind. It is changing sides in the cosmic struggle. In the ancient Church, candidates actually turned around to face the east when they responded to this question, symbolizing their inward and spiritual conversion by their visible turning.

Once the candidates have responded to both sets of questions, they are ready to enter the baptismal covenant. But first the celebrant asks us, the congregation: "Will you who witness these vows do all in your power to support *these persons* in *their* life in Christ?" (BCP: 303). *Our* witness is of great import, because the initiation of new members is the concern of the *entire assembly.* We must be the supportive community in which the newly baptized will develop as members of the Body of Christ, the Church.

To emphasize the ecclesial nature of the sacrament, the Baptismal Covenant is renewed by all the baptized Christians who are present. They join with those being baptized in reciting the Apostles' Creed and in responding to the Covenant's other questions (BCP: 303-5). Originally the baptismal promises were made while the candidates stood in the water. They were asked three questions, an interrogative form of the creed, and as they responded to each question with "I believe," they were immersed.[5] The Prayer Book follows the universal custom of later rites by asking the questions of all assembled first, and then the candidates are baptized with the Matthean formula naming the three persons of the Trinity.

The manner in which the Apostles' Creed is used in the rite does not so much imply that the Apostles' Creed has been inserted into the baptismal liturgy as that the creed developed out of the baptismal covenant. In the Prayer Book rite, the assembled people respond to the first three questions of the covenant by reciting the three paragraphs of the Apostles' Creed. What does it mean to be baptized "in the Name of the Father, and of the Son, and of the Holy Spirit?" It certainly means more than having that formula recited over the newly baptized. The baptismal *symbolum*, or creed, has been—and continues to be—the traditional expression of the faith in the Father, Son and Holy Spirit into which the candidates are baptized. The Church has called those who recited a different *symbolum* heretics, for quite literally they had a different baptism, because they baptized into a different faith. The baptismal creed, then, is the Church's primary liturgical statement of faith in the Triune God into which Christians are baptized.

Since the fourth century the content of the creed has provided the topic headings for the instruction of candidates for baptism; thus, that content is itself a syllabus for a secondary theology. Thorough discussion of the content of the baptismal creed could fill several volumes, and frequently has. What is important for this study is to note that the creed is a statement intended to proclaim the faith into which Christians are baptized. It is a very selective statement. It contains no mention of the sacraments, for they were not a part of the ancient baptismal catechesis, but rather formed the content of the mystagogical catechesis given to the newly baptized in the days and weeks following their baptism.[6] Neither does the statement mention the Scripture, which had been the basis of the earlier portion of the baptismal catechesis. What then are the topics included in the statement? They deserve some mention.

The first paragraph of the creed affirms belief in God as omnipotent Father and creator of all that is. The second affirms belief in Jesus as Messiah, or Christ, and declares that he is Lord and "only Son" of God. The Christological controversies of the fourth and fifth centuries, and many since, were waged over the precise interpretation of these words, which the more technical language of the Nicene Creed was intended to clarify. At the very least, these words mean that Jesus the Lord is a proper recipient of the prayers of Christians, and that he is not a deity separate from the Father of the previous paragraph.

The creed gives no account of the ministry of Jesus, but it does provide a narrative of the saving acts of God in Christ: his conception "by the power of the Holy Spirit," his birth to the Virgin Mary, his suffering, death, resurrection, ascension, exaltation to the place of honor "at the right hand of the Father" and his coming again. With the exception of the Virgin birth, these are the elements of the apostolic preaching. The Davidic descent and divine origin of Jesus are clearly a part of the New Testament narrative and were quite prominent in the writings of the apostolic fathers.[7] Ignatius of Antioch, for example, writes:

> For our God Jesus Christ was conceived by Mary according to God's plan, of the seed of David and of the Holy spirit; Who was born and baptized that by His passion He might cleanse water.

The creed's third paragraph yokes the belief in the Holy Spirit with the holy catholic Church, the principal sphere of the Spirit's activity. In baptism we receive the Spirit. Baptism makes us members of the Church, unites us with one another in a fellowship of saints or holy communion, forgives our sins and gives us resurrection and life. The creed states simply the faith into which the Christian is baptized, keeping closely to the Scripture and the apostolic preaching. The creed is not intended to be a systematic theology but an expression of baptismal faith.

Five questions framed by the drafting committee for the present Prayer Book follow the traditional recitation of the creed. The questions are intended to spell out the most important implications of living the baptismal life in our time and place. The first question is based on Acts 2:43, which describes the manner of life of the first Christian converts who were baptized in response to the preaching of Peter on the day of Pente-cost. The second asks that the baptized persevere in resisting evil and repent and return to the Lord when-ever they fall into sin. It recognizes that the baptized are not perfected and that they will fall again into sin. However, it holds out to them the promise of forgive-ness if they repent and return to the Lord. The third question asks Christians to witness to God in Christ by word and example. The duty to proclaim the Good News to others has always been a part of the baptismal life. It is the mission on which Christians are sent, and it is here articulated both for the candidates for baptism and for those renewing their baptismal vows. The fourth and fifth questions deal with the social implica-tions of baptism: seeking and serving Christ in all per-sons, loving neighbor as self, striving for justice and peace and respecting the dignity of every human being. Baptism is not a private religious activity without impli-cations for life in the world. The baptismal covenant commits Christians to living out their baptism in their daily lives.

The questions and answers of the covenant lay the basis for living the baptismal life, and baptized Chris-tians renew their commitment to this life whenever they participate in a baptism and join in these promises. In fact, whenever they say the creed, whether at the eucha-rist, in the Daily Offices or in private prayer, Christians renew the commitment of their baptism.

The making of the baptismal promises, which might be considered either as the marriage vows of the believ-ers' spiritual marriage to the Lamb or as the ordination vows of the priesthood of all believers, completes the preparation of the candidates for the reception of the sacrament. Congregational prayer for the candidates in the form of a litany forms a transition to the action at

the font (BCP: 305f). The petitions of the litany enu-
merate the benefits which the Church asks for those
about to be baptized: to deliver them from sin and
death; to open their hearts to God's grace and truth; to
fill them with the Holy Spirit who will keep them in the
faith and communion of the Church, teach them to love
others, send them into the world as witnesses to the love
of Christ, and fill them with peace and glory. The final
collect of the litany prays that all who are baptized into
Christ's death may live in the power of his resurrection
and await his coming again in glory. The collect sets
baptism once again in the context of the resurrection
and the eschatological hope of Christians.

The Thanksgiving
over the Water

The principal prayer of the baptismal liturgy is the
Thanksgiving over the Water. Like the Great
Thanksgiving at the eucharist, it is the Church's formal
proclamation before God of what it is about. It is proclaimed by the celebrant as leader of the congregation,
who are invited to join in it through the bidding "Let us
give thanks to the Lord our God" (BCP: 306).[8]

The prayer begins by thanking God for the gift of
water, using scriptural allusions to the Spirit moving
over the water at creation (Genesis 1:2) and Israel passing through it in the Exodus (Exodus 14:22), both of
which accounts are read at the Great Vigil.[9] The prayer
then turns to the New Testament and mentions the
baptism of Jesus in the Jordan and his anointing with
the Spirit "to lead us, through his death and resurrection, from the bondage of sin into everlasting life." The
reference is, of course to the synoptic accounts of the
baptism of Christ in which the Holy Spirit is seen to
descend upon him, which descent, in turn, is described
in Acts 10:38 and elsewhere as an anointing. The early

Church used the Gospel account (Mark 1:9-11) as a model for its baptismal liturgies: as Jesus went down into the water of Jordan, so the Christian goes down into the water of the font; as when Jesus came up from the water, the Holy Spirit descended upon him, so the Christian comes up from the water of baptism and is sealed with the Holy Spirit; as the voice of the Father proclaimed Jesus his Son, so, too, is the Christian proclaimed to be the child of God by adoption and grace.

The second paragraph of the Thanksgiving over the Water is more explicit. It says that in baptism we are buried with Christ in his death and share in his resurrection (see Romans 6:4-5; Colossians 2:12). Through the water of baptism we are reborn by the Holy Spirit (John 3:5) and sent in express obedience to the great commission of Matthew 28:19 to bring others into the Christian fellowship. Thus the prayer sets forth participation in Christ's death and resurrection, new birth in the Holy Spirit (or baptismal regeneration), and commissioning to preach the Good News to the world as the effects of the sacrament.

The third paragraph invokes the Holy Spirit to sanctify the water, speaks of the baptized as "cleansed from sin and born again" and prays that they may continue for ever in the risen life. The most important teachings of the Church concerning baptism are set forth in this prayer. "Reborn" is used instead of the Latinate "regenerate," but the meaning is the same. The phrase "born again," so dear to the hearts of Evangelicals, makes it clear that this is what the Church believes happens in the Paschal sacraments. Birth, death and rebirth or resurrection are the great events celebrated in the Paschal Mystery, in baptism, and in the eucharist. The salvation won for all by Christ in his death and resurrection is made available to each individual believer in the sacraments. Once for all in baptism, and week by week in the eucharist, the Christian is united with Christ in the power of his dying and rising. This we call the Paschal Mystery.

The structure of the Thanksgiving over the Water is deliberately parallel to that of the Great Thanksgiving at the eucharist. It begins with thanksgiving for creation and redemption, includes the Great Commission as its "institution narrative," continues with specific reference to our present action, invokes the Holy Spirit to sanctify the baptismal water and concludes with a doxology. The structure is not artificial. The Church has traditionally used the *eucharistia* form for its most important prayers of blessing. The prayer also is placed at the focal point of the baptismal liturgy, between the entrace into the baptismal covenant and the sacramental washing.

The Consecration
of the Chrism

The prayer for the consecration of chrism (BCP: 307) is used only when the bishop presides and desires to consecrate the holy oil to be used to sign the cross on the foreheads of the newly baptized. The Prayer Book expects the bishop to consecrate the chrism in the parishes where it will be used at the time of his visitation and leave it in the parishes for the use of the parish priest at other baptisms throughout the year. Only the bishop may consecrate chrism (BCP: 298). The Prayer Book also permits (BCP: 419) the bishop to consecrate chrism for use at baptisms when he makes a confirmation visitation, even if there are no baptisms celebrated at the confirmation. *The Book of Occasional Services* gives further directions for doing the consecration and includes an introductory address which the bishop may read before the consecration prayer. This excellent address, which would be perfectly appropriate when

chrism is consecrated at baptism, summarizes much of
the rationale for baptismal anointing:

> Dear Friends in Christ: In the beginning, the Spirit of
> God hovered over the creation; and, throughout his-
> tory, God, by the gift of the Holy Spirit, has empowered
> his people to serve him. As a sign of that gift, the priests
> and kings of Israel were anointed with oil; and our Lord
> Jesus Christ was himself anointed with the Holy Spirit at
> his baptism as the Christ, God's own Messiah. At Bap-
> tism, Christians are likewise anointed by that same Spirit
> to empower them for God's service. Let us now set
> apart this oil to be the sign of that anointing. (BOS: 210)

In the baptismal rite, the prayer over the oil begins:

> Eternal God, whose blessed Son was anointed by the
> Holy Spirit to be the Savior and servant of all. . . .
> (BCP: 307)

This is a reference to Isaiah 61, the passage read by
Jesus in the synagogue in Nazareth (Luke 4:18f), interpreted in the light of the events of his baptism (Luke
3:21-22). The prayer then refers to the general fact
that Christ, or Messiah, means "Anointed":

> . . . we pray you to consecrate this oil, that those who
> are sealed with it may share in the royal priesthood of
> Jesus Christ. . . .

In the Old Testament only kings and priests were
anointed. Christians from the earliest centuries interpreted their baptismal anointing both in the light of the
Old Testament anointings and in the light of 1 Peter 2:9
and 1 John 2:20:

> You are a chosen race, a royal priesthood, a holy nation,
> God's own people, that you may declare the wonderful
> deeds of him who called you out of darkness into his
> marvelous light. (1 Peter 2:9)

> You have been anointed by the Holy One. (1 John 2:20)

The word "chrism" is from the Greek word for anointing and is cognate with "Christ." Chrism is the Western name for the oil which the Greeks call *myron*, a compound of olive oil and aromatic spices traditionally referred to as "balsam." We do not know exactly how old the anointing with chrism at baptism is. It may well go back to New Testament times, but it was certainly well established by the end of the second century.[10] One writer of that period, Theophilus of Antioch, wrote:

> We are called Christians because we are anointed with the chrism of God. (*Apologia ad Autolycum* 1.12)

The anointing with chrism was a part of the baptismal rite of the First Prayer Book of 1549, but disappeared from Anglican practice in 1552. It is restored, for optional use, in this Prayer Book and in the contemporary rites of other Anglican Churches. It is also an option in the rite of *The Lutheran Book of Worship*.

The use by priests of episcopally consecrated chrism has always been seen as binding the presbyter who presides at a baptism to the bishop. The bishop, as chief priest and pastor of the local church, is the normative chief celebrant of both baptism and eucharist (BCP: 298). When the presbyter replaces him in this role, the use of chrism which the bishop has consecrated signifies that the presiding priest is acting with the consent of and in communion with the bishop who both consecrated the chrism and delivered it to the presbyter to use at baptism.

The Book of Occasional Services also provides a set of propers for use *"if there is a need to consecrate Chrism at a separate, diocesan service"* (BOS: 211), as has been the custom in many dioceses.

The Baptism

The blessing of the water and chrism leads directly to the baptism itself. *"Each candidate is presented by name to*

*the Celebrant, or to an assisting priest or deacon, who then
immerses, or pours water upon, the candidate"* (BCP: 307).
The naming of the newly baptized has always been an
important part of the baptism of infants. In the case of
adults,

> Admission to the catechumenate is an appropriate time
> to determine the name by which one desires to be
> known in the Christian community. This may be one's
> given name, a new name legally changed, or an addi-
> tional name of Christian significance. (BOS: 113)

At their admission to the catechumenate, the cross is
traced on the foreheads of the adults. Later, at their
enrollment, the adult catechumens write their names in
the register. In the case of both infants and adults,
sponsors present the candidates by name to the celebrant before their examination (BCP: 303) and again at
the font for baptism. The rite does not suggest that the
unbaptized are somehow nameless, but it does imply
that the given name of the candidate becomes his or her
Christian name within the context of Christian
initiation.[11]

Although the bishop, or in his absence the parish
priest, is assumed to be the celebrant of baptism (BCP:
298), the actual baptismal washing may be performed
by "an assisting priest or deacon." This practice is analogous to the tradition at the eucharist, where the presiding bishop or priest proclaims the eucharistic prayer but
other ministers assist in distributing communion. Pas-
torally, the bishop might wish the local pastor to perform the baptismal action; or practically, if there are a
large number of candidates, several ministers might
baptize simultaneously.

The number of Episcopal Churches which actually
baptize by immersion is probably quite small, but the
Prayer Book has always named immersion as the pre-
ferred method of baptism, with pouring water upon the

candidate as an alternative. We do not accept the position of those who contend that full immersion in the water is necessary for baptism, but immersion certainly enhances the symbolism of the water by making it much clearer what is happening. We *go down* into the water and are buried with Christ, we *come up* out of the water and are raised to newness of life in him. The same concern for the fullness of the sacramental sign expressed in the desire to use one loaf of bread and one cup of red wine for the eucharist finds baptismal immersion preferable to pouring.

The baptismal formula, based on Matthew 28:19, is intended to state in brief compass the meaning of the sacrament. Its use during baptism is first recorded in the 4th-century baptismal homilies of St. John Chrysostom and was apparently intended to shorten the service by permitting the candidates to respond to the creedal questions of the baptismal covenant all together before the baptism instead of individually as they stood in the water.[12] In the Eastern churches the form is normally "N. is baptized. . . ," while the Western churches use the active "I baptize you. . . ." The passive form may perhaps make it clearer that it is God who acts in the sacrament, while the active form stresses the ministerial role of the baptizing minister. No matter the formula, it is through the words and actions of the minister that God acts in the sacraments, and Eastern and Western theology have usually arrived at the same conclusion through different linguistic approaches.[13]

A lighted candle may be given to each of the newly baptized after the baptism (BCP: 313). The suggestion that it be lighted from the Paschal Candle reinforces the symbolism of rite. The lighted candle is explanatory in nature, calling attention to one aspect of what happens in baptism: we come to participate in the light of the risen Christ that now shines in our hearts. The Prayer Book does not suggest that this ceremony is a necessary

part of baptism, but it is both ancient and commonly
done. Neither does the Prayer Book mention the even
more traditional and widespread practice of clothing
the newly baptized in white robes, which symbolizes
forgiveness of sin and newness of life. The Drafting
Committee, at least, did not intend to abolish this custom but merely to avoid raising it to the status of a
recommended ceremony which might deflect attention
from the consignation and chrismation.

Consignation

When all the candidates have been baptized, the bishop
or celebrating priest *"at a place in full sight of the congregation"* prays over the newly baptized, asking the sevenfold gifts of the Holy Spirit (BCP: 308). The prayer
gives thanks that God has forgiven the sins of the newly
baptized and has raised them to the new life of grace
"by water and the Holy Spirit," prays that God will
sustain them in the Holy Spirit and asks for God's gifts:

> Give *them* an inquiring and discerning heart, the cour-
> age to will and to persevere, a spirit to know and to love
> you, and the gift of joy and wonder in all your works.

At the conclusion of the prayer *"the Bishop or Priest
places a hand on the person's head, marking on the forehead
the sign of the cross [using Chrism if desired]."*

The most obvious reading of the prayer and of the
preceding and following rubrics indicates that the baptismal action (immersion or pouring of water) through
which God has forgiven the sins of the candidates and
raised them to new life has now taken place (*"When this
action has taken place for all candidates. . ."*). The prayer
also indicates that through another action about to take
place—the placing of a hand on the head of the newly
baptized and the signing of their foreheads with the

cross—God will give the gifts of the Spirit to the neo-phytes. The two actions (water and consignation), how-ever, are closely connected and may equally well be considered to be two parts of a single action. One theo-logical expression of this view is that of St. Isidore of Seville: "These are sacraments: baptism and chrism, body and blood" (*Etymologium Libri* VI:39). Thus, St. Isidore names both the baptismal washing and the anointing as sacramental acts, analogous to the two parts of the sacrament of the eucharist.

The prayer for the gifts of the Spirit appeared in the Order for Confirmation in previous editions of the *Book of Common Prayer*, where it immediately preceded the imposition of the bishop's hand.[14] The prayer itself is found in the classic Latin sacramentaries to be used by the bishop after the baptismal washing.[15] The medieval separation of baptism and confirmation obscured the relationship of confirmation to baptism. Confirmation's direct association with the baptismal washing is one of the principal, theologically significant changes made by the 1979 *Book of Common Prayer*. Price and Weil in *Liturgy for Living*, the volume on the liturgy in the semi-official Church's Teaching Series, speak of "the divided Anglican tradition about confirmation" and offer two interpretations of the rite.[16] The first, which they them-selves hold, seems more obviously to come out of the liturgy itself:[17]

> One notices that the prayer for the sevenfold gifts of the Spirit, a formula for the laying on of hands by the cele-brant, and a welcome into the church have been added at the baptismal rite, after the water rite. The material is a slightly modified form of the old confirmation ser-vice, which earlier Anglican Prayer Books reserved to the bishop. One might conclude that baptism has been restored to the full form which it had in Hippolytus, and which it still has in the Eastern Orthodox liturgies. . . .

On this showing, our rite of initiation has been reunited
after its millennium-long fragmentation.[18]

The second interpretation given by Price and Weil
seeks to interpret the rite as "not significantly different
from that of prior Anglican Prayer Books":

> There is a service of baptism with water. In the new
> book this service concludes with laying on of hands and
> possible anointing by a presbyter, or even by a bishop if
> present. But from the earliest times there has been a
> concluding ceremony after the water baptism *and before
> the candidate comes to the bishop for the conclusion of the
> service.* One may interpret the end of the baptismal rite
> in the new book as corresponding to the anointing with
> the oil of thanksgiving by the presbyter in Hippolytus.[19]

It is the expressed intention of the Prayer Book that
its baptismal rite be "full initation by water and the
Holy Spirit" (BCP: 298). The fullness of the initiatory
rite has been seen from very early times to include more
than simply the water rite. The Faith and Order Commission of the World Council of Churches in its Lima
document *Baptism, Eucharist, and Ministry,* for example,
writes:

> Within any comprehensive order of baptism at least the
> following elements should find a place: the proclama-
> tion of the scriptures referring to baptism; an invocation
> of the Holy Spirit; a renunciation of evil; a profession of
> faith in Christ and the Holy Trinity; the use of water; a
> declaration that the persons baptized have acquired a
> new identity as sons and daughters of God, and as mem-
> bers of the Church, called to be witnesses of the Gospel.
> Some Churches consider that Christian initiation is not
> complete without the sealing of the baptized with the
> gift of the Holy Spirit and participation in holy
> communion.[20]

All of these elements are a part of the rite of Holy
Baptism in the 1979 *Book of Common Prayer.* Thus, Holy

Baptism can claim to be a complete rite of Christian initiation. Whether or not the post-baptismal consignation is a necessary part of the complete rite of baptism, it is certainly a normative part of the rite and has been since the second century. Baptismal anointing was a part of the rite of the 1549 Prayer Book, and the signing with the cross has been specifically included in all Prayer Books since 1552. Some consider the anointing and signing to be explanatory ceremonies—like the giving of a lighted candle—which illuminate the meaning of what is done in baptism. Others see them as a separate sacramental act by which the Holy Spirit comes to dwell in the newly baptized. The Prayer Book does not attempt to settle this question, but by including both washing and consignation in its baptismal rite the Episcopal Church has produced a rite which all Christians should be able to regard as containing all things necessary for the celebration of the sacrament of Christian initiation.

I believe that the first explanation of the meaning of confirmation offered by Price and Weil is the most natural understanding of the Prayer Book liturgy, and one which places the liturgy in the *Book of Common Prayer* in the great tradition of the patristic Church. The authors' second explanation, I believe, results from what I have called "an attempt to read theological meaning into rather than out of the Prayer Book."[21] Specifically, it views the rites of the *Book of Common Prayer* in the light of Latin Medieval theology which was attempting to find meaning in separated rites of baptism and confirmation. It is undoubtedly a theology which was held by many in the Church of England at the time of the Reformation and continues to be held by many Episcopalians today. However, Marion Hatchett has demonstrated that such was not the theology Cranmer sought to embody in the First and Second Prayer Books of Edward VI, nor is it the most obvious interpretation of the rites of either the 1928 or 1979 *Book of Common Prayer.*[22]

The formula provided for the bishop or priest to use while marking the sign of the cross on the foreheads of the newly baptized—the action called consignation—makes it clear that what is being done is intimately related to baptism and is in fact a part of the baptismal rite:

> N., you are sealed by the Holy Spirit in Baptism and marked as Christ's own forever. (BCP: 308)

The signing with the cross is clearly related to the sealing of the servants of the living God upon the forehead in Revelation 3:7. However, it is impossible to tell if Revelation is describing an existing liturgical practice or if the practice is derived from the biblical account.[23] G.W.H. Lampe, in his monumental study *The Seal of the Spirit* (London: Longmans, Green and Co., 1951), p. 307, says,

> In the New Testament the "seal" is the inward mark or stamp of the indwelling Spirit of God which is received by the convert who is justified by faith in Christ and through baptism is sacramentally made a partaker of Him in His death and resurrection.

The patristic writers tend to identify "the seal" with the consignation: the Good Shepherd places his seal on his own sheep; the King of kings seals his servants with the royal signet; the elect are sealed on the forehead unto the day of redemption; the devil will see the cross shining on the foreheads of the baptized and will have to turn away his eyes. These are the images by which the fathers explain the seal of the cross.

The Prayer Book uses the verb "seal" at the consignation but does not actually identify the "seal" with that consignation. The "seal" is given in baptism, but whether it is the inward grace of the baptismal washing, as Lampe interprets the New Testament, or the consignation itself, as the fathers thought, is left undetermined. Academic theologians may continue to discuss the question, but advocates of both sides acknowledge that in baptism we are sealed by the Holy Spirit.

Chrismation

The Prayer Book permits, but does not require, the use of chrism to mark the cross. Many of the fathers describe chrism simply as the "paint" with which the cross is marked on the Christian's forehead, but chrism itself is an important symbol, even apart from the consignation. We have already dealt with the meaning of baptismal anointing in discussing the form for the consecration of the chrism.

Many Episcopalians would be happier if the use of episcopally consecrated chrism for the post-baptismal consignation were required, but it would be most difficult to maintain that the use of chrism at baptism is necessary in the light of the slight evidence for its use in the New Testament and the obvious fact that it has not been a part of the official Anglican liturgy for four hundred years. Other Episcopalians, finding no clear warrant for the use of chrism at baptism in the New Testament and no continuous tradition of its use in the Anglican Church, prefer not to introduce it.

Participation in the Eucharistic Assembly

When all have been baptized and signed, they are welcomed into the congregation and begin to function as members of the Church. Celebrant and people say together:

> We receive you into the household of God. Confess the
> faith of Christ crucified, proclaim his resurrection, and
> share with us in his eternal priesthood. (BCP: 308)

This verbal welcome is accompanied by the ritual
action of the exchange of the peace. In this exchange
the newly baptized are greeted as brothers and sisters in
Christ, and they, in turn, so greet the other members of
the congregation. As members of the Church they take
their places as participants in the eucharistic assembly.
This may be ritualized by their presenting the eucharistic oblations of bread and wine (BCP: 313).

The participation by the newly baptized in the celebration of the eucharist is historically and theologically
the climax and completion of the rite of baptism, and
the Prayer Book expects that the eucharist will normally
form the concluding act of the liturgy of Christian initiation. The permission to omit it is exceptional and seriously truncates the rite. The eucharist is, in one sense,
the final repeatable act of the sacrament of Christian
initiation. The bond established between the Christian
and the dying and rising Christ in baptism is renewed
week after week by Christians' common participation in
the eucharist and communion with one another in the
Body of Christ. Conversely, the interrelation of baptism
and eucharist and their coinherence in the Paschal Mystery are obscured unless those who are baptized participate in the eucharist and receive communion.

The Prayer Book remains silent on the subject of the
reception of communion by the newly baptized. A
rubric on the subject disappeared from the 1975 version of the rite before its inclusion in the Prayer Book.[24]
There is no doubt that every baptized adult (including
the newly baptized) should receive communion at the
baptismal eucharist, and in many places it is increasingly
recognized that the theological connection of the two
sacraments should be expressed by communicating all

of the baptized, regardless of age. There are no theological reasons why baptized Christians who are not excommunicate (BCP: 409) should be forbidden to receive communion, and there are many good theological reasons why they should be encouraged to do so.

Infant communion was practiced in the Western Church from the earliest times until the 13th century, and it remains the practice of the Eastern Church. The objections often raised today against infant communion are really objections to infant baptism. Our principal, and by no means insignificant, difficulty is that we have become accustomed to a different practice, one which has developed a supporting rationale over seven centuries. We need to consider as a Church the serious question of the theological and pastoral statement which we make in excluding children from the eucharist but not baptism, while solemnly declaring that both are "necessary for all persons" (BCP: 860). There is, of course, no suggestion in the Book of Common Prayer that not all baptized persons should receive communion. Much of the confusion is caused by the fact that the Episcopal Church formerly forbade the reception of communion by the unconfirmed (BCP 1928: 299). This regulation in the Church of England goes back to John Peckham, a reform-minded 13th-century Archbishop of Canterbury who wished to encourage his bishops to do more confirming, a practice they were neglecting. He hoped that by forbidding communion before confirmation he would put pressure on both bishops and parents to bring children to confirmation.[25] Although the regulation has been freqently so used in subsequent centuries, its purpose was neither to exclude Protestants (of whom there were none in the 13th century) nor children (since confirmation was then generally administered to infants). The requirement was abandoned by the Episcopal Church in 1970.[26]

Confirmation

The Prayer Book provides both in the baptismal rite (BCP: 303, 309f) and in a separate service printed among the Pastoral Offices (BCP: 412-19) for confirmation, reception and reaffirmation of baptismal vows by persons who have been previously baptized. The baptismal rite celebrated by the bishop at the time of his parochial visitation is the primary *locus* for confirmation. The presentation of the candidates for confirmation takes place after the presentation of the baptismal candidates (BCP: 303), and the confirmation itself follows the verbal welcome of the newly baptized and precedes the peace (BCP: 308-10).

The separate service (BCP: 412-19) is included for the pastoral convenience of participants on those many occasions at which no baptisms are to be celebrated. It contains no material not found in the baptismal rite, except in the opening and closing rubrics. Most of these rubrics deal strictly with ceremonial matters, but the first two under the heading "Concerning the Service" state the Episcopal Church's understanding of the use of confirmation. The first is:

> In the course of their Christian development, those baptized at an early age are expected, when they are ready and have been duly prepared, to make a mature public affirmation of their faith and commitment to the responsibilities of their Baptism and to receive the laying on of hands by the bishop. (BCP: 412)

This rubric describes confirmation as "a mature public affirmation" of baptismal faith and commitment and the reception of episcopal laying on of hands. Thus, the rite that follows is designed to be just that. It gives no suggestion that confirmation is the completion of baptism. In fact, that possibility is excluded by the opening rubric of the baptismal rite which declares baptism to be "full initiation by water and the Holy Spirit" (BCP:

298). The meaning of confirmation is further expli-
cated in the prayer said by the bishop following the
renewal of baptismal vows (and the baptismal washing
and consignation) and before the laying on of hands:

> Almighty God, we thank you that by the death and
> resurrection of your Son Jesus Christ you have over-
> come sin and brought us to yourself, and that by the
> sealing of your Holy Spirit you have bound us to your
> service. (BCP: 309)

This first sentence of the prayer refers to what has
already happened in baptism: forgiveness of sins, sealing with the Spirit, binding to God's service. Since sealing with the Spirit and commissioning for Christian
service have sometimes been put forward as effects of
confirmation, it is important to note that in the Prayer
Book these are parts of baptism.[27] The prayer
continues:

> Renew in *these* your *servants* the covenant you made with
> *them* at *their* Baptism. Send *them* forth in the power of
> that Spirit to perform the service you set before
> *them*. . . . (BCP: 309)

Confirmation is the renewal of the baptismal covenant, not its completion. Confirmands affirm their baptismal commitment, and God renews the covenant and
empowers them with the Holy Spirit to fulfill their baptismal promises and live the baptismal life to which they
are committed. The Prayer Book provides two alternative formulas to accompany the laying on of hands. One
has been in every Anglican Prayer Book since 1552.
The other was newly drafted by the late Urban T.
Holmes:

> Strengthen, O Lord, your servant N. with your Holy
> Spirit; empower *him* for your service; and sustain *him* all
> the days of *his* life. (BCP: 309)

The traditional form speaks of a "daily increase in your Holy Spirit more and more, until *he* comes to your everlasting kingdom" (BCP: 309). Neither speaks of a specific outpouring of the Holy Spirit at the moment of confirmation, and both speak of an ongoing sustenance and strengthening or defense by the Spirit.

For those baptized at an early age, this is a significant event. They did not make the baptismal promises themselves, and confirmation provides a public opportunity for them to own their baptismal faith by making an adult commitment in the presence of the bishop and to receive, through the laying on of the bishop's hand, the renewal of the power of the Holy Spirit in their lives.

The "Statement of Agreed Positions . . . Concerning a post-baptismal Affirmation of Vows" prepared by an ad hoc committee following a joint meeting of the Standing Liturgical Commission and the Theological and Prayer Book Committees of the House of Bishops provides a valuable background for understanding what the Prayer Book is saying about confirmation. This statement is preceded by "Agreed Positions" concerning baptism, the first of which is "There is one, and only one, unrepeatable act of Christian initiation, which makes a person a member of the body of Christ" (PBS 26:3). The most significant positions for our purpose are these:

> 1. An act and occasion for (more or less) mature personal acceptance of promises and affirmations made on one's behalf in infancy is pastorally and spiritually desirable.
> 2. Such an act and occasion must be voluntary: but it should be strongly encouraged as a normal component of Christian nurture, and not merely made available.
> 3. It is both appropriate and pastorally desirable that the affirmations should be received by a Bishop as representing the Diocese and the world-wide Church; and that the Bishop should recall the applicants to their

Christian mission, and, by a laying-on-of-hands, transmit his blessing, with a prayer for the strengthening graces.

4. The rite embodying the affirmations should in no sense be understood as being a "completion of Holy Baptism," nor as being a condition precedent to admission to the Holy Communion, nor as conveying a special status of Church membership.

5. The occasion of the affirming of baptismal vows and obligations that were made by parents and godparents on one's behalf in infancy is a significant and unrepeatable event. It is one's "Confirmation Day."

6. The rite, however, is suitable, and should be available on other occasions in the lives of Christian people. For example, (1) when a person who has been baptized in some other fellowship of Christians wishes to become a member of The Episcopal Church, it is desirable and appropriate that this person be presented to the Bishop, as representing the world-wide episcopate, and that the new relationship be blessed with the laying-on-of-hands and a recommissioning to Christian service; and (2) when a person whose practice of the Christian life has become perfunctory, or has completely lapsed, awakens again to the call of Christ and desires to signalize his response publicly, and to receive the strengthening gifts of the Spirit for renewal. (PBS 26: 4f)

In publishing these statements, the Standing Liturgical Commission commented, "It is hoped that this statement of agreed positions will make clear what the rites are designed to do" (PBS 26:5). The commission also published a *Supplement to Prayer Book Studies 26* "under the signature of its principal author, the Rev. Dr. Daniel Stevick," as a detailed commentary on the rites then proposed. The rites appearing in the *Book of Common Prayer* are revised versions of those proposed in *Prayer Book Studies 26*, but they do what the statement of agreed positions said they intended to do—in some ways more clearly than the earlier proposals—and both the agreed principles and the commentary remain valuable resources for those who wish to understand what those who drafted and proposed the rite understood it to mean. We need to beware, however, of confusing the intentions of the drafters with the *lex orandi,* the theology which the liturgy itself proclaims.

The opening rubric of the confirmation rite clearly does teach that those baptized in infancy are "expected" to be confirmed. The rite is not simply made available. Readiness and due preparation are required, but no interpretation is given of what that involves. No particular age for candidates is suggested, but they must be old enough to make a "mature public affirmation." It is not a "puberty rite" for adolescents but the appropriate liturgical and sacramental act by which a baptized person personally accepts the faith into which he or she has been baptized and renews the promise to live the baptismal life. The promises of the baptismal covenant are renewed before the bishop who lays on hands invoking the power of the Holy Spirit upon the confirmand and renewing the call to Christian mission. Confirmation so understood remedies what might otherwise be considered a pastoral and theological deficiency in infant baptism: the impossibility of the candidates' taking the baptismal covenant personally.

The second opening rubric (BCP: 412) goes beyond the statement of agreed principles and raises new theological and pastoral questions.[28] If baptism is, as the Prayer Book teaches, "full initiation by water and the Holy Spirit" (BCP: 298), it is unclear why an adult who has been baptized by the parish priest after making the promises of the baptismal covenant before the congregation, anointed and signed by the priest with the laying on of hands, and strengthened by the reception of the Body and Blood of Christ in the Holy Eucharist, should be expected to make a second profession of faith before the bishop and receive the laying on of episcopal hands.

The obvious intention of the rubric is to maintain the Anglican practice of having every adult Church member confirmed by the bishop. There is clear pastoral merit in having every Episcopalian come into personal contact with the bishop, and the rubric may be seen as enjoining an "old Anglican custom," but it is difficult to see its theological significance.

One possible theological explanation would be that it is the baptism, not the person, which is being confirmed. This view is not without historical precedent. Its origin lies in the recognition that the bishop is the normative minister of baptism and that when the priest baptizes in his place, it is the bishop's prerogative to "confirm" that action by personally receiving the baptizand's profession of faith and adding an episcopal benediction through the imposition of hands. This theology is not widely held, or even known, in the Episcopal Church, however, and it is more reasonable to assume that the General Convention simply wished to maintain the practice to which the Church was accustomed.

The theology of Christian initiation is most clearly expressed when the bishop presides at the baptism of adults, receives their profession of faith, prays for the gifts of the Holy Spirit, places a hand upon their head, signs them with the cross (using chrism if desired), and ministers to them the Holy Communion (BCP: 298). In such a case, as the rubric recognizes (BCP: 412), there is no further confirmation. If bishops were encouraged to undertake this practice in their cathedrals at the Great Vigil of Easter and throughout the parishes of the diocese at their visitations, it would not only be most impressive for the candidates but would be a significant manifestation to the congregation of the Episcopal Church's theology of baptism, ministry and the Church.

Reception and Reaffirmation

The "Agreed Positions" state that the rite of confirmation is suitable both "when a person baptized in some other fellowship of Christians wishes to become a member of The Episcopal Church" and when one who has lapsed wishes to return to Christian faith and practice (PBS 26:4). Separate formulas are given in the Prayer Book "For Reception" and "For Reaffirmation" (BCP: 310). Although it was the expectation of the statement of agreed principles that the persons taking part would also receive the laying on of hands, the Prayer Book does not specify the ritual gesture to be used, nor does it specify the conditions for the use of its formulas. This permits a diversity of practice, which in fact exists.

The form for reception recognizes that the person being received is already a member of the one, holy, catholic and apostolic Church, and it receives the baptized Christian "into the fellowship of this Communion" with a Trinitarian blessing (BCP: 418). The previous baptism and church membership of the person is clearly recognized, and there is no demand that former allegiances be renounced or denied. The bishop, as representative of the world-wide episcopate and the Episcopal Church, accepts jurisdiction over the person baptized in another communion and brings that person into communion with the bishop. The imposition of hands is the traditional and appropriate gesture for the bishop to use when receiving or restoring people to this communion and fellowship. The right hand of fellowship is an appropriate gesture to welcome the newly baptized or to greet the confirmands at the peace, but it does not have the sacramental or sacerdotal significance of the imposition of hands.[29] The final prayer said by the bishop after confirmation, reception and reaffirmation asks that the "fatherly hand" of God may be over those who have received the rite, and the Holy Spirit

ever with them (BCP: 319). This makes it even more
obvious that the ritual act to accompany the blessing of
the Church on those entering this communion should
be the imposition of hands.

The formula for reaffirmation asks that the Holy
Spirit, "who has begun a good work in you, may direct
and uphold you in the service of Christ and his kingdom" (BCP: 310). It is difficult to see what the theological difference is between this and the formula for
confirmation. The late Dean Holmes called this distinction "the argument from subjective intentionality" and
argued:

> The insistence that we must distinguish Confirmation
> and subsequent reaffirmation is more the result of our
> own inherited tradition coloring our thought than any-
> thing that can be supported by the data.[30]

Holmes may well be right that we have made a distinction without a difference, but the distinction is
nonetheless real in our inherited tradition. We have
already seen that Price and Weil recognize two distinct
interpretations of the initiation rites of the Prayer
Book, and our understanding of both reception and
reaffirmation will, to a large extent, depend on which
interpretation we follow. Price and Weil, and I, prefer
the following version:

> These [reception and reaffirmation] are coordinate ele-
> ments of the new service of confirmation. Thus, the
> strengthening gifts of God's grace are available also
> when a person joins the Episcopal family or when bap-
> tized and confirmed Episcopalians especially need the
> power of the Spirit at a time of particular significance in
> their lives.[31]

As has been already stated, I believe that this interpretation is the more obvious explanation of the rites.
It is certainly so if the rites are interpreted in the light of
the 1973 statement of agreed principles. The second

interpretation, which may well be the view of the authors of the second introductory rubric on the confirmation of those who are baptized as adults, sees the situation in a quite different light:

> The rite of confirmation appears in the new book as it has for a thousand years in the Catholic churches of Western Christendom, as the act of the bishop. . . . The added features of the confirmation service— Reception of new members and Reaffirmation of Baptismal Vows—are indeed useful liturgical expressions of the continued availability of the Spirit, but they are not coordinate with confirmation. New Episcopalians would be confirmed unless they come from the Roman Catholic or Orthodox churches, in which case they should be *received*. Episcopalians may *reaffirm their baptismal vows*. Confirmation is always signified by the laying on of hands. In the other two cases, other gestures could be used.[32]

If this interpretation of the rites is followed, Holmes is wrong and there is a substantial theological difference between confirmation and reaffirmation. Yet the differences between these two views is no greater than other differences of opinion among Anglican theologians throughout the years. Both are secondary theological expositions of the primary theology of the liturgy itself, the *lex orandi*.[33]

There is no way we can be certain of the motives of all of those who prepared or voted to adopt the rite of the *Book of Common Prayer*, nor is there any reason why we should attempt to discover "the mind of the Church" in this manner. Liturgical rites may be proposed by committees of experts and authorized by General Convention, but it is only in their use by Christian congregations, as they are chewed and digested by the Church and by individual worshiping Christians and become a part of their way of praying and believing, that they become true liturgy, the *lex orandi* which establishes the *lex credendi.* When this has had time to happen, we shall be better able to explain the theology of confirmation in the Episcopal Church.

Chapter Six:
The Holy Eucharist

The eucharist is, as we saw in Chapter One, the chief act of Christian worship on the Lord's Day (BCP: 13) and, as we saw in Chapter Five, the climax and conclusion of the sacrament of Christian initiation (BCP: 298). As Gregory Dix wrote in one of the truly great passages in 20th-century liturgical literature:

> At the heart of it all is the eucharistic action, a thing of absolute simplicity—the taking, blessing, breaking and giving of bread and the taking, blessing, and giving of a cup of wine, as these were first done by a young Jew before and after supper with His friends on the night before He died. . . . He had told His friends to do this henceforward with the new meaning for the anamnesis of Him, and they have done it ever since.
>
> . . . week by week and month by month, on a hundred thousand successive Sundays, faithfully, unfailingly, across all the parishes of christendom, the pastors have done this just to *make* the *plebs sancta Dei*—the holy common people of God.[1]

It is in the celebration of the eucharist that the Church most clearly acts as the Body of Christ, the people of God. Like baptism, the eucharist is rooted and grounded in the Paschal Mystery and finds its fullest context in the Great Vigil of Easter. Yet every Lord's Day is the celebration of the resurrection, and it is the Sunday eucharist which gives its paschal character to Sunday, for it is in the eucharist that the Church proclaims and lives out the Paschal Mystery of Jesus' dying and rising again. Easter, the Lord's Day and the celebration of the eucharist are inextricably bound together.

If the eucharist is a manifestation of the nature of the Church, it is best seen when the bishop is the chief celebrant. We are an Episcopal Church, and our bishops are not primarily bureaucrats and administrators but priests and pastors. The first rubric at the beginning of the eucharist, therefore, declares:

> It is the bishop's prerogative, when present, to be the principal celebrant at the Lord's Table, and to preach the Gospel (BCP: 354)

But the eucharist is not the action of one person, not even of the bishop. It is the action of the Body of Christ, Head and members. God in Christ is the principal actor. We all, in our various ministries, play our own parts. The catechism makes it clear that "the ministers of the Church are lay persons, bishops, priests, and deacons" (BCP: 855) and that all have their roles in the eucharist.

When other priests are present, they "stand with the chief celebrant at the Altar, and join in the consecration of the gifts" (BCP: 354). Deacons read the Gospel, lead the prayers of the people and prepare and serve the Lord's table (BCP: 354). Lay persons read the lessons, exchange the peace, receive communion, offer their prayers and gifts, and bring the offerings of bread and wine and money to the altar (BCP: 354, 361). By far the most important role for everyone is to be the celebrant community, the Body of Christ offering "the Church's sacrifice of praise and thanksgiving [as] the way by which the sacrifice of Christ is made present, and in which he unites us to his one offering of himself" (BCP: 859). We who are the Church assemble to do this "in Christ," and he is present and acts in us. We are united with him in the Paschal Mystery of his dying and rising.

This multiplicity of ministers and of liturgical roles is theologically significant, not simply liturgically impressive. It signifies the unity in the Body of Christ of a diversity of gifts and ministries (1 Corinthians 12:4-31; Ephesians 4:4-16). In the past, the eucharist has often appeared to be a "one-man show." A single priest "said mass" or "celebrated Communion," while all others watched and prayed their own prayers. Although this may have been common practice in a variety of both Catholic and Protestant Churches, it fails to present a true picture either of the Church or of the eucharist. Rather, such practice is the icon of a clerically dominated church in which lay people are expected to be passive spectators, or at best active supporters, of hierarchical leadership. In fact, however, the eucharist is the action of the *whole* Church and cannot be usurped by a priest or even by a bishop. People experience the structure of the Church by what they experience when they attend Sunday worship, not from what they read in books of canon law and church polity. The Prayer Book catechism teaches:

> The mission of the Church is to restore all people to unity with God and each other in Christ.

> The Church pursues its mission as it prays and worships, proclaims the Gospel, and promotes justice, peace, and love.

> The Church carries out its mission through the ministry of all its members. (BCP: 855)

If not obscured by the *manner* in which it is celebrated, the Sunday eucharist best expresses these values: the Church assembles in the name and presence of Christ, and the bishop presides surrounded by the presbyters and assisted by deacons and lay people, as the Body of Christ actualizes itself by proclaiming and celebrating the Paschal Mystery. The visual image is that of

Revelation 4, where all join in the worship of God enthroned in glory.

The Structure of the Eucharistic Liturgy

The structure of the eucharist is traditional in the fullest sense of the word. We can trace it back at least to the middle of the second century.[2] It is composed of two interrelated parts which the Prayer Book calls The Word of God (BCP: 355) and The Holy Communion (BCP: 361). The core of the celebration of the Word of God is the reading of Scripture. We have looked extensively at Scripture readings in the context of the Great Vigil, but it is important to recognize that the liturgy of the Word is not simply a preparatory service, but an integral part of the eucharistic celebration. It is in the context of the liturgy of the Word of God that baptism is celebrated, ordinations performed, marriages celebrated and blessed, and God's Word proclaimed to God's people.

It was in connection with the reading of the Gospel that Christians first came to speak of the presence of Christ in the eucharist. Christ is present in the proclamation of the Word. He is present "when two or three are gathered together" in the assembly of the faithful (BCP: 102). Only when we have said this can we speak of Christ's presence in the eucharistic bread and wine. Today everyone stands for the reading of the Gospel (BCP: 357). Members of the early Church carried lights and incense before the Gospel book when it was brought down to the ambo, or reading desk, for the proclamation of the Gospel. For they saw in the book the symbol of the presence of the living Word of God, Jesus Christ, in the midst of the congregation.

It is generally recognized today that Christians should not be required to choose between the hearing of the Word and the celebration of the Sacrament at Sunday worship. Normative Sunday worship involves both in a single service called simply "the Eucharist." The Lima document of the World Council of Churches, for example, affirms:

> The eucharistic liturgy is essentially a single whole. . . . In the celebration of the eucharist, Christ gathers, teaches and nourishes the Church. It is Christ who invites to the meal and who presides at it. He is the shepherd who leads the people of God, the prophet who announces the Word of God, the priest who celebrates the mystery of God. . . . As the eucharist celebrates the resurrection of Christ, it is appropriate that it take place at least every Sunday. As it is the new sacramental meal of the people of God, every Christian should be encouraged to receive communion frequently. (WCC 1982: 15f)

The Prayer Book contains two forms of the Holy Eucharist—as it does of the daily offices—Rite One in traditional language and Rite Two in contemporary language. The structure of the two rites is the same, and we shall use Rite Two as the basis for our discussion. There are no real theological differences between the rites, but there are differences of emphasis, and reference will be made to prayers of Rite One whenever they make theologically significant additions to our discussion.

The Entrance Rite

The celebration of the Word of God actually begins with an entrance rite (BCP: 355f). It is worth noting that many elements of the entrance rite are optional for the celebration of Holy Eucharist. Still, we shall deal with all of these elements, not because they are required for a valid service, but because we are concerned with their *meaning* for the service. The entrance song, for example, whether hymn, psalm or anthem, is more than simply incidental music to cover the entrance of the liturgical ministers. The entrance song has a much deeper meaning: Singing together is a means of involving and unifying the congregation so that it is able to respond corporately, and not as an aggregation of isolated individuals, to the opening acclamation of the chief celebrant.

The collect for purity (BCP: 355) is a preparatory prayer of the priest and people that calls upon God, who knows the condition of our inner beings, to cleanse our hearts "by the inspiration of [the] Holy Spirit, that we may perfectly love [God], and worthily magnify [God's] holy Name." Whether it is better said aloud by the priest or silently by everyone as a personal act of preparation before the beginning of the service, it voices the sentiments with which all should approach the Lord in public worship. Indeed, this prayer has been used for such purpose at the opening of the Anglican eucharist since 1549.

The Sunday eucharist normally continues with a song of praise, such as the *Gloria in excelsis* (BCP: 356). Alternatively, the eucharist moves to a penitential act with a general confession (BCP: 351-3). Like the collect for purity, the general confession is a preparatory action readying the congregation for the eucharistic celebration. Many feel that the general confession should regularly be included in the service at this point. However, its use at this point sets a penitential tone for what follows, just as the use of *Gloria in excelsis* or *Te Deum laudamus* at this point sets a festal tone. A third option, for ordinary occasions, is to follow the collect for purity with either *Kyrie eleison* ("Lord, have mercy") or *Trisagion* ("Holy God, Holy and Mighty"). Both are ancient hymns of praise, but they are less obviously festive than the *Gloria*. Whether the Penitential Order has been

included or not, the singing of the hymn of praise concludes the entrance rite.

The Liturgy of the Word

The ancient greeting "The Lord be with you," again
bringing the people into dialogue with the chief celebrant, begins the central portion of the liturgy of the
Word of God and introduces the collect of the day.
"Collect," from the Latin *collecta,* has become the technical term for a particular prayer structure,[3] but its original meaning is the collecting of the petitions of the
members of the congregation into a single short prayer.
The chief celebrant invites the people to pray and, after
they have done so, "collects" their petitions in the
prayer called the collect. This is most obvious in the
collect recited at the conclusion of the prayers of the
people (BCP: 394f) and in the collect at the end of a
litany; but at the eucharist, too, the invitation "Let us
pray" is issued, and if time is allowed for the people to
offer their own prayers at least briefly (aloud or in
silence), the collect of the day may collect and offer the
petitions of the people.[4]

The collect frequently specifies the occasion being
celebrated, or introduces the theme of the readings
which follow. The Prayer Book provides proper collects for Sundays, holy days, and various other occasions, in both traditional (BCP: 159-210) and
contemporary (BCP: 211-261) language. The content
of some specific collects was discussed in Chapter Two.

The lessons, or readings, are indicated in the Lectionary (BCP: 887-931) and follow a three-year cycle used
also by the Roman Catholic Church, most other
Anglican Churches, and major North American Protestant Churches.[5] For Sundays and major holy days, three
readings are assigned. On weekdays there are usually
only two. The psalm appointed for use between the first

two readings, traditionally called the Gradual because it was led by a cantor from the *gradus* or steps of the ambo, is a part of the scriptural content of the liturgy of the Word, not simply a musical interlude. St. Augustine of Hippo frequently quotes portions of the psalm in his sermons.

The lessons before the Gospel are normally read by lay persons appointed by the celebrant (BCP: 354). The reading of the Scripture in church is a lay ministry which was usurped by the clergy at a period when few lay people were able to read. The Prayer Book does not require the lectors to be licensed lay readers, but simply people who are able to read aloud intelligibly.

The Gospel holds the place of honor as the final reading. It is read by the deacon (BCP: 354), the chief liturgical assistant at the liturgy, from the pulpit or lectern, or from the midst of the congregation (BCP: 406). The Gospel procession, carrying the book to the place where the Gospel will be read, has often been seen as symbolic of the Word coming to the people, and has been accompanied by music, lights, and incense. It is, at least, dramatic, and it calls attention to the Gospel reading and the honor paid to the Gospel as the Word of God. In the same way, standing to hear the Gospel, like standing during the playing of the national anthem, honors the reality behind what is heard: in one case, the nation; in the other, the Lord.

The Sermon

The Gospel reading is immediately followed by the sermon, which is intended to be an exposition of the Gospel that applies the scriptural text to the actual situation of the congregation. The bishop is the primary preacher of the Gospel (BCP: 354), but he may ask other ministers, ordained or lay, to preach. Priests are authorized by their ordination to preach (BCP: 531).

Deacons have usually, though not necessarily, been permitted to preach, and the bishop may license lay readers to preach.

Sermons are not inspirational talks but the breaking open of the Word of God so that God's people may be fed with it.[6] Sermons are not interruptions of the liturgy but integral parts thereof. They are clearly intended to be a part of every Sunday and holy day eucharist, and many suggest that the eucharist should never be celebrated, even for a small group on a weekday, without some exposition of the Word. No rubric requires that a sermon be preached, but "The Sermon" is simply listed a a component part of the service.

No provision is made for a hymn or anything else to come between the Gospel and the sermon which expounds it (BCP: 358). Clergy normally preach in their liturgical vestments to symbolize the formal liturgical nature of the sermon and its intimate relationship to the pastoral ministry. Often sermons begin with a prayer or the invocation "In the Name of the Father, and of the Son, and of the Holy Spirit," although some preachers feel that this usage separates the sermon from the rest of the liturgy and prefer to begin directly.

The Creed

The movement of the first part of the liturgy has been primarily from God to humankind through Christ. The Word is read in the Scripture and proclaimed in the sermon. "Faith," says St. Paul, "comes from what is heard, and what is heard comes by the preaching of Christ" (Romans 10:17). The response of faith is exemplified by the corporate recitation of the Nicene Creed. The creed which is recited at the eucharist is not the baptismal creed, usually called the Apostles' Creed, but the official ecumenical statement of the faith of the universal Church accepted by the Councils of Nicea and

Constantinople in the fourth century (BCP: 852). Its plural form affirms the corporate faith of the Church catholic as it was defined by the ecumenical councils and reminds us that it is into this faith that we were baptized. It is not intended to be a test of individual orthodoxy, but a corporate affirmation of faith and allegiance to the Lord and the Church.

The creed is, nevertheless, the most formal theological statement in the liturgy, which more naturally expresses its theology in the eucharistic prayer. The Nicene Creed, proclaiming in propositional form our most basic beliefs about God (BCP: 851), provides the material for both an historical and a systematic theology.[7] It is based on the ancient baptismal creeds, expanded by the councils to negate the classic Trinitarian and Christological heresies. Its liturgical use on Sunday and major feasts (BCP: 358) is both a sign of the unity of the Church which professes the creed and which now makes eucharist, and a renewal of the baptismal covenant by the assembled congregation as a faith response to the hearing of the Word.

The Prayers of the People

After the creed, or after the sermon on days when the creed is not said, the deacon leads the prayers of the people (BCP: 383). Corporate prayer is itself a most fitting faith response to the proclamation of the Word. An important part of the deacon's ministry is "to serve all people, particularly the poor, the weak, the sick, and the lonely" in the name of Jesus Christ and "to interpret to the Church the needs, concerns, and hopes of the world" (BCP: 543). To lead the prayers of the people is a part of this diaconal ministry. Deacons lead the people of God in praying for those people they have been ordained to serve and for those needs and concerns of the world they are charged to interpret to the Church.

If there is no deacon present to lead the prayers, another person, ordained or lay, engaged in this ministry is the appropriate leader (BCP: 354). The celebrant may introduce the prayers (BCP: 383) and normally concludes them with an appropriate collect (BCP: 394).

The prayers of the people are the principal occasion for the common prayer of the people of God in the eucharistic liturgy. They are, as their name indicates, the people's prayers, and the leader must allow others in the assembly of the people of God, as members one of another in the Body of Christ, to offer their own petitions, intercessions and thanksgivings. The Prayer Book permits the utmost flexibility in the prayers, requiring only that certain basic topics, encompassing the concerns of the Church, the nation and the world, as well as those of the local community, be included (BCP: 383). The use of the litany form makes it possible for the people to respond to any petition offered by the leader which ends with a fixed formula, such as, "Let us pray to the Lord."

General Confession

If the general confession was not used in the Penitential Order at the beginning of the service (BCP: 352), it may form the concluding act of the prayers of the people (BCP: 359f). The confession of sin is an integral part of our common prayers and an important preparation for worship. When it is used in this position in the liturgy, it forms a part of our response to the Word, just as Isaiah's response to God's initiative was the acknowledgment of his sinfulness (see Isaiah 6:5).

The exhortation (BCP: 316f), which "*may be used in whole or in part, either during the Liturgy or at other times,*" is quite explicit about the importance of self-examination and confession as preparation for communion:

> Examine your lives and conduct by the rule of God's commandments, that you may perceive wherein you have offended in what you have done or left undone, whether in thought, word, or deed. And acknowledge your sins before Almighty God, with full purpose of amendment of life, being ready to make restitution for all injuries and wrongs done by you to others; and also being ready to forgive those who have offended you, in order that you yourselves may be forgiven. And then, being reconciled with one another, come to the banquet of that most heavenly Food.

This is the pattern into which the general confession fits. Each Christian is expected to come to the eucharist having made this self-examination and confession to God. The confession of sin in corporate worship is the verbalization of that private, personal confession and the recognition of our participation in the corporate sinfulness of the society of which we are a part. Sin is seldom an individual undertaking, and in the general confession we acknowledge not only our individual sin but our solidarity in corporate sinfulness.

The Litany of Penitence in the Ash Wednesday liturgy (BCP: 267-9) is the fullest statement of our involvement in the web of sin, but the forms of general confession used ordinarily in the eucharist (BCP: 320-21, 331, 360) make the substance of sin explicit:

> . . . in thought, word, and deed, by what we have done, and by what we have left undone. We have not loved you with our whole heart, we have not loved our neighbors as ourselves. (BCP: 360)

In the face of our sin, we can only acknowledge our fault and pray:

> We are truly sorry and we humbly repent. For the sake of your Son Jesus Christ, have mercy on us and forgive us. . . .

This is the core of the Gospel's promise of forgiveness. Repent, confess, and through Jesus Christ, God
will forgive. This is what the priest declares in the absolution (BCP: 360): forgiveness through our Lord Jesus
Christ. An older Anglican form preserved in the Ash
Wednesday liturgy is more explicit still:[8]

> Almighty God, the Father of our Lord Jesus Christ, who
> desires not the death of sinners, but rather that they
> may turn from their wickedness and live, has given
> power and commandment to his ministers to declare
> and pronounce to his people, being penitent, the absolu-
> tion and remission of their sins. He pardons and
> absolves all those who truly repent, and with sincere
> hearts believe his holy Gospel. (BCP: 269)

This form is not a prayer but a declaration of God's
forgiveness to all who repent and believe the Gospel.
Pronouncing this forgiveness to God's people is the
duty and responsibility of the priest, who has God's
"power and commandment" to do so. The forms of
absolution in the eucharist, both that in Rite One (BCP:
332) and that in Rite Two (BCP: 360), are precatory,
asking God to forgive sins as God has promised. The
effect of both forms is the same.

The efficacy of this general absolution is frequently
questioned. Is it simply a prayer that God will forgive,
or an exercise of the priestly power of absolution? This
is not really the critical question. God has promised to
forgive, and God will forgive the penitent sinner. Both
the precatory forms of absolution found in the eucharist
and the daily offices and the declarative forms in the
Ash Wednesday liturgy and the Reconciliation of
Penitents (BCP: 451) invoke this forgiveness. A better
questions is whether or not the general confession is
efficacious. If it is used as the exhortation suggests,
following self-examination and confession to God with
full purpose of amendment of life, it undoubtedly does

what God has promised it will do. On the other hand, if the confession is merely a general acknowledgment that we might have done better and have, no doubt, failed in specific instances, and if it lacks specificity as to how or when this failure might have occurred, then it would seem to follow that the absolution, too, would be a generalized statement of divine forgiveness, promising God's forgiveness of specific sins when they are acknowledged and confessed. God gives more than we ask, but we dare not presume on God's giving.

The intention of the Church that these forms be priestly absolutions seems clear from the many rubrics forbidding deacons or lay persons to use them. When the forms are said by the celebrating priest or bishop, who *stands* and *faces* the people, as the Prayer Book directs both in the offices (BCP: 80) and in the eucharist (BCP: 360), the manner of their use expresses the exercise of priestly authority. When the forms are pronounced by a deacon or lay person, by contrast, he or she remains *kneeling* and uses the first person plural rather than the second person in address (BCP: 80, 117). The leader is praying that God will grant us all the forgiveness which God has promised to the penitent in the Gospel.

Although there is no dispute about the importance of confession both as a preparation for communion and as a regular component of the daily prayers of Christians, it is not self-evident that reciting a simple form of general confession at every service is the best way to move the congregation to penitence, contrition and resolution to amend their lives. Nor is it necessarily the best way to assure them of the reality of God's forgiveness. Some would argue that less frequent use of the general confession would call attention to it on those occasions when it is used and would make it more psychologically effective. This is almost certainly true for those who attend the eucharist daily, and the Prayer Book permits

the confession to be omitted "on occasion" (BCP: 359);
it does not specify upon how many occasions it may be
omitted. Except on the basis of personal inclination, it is
exceedingly difficult to attempt to answer the question
"How much is too much?" Certainly the confession of
sin is a regular, although not an invariable, part of the
eucharistic celebration.

People of the late middle ages were preoccupied with
sinfulness and the need for absolution. That preoccu-
pation is reflected in the liturgies of the 16th century,
including, of course, the first several versions of the
Book of Common Prayer. Nevertheless, neither that pre-
occupation with sin nor our avoidance of it makes the
horror of sin less real. The question of how to use
general confession most effectively in public worship is
one of tactics, not theology.

The Peace

The exchange of the Peace is the bridge between the
liturgy of the Word of God and that of the Holy Communion. It is not a "folksy" greeting of one's friends
and neighbors but a solemn liturgical rite. It is the final
act of the Liturgy of the Word. The people conclude
their common prayers by greeting one another in
peace.

If the eucharist were not being celebrated, the people
would depart, as they do following the exchange of the
Peace at the end of the Order for Evening (BCP: 113).
But the exchange of the Peace also defines the eucharistic community ritually and so binds the two parts of the
service together. Those who greet each other in peace
are those who will offer the eucharist together so that
they may become one in Christ.

The recitation of the general confession and the
exchange of the Peace express ritually what is implied
verbally in the 16th-century invitation to communion

included before the Confession of Sin in Rite One: "Ye who do truly and earnestly repent you of your sins, and are in love and charity with your neighbors . . ." (BCP: 330).

The Pauline epistles testify that Christians have greeted one another with a "holy kiss" (1 Corinthians 16:20; 2 Corinthians 13:12) from the earliest times, and in our oldest liturgical records the Kiss of Peace is used liturgically to greet the newly baptized. Its placement between the confession of sin and the preparation of the eucharistic gifts is obviously intended to reflect the teaching of Matthew 5:23-4, which is included among the Offertory Sentences:

> If you are offering your gift at the altar, and there remember that your brother has something against you, leave your gift there before the altar and go; first be reconciled to your brother, and then come and offer your gift. (BCP: 376)

The Prayer Book also permits the Peace immediately before the administration of communion (BCP: 407), following the historic tradition of the Roman Church. In this latter position the Peace also defines the eucharistic community, but it tends to reduce the role of the laity to receiving communion. The earlier placement marks them as the celebrant community for the entire eucharistic action.

When There Is No Priest

The eucharistic community, as we have seen, assembles under the presidency of the bishop or of a priest. What happens when there is no priest to preside? Apparently when the early Church faced the question of what to do when the bishop was not present to preside, it responded by authorizing one of the presbyters to preside in his place.[9] The term "priest," which had originally been applied only to Christ and to the priestly people, his Body, but had become the regular title of the bishop as chief celebrant of the liturgy, was then applied to the presbyter, the new chief celebrant of the eucharist.

Following the path opened by Edward Schillebeeckx,[10] some contemporary Christians have suggested that since the Church is prior to the ministry and the ministry exists for the Church, the local Church should designate someone to preside at the eucharist so that the community may make eucharist as Christ commanded.[11] According to this view, such a practice would be an extension of the earlier authorization of presbyters to preside, and analogous to the permission given by the Prayer Book (BCP: 408) and the Canons of the Episcopal Church (III. 27.5) for the licensing of lay readers to administer the chalice "in the absence of sufficient deacons and priests." It is only fair to note that the clear restriction of the Prayer Book to cases of necessity is widely ignored, as is the similar restriction on lay presidency at the eucharist in those denominations which permit it. Throughout liturgical history, permission to do something in particular situations understood to be extraordinary has frequently resulted in the exception becoming the usual state.

The Prayer Book, however, does not permit lay presiders at the eucharist; instead it permits a deacon, or in the absence of a deacon, a lay reader to preside at the liturgy of the Word of God as the Sunday *synaxis* of the people (BCP: 407). The liturgy of the Word has always maintained an independent existence alongside of its incorporation into the eucharist and has been used throughout the centuries as the community's worship service on those occasions when it was impossible or undesirable to celebrate the eucharist. The bishop may also "authorize a deacon to distribute Holy Communion to the congregation from the reserved Sacrament" (BCP: 408) after the liturgy of the Word. This rubric is an attempt to meet the needs of congregations which are deprived of the ministry of a priest. It provides a substitute for the eucharist, which includes both the ministry of the Word and the opportunity to receive communion.

These are emergency measures. The permanent existence of a Christian community without a priest is an anomaly. One approach to ending the anomalous situation is to ordain non-stipendiary priests for those congregations unable to support a "full-time" pastor. In the words of Schillebeeckx:

> Given the specific and sometimes "extraordinary" circumstances which can prevail, the laying on of hands, as acceptance by the church, bestowed on a member who is to be a leader in the community, seems to me to be the normal liturgical accreditation, in line with the first and second Christian millennia—for someone who is to preside over a community, and thus over its eucharist. From a theological point of view this means that actual leaders of the community, who are also accepted by it, must also be given *ordinatio* or liturgical accreditation.[12]

The Holy Communion

The Peace, as we have said, is the structural hinge which connects the liturgy of the Word of God to the liturgy of the Holy Communion, forming a single liturgy of Word and Sacrament. The liturgy of the Holy Communion is the sacramental meal "commanded by Christ for the continual remembrance of his life, death, and resurrection, until his coming again" (BCP: 859). As Gregory Dix so eloquently pointed out in *The Shape of the Liturgy*, "The last supper of our Lord with His disciples is the source of the liturgical eucharist, but not the model for it. We are," he reminded us, "so accustomed to the liturgical shape of the eucharist as we know it that we do not instantly appreciate the fact that it is not based in practice on [the scheme of the actions of Jesus at the Last Supper] but on a somewhat drastic modification of it."[13] Dix's point, which is central to his great book, is that although the New Testament texts all describe our Lord as taking bread, giving thanks over it, breaking it, and distributing it, and then taking the cup, blessing it, and distributing it, the present liturgy does not follow this sevenfold structure:

> With absolute unanimity the liturgical tradition reproduces these seven actions as four: (1) the offertory; bread and wine are "taken" and placed on the table together. (2) The prayer; the president gives thanks to God over the bread and wine together. (3) The fraction; the bread is broken. (4) The communion; the bread and wine are distributed together.[14]

It is this "four-action shape" so clearly described by Dix that underlies the eucharistic liturgy of the *Book of Common Prayer* and most other rites. He took, he blessed, he broke, he gave: offertory, consecration, fraction, communion. We do not know exactly how or why the liturgical tradition came to ignore the witness of the New Testament on this point, but that it did so without exception for 1400 years cannot be denied. Dix is probably right that it "must be connected in some way with the severance of the eucharist proper from its original connection with a meal"[15] and its subsequent attachment to the Liturgy of the Word.[16]

There is almost universal recognition today that Dix's analysis of "the four-fold shape of the liturgy" is correct. Contemporary liturgies, such as Rite Two in the Prayer Book, are composed in the light of this understanding, accenting the "shape" and treating other elements as subordinate to it. In the words of

Kenneth Stevenson, "It could almost be said that every rite that has been compiled since manifests the work of Dix in its revised structure, and this does not apply simply to new rites, it also applies to old ones which are rearranged in order to make their 'shape' clearer."[17] But Dix did not invent the "shape"; he recognized and identified it in the liturgies he studied. And Rite One, like all traditional liturgies, manifests the "four-fold shape" as surely as Rite Two. Archbishop Cranmer and those who worked with him in the 16th century to craft the *Book of Common Prayer* were undoubtedly unaware of "the four-fold shape," but they were very aware of the traditional structure of eucharistic liturgies and preserved that structure in the new English service.

Subsequent scholarship has nuanced Dix's work slightly. It is generally held today that the four elements are not coordinate. The prayer of thanksgiving and communion are primary. The preparation of the gifts and the breaking of bread are significant but secondary actions.

The Offertory

The first action of this second part of the eucharist consists of preparing the gifts of bread and wine and placing them on the altar. The Prayer Book calls this "the Offertory" (BCP: 361), which is its traditional name. The name has been abandoned by the Church of England's *Alternative Service Book 1980* and by the *Sacramentary of the Roman Missal* of Paul VI, which speak merely of the preparation of the gifts, although the *Sacramentary* continues to refer to the "offertory song."[18] The offertory is essentially action. Words, if there are any, are strictly secondary.

Representatives of the congregation bring the people's offerings of bread and wine, and money and other gifts, to the deacon or

*celebrant. The people stand while the offerings are presented
and placed on the altar.* (BCP: 361)

The action is the "taking" of the bread and wine.
The action involves the people, the deacon, and the
priest. The congregation, through their representatives, bring forward the gifts; the deacon prepares them
and places them on the altar; and the priest offers them
in the Great Thanksgiving. At one level, this is simple
utilitarian action. The people who have either prepared or bought the bread and wine bring them to the
deacon, who "sets the table" for the paterfamilias of the
Christian family, the bishop or priest, to give thanks
over them. But the tradition has generally seen it as
more than this. The Prayer Book speaks of "gifts" and
"offerings" and their being "presented." The people
are bidden, "Let us with gladness present the offerings
and oblations of our life and labor to the Lord" (BCP:
377), and several of the recommended offertory
sentences use sacrificial terminology, especially Romans
12:1 (I appeal to you, brethren, by the mercies of God,
to present yourselves as a living sacrifice, holy and
acceptable to God, which is your spiritual worship),
Psalm 50:14 (Offer to God a sacrifice of thanksgiving,
and make good your vows to the Most High), and Matthew 5:23, 24 (If you are offering your gift at the
altar. . .) (BCP: 376f).

The language and ceremonial of the Prayer Book
(BCP: 361) reflect the Greek liturgical terminology of
the ante-Nicene Church which speaks of the *prosphora*,
the things offered, or oblations, which the people are
said to bring (*prosenegkein*), the deacons to present
(*anapherein*), and the bishop to offer (*prospherein*).[19] The
congregation, who stand while their representatives
bring forward the gifts, the deacon who prepares them,
and the priest who offers them, all in different ways

participate in the action. In Dix's understanding the offertory is a true self-offering of the Church:

> The whole rite was a true corporate offering by the church in its hierarchical completeness of the church in its organic unity. . . . The primitive layman's communion, no less than that of the bishop, is the consummation of his "liturgy" in the offering of the Christian sacrifice.

> The offertory, in the original view of the rite, is therefore something much more than a ceremonial action, the placing of bread and wine upon the altar by the clergy as an inevitable preparation for communion. It is as the later liturgies continued to call it—even when it had lost all outward signs of its previous meaning—the "rational worship" by free reasonable creatures of their Creator, a self-sacrificial act by which each Christian comes to his being as a member of Christ in the "recalling" before God of the self-sacrificial offering of Christ on Calvary. "There you are upon the table," says S. Augustine to the newly confirmed communicants at the Easter liturgy, "there you are in the chalice."[20]

The offertory in the Prayer Book eucharist expresses symbolically and ritually the self-offering of the people of God. This is implied in the inclusion of money as well as bread and wine among the gifts to be presented at the altar. It is also implied in the selection of Romans 12:1 (BCP: 376) as an offertory sentence. In the words of Price and Weil:

> In placing on the altar money and bread and wine, the congregation offers *itself* and *its world*. Money represents the work of the congregation. . . . Symbolically, we offer bread to become the body of Christ. But the underlying reality of the action is that we offer our lives, individually and corporately, to become his body in this world.[21]

It is also worth noting that the eucharistic gifts are not wheat and grapes but bread and wine, products not only of God's natural bounty but also of the human labor which prepared them, and therefore symbols of human society in dependence upon God.

This "offertory theology" has been severely criticized on both theological and historical grounds.[22] Certainly, Dix's interpretation is not the only one possible either of the Prayer Book offertory or of the patristic evidence. Considerable care needs to be taken to avoid not only the suggestion that Christians have an offering to make, whether of bread and wine and money, or of themselves—their souls and bodies—which can be separated from the sacrifice of Christ, but also to avoid the temptation to see in the offertory some offering separate from the oblation of all these things in the eucharistic prayer, which is the *anaphora,* the "great offering," as well as the Great Thanksgiving. It is in the eucharistic prayer itself that the actual offering of the gifts to God takes place. It is only as Christians are the Body of Christ, united to their crucified and risen head, that their self-offering can be taken up into his perfect self-offering and presented. Of ourselves, we have literally nothing to offer, yet as the baptized people of God we make this eucharistic offering of "our bounden duty and service" (BCP: 336).

The Great Thanksgiving

When the gifts have been presented and placed upon the altar, the chief celebrant begins the eucharistic prayer, or Great Thanksgiving. The Greek name for this prayer is *anaphora,* the offering. The Latins called it simply *prex,* the prayer. Since 1662, the Prayer Book has used the title Prayer of Consecration, which focuses on the consecration of the gifts but neglects the wider eucharistic aspects of the prayer. In the Middle Ages the *canon actionis* or *canon missae* came to be seen as beginning after the *Sanctus*, and that is where the title was placed in earlier prayer books.[23] The Great Thanksgiving, as the present Prayer Book indicates, properly begins with the dialogue generally called by its Latin incipit *Sursum corda* (BCP: 333, 361).

The dialogue begins with the traditional greeting of the chief celebrant, "The Lord be with you," and the people's response. "Lift up your hearts" (*Sursum corda*) is the invitation to the congregation to join in the *anaphora*, or eucharistic offering. It is an invitation to the baptized people of God to raise their minds to "things that are above, where Christ is, seated at the right hand of God" (Colossians 3:1-3). In the 4th century Cyril of Jerusalem commented:

> For at that most awesome moment we must indeed raise our hearts high to God, not keep them intent on the earth and on earthly matters. So the priest is virtually commanding you at that moment to lay aside the cares of this life, your domestic worries, and to keep your heart in heaven on God who loves men. (*Mystagogical Catecheses* 5.4)[24]

In the 16th century John Calvin was even more explicit in his Geneva liturgy. The following passage has found its way into the eucharistic liturgies of most churches of the Reformed tradition:

> Let us raise our hearts and minds on high, where Jesus Christ is, in the glory of his Father. . . . Our souls will only then be disposed to be nourished and vivified by his substance, when they are raised high as heaven, to enter the kingdom of God where he dwells.[25]

All of this "uplifting" commentary suggests that in the eucharist we are brought into the presence of God in Christ, not by our bringing Christ "down" to our eucharistic assembly, but by God's lifting us "up" to heaven.

The dialogue continues with "Let us give thanks," a direct invitation to participate not only in the earthly action of the celebrant in making eucharist but also in the heavenly action of Christ the Great High Priest, the true offering of which the eucharist is the earthly sacrament (see Hebrews 8:1-2; 9:10-11). The proclamation of the Great Thanksgiving is the specific liturgy of the chief celebrant, but it is also the action of the entire congregation, who respond to the invitation by giving their assent. In the eucharistic prayer the priest acts in the name of the Church, offering praise and thanksgiving to the Father, through Jesus Christ, in the power of the Holy Spirit.

Structure of the Eucharistic Prayer

Eight alternative eucharistic prayers are included in the *Book of Common Prayer*: two in Rite One, four in Rite Two, and two in An Order for Celebrating the Holy Eucharist. Six of these prayers have a common structure, that adopted by the First American Prayer Book of 1789 from the Scottish Nonjurors who found it in the liturgy of the Apostolic Constitutions (Book 8) and the Liturgy of St. James. The structure is called West Syrian by students of comparative liturgy. The other two prayers (Eucharistic Prayer C and Form 1) contain the same elements but follow the structure of the Alexandrian Liturgy of St. Mark, which is also the structure of the eucharistic prayers of the *Alternative Service Book* in the Church of England and of the new Roman Catholic eucharistic prayers. The Episcopal Church has an historical commitment to the West Syrian-Scottish form of eucharistic prayer, and the inclusion of two prayers in another structure can be seen as not only a recognition of the validity of other structures but also a reaching out to both Roman Catholics and English Anglicans.

The outline of the West Syrian *anaphora,* followed by Eucharistic Prayers I and II, A, B, D, and Form 2 with only minor variations, will provide a structure for our discussion of the eucharistic prayers. Since the prayers are alternatives, they should be examined together. No single prayer can say everything which might be desirable to say in a eucharistic prayer. Each has its own emphases, but collectively the prayers present a balanced picture of eucharistic theology.

Thanksgiving for Creation

Following the opening dialogue, all the prayers begin by giving thanks. "It is right, and a good and joyful thing, always and everywhere to give thanks to you, Father Almighty, Creator of heaven and earth" (BCP: 367). It is this opening thanksgiving, or *eucharistia,* which gives its name to the Great Thanksgiving. In most Western eucharistic prayers a variable proper preface permits the inclusion over the course of the year of many specific grounds for thanksgiving. The proper prefaces as a group (BCP: 377-382) bear witness to the mighty acts of God in creation and redemption. Eucharistic Prayers C and D do not include proper prefaces but accomplish this same witness with a single narrative.

Eucharistic Prayers C and D present the most extensive thanksgiving for creation. Eucharistic Prayer I, which has been in the American Prayer Book since 1789, does not mention creation at all, but begins after the *Sanctus* by giving thanks for the crucifixion (BCP: 344). This eucharistic prayer's narrowing of focus to the atonement and the consecration of the gifts was typical of the religious climate of the Late Middle Ages. The same is true of Cranmer's eucharistic prayer in the 1549 Prayer Book, on which Eucharistic Prayer I is based. This narrowing must be considered a defect in the prayer, but it can be partially remedied by using the first Preface of the Lord's Day (BCP: 344) whenever possible. Eucharistic Prayer II, a conservative revision of Eucharistic Prayer I by the Standing Liturgical Commission, includes thanksgiving for creation in its first sentence after the Sanctus:

> All glory be to thee, O Lord our God, for that thou didst create heaven and earth, and didst make us in thine own image. . . . (BCP: 341)

Eucharistic Prayer D, a contemporary ecumenical composition based closely on the 4th-century Alexandrian *Anaphora* of St. Basil, gives thanks to God as "fountain of life and source of all goodness":

> . . . you made all things and fill them with your blessing; you created them to rejoice in the splendor of your radiance.

> You formed us in your own image, giving the whole world into our care, so that, in obedience to you, our Creator, we might rule and serve all your creatures. (BCP: 373)

Eucharistic Prayer C, an original contemporary prayer drafted by Howard E. Galley, includes "galaxies, suns, the planets in their courses, and this fragile earth, our island home" in its catalogue of creation, and gives thanks that God has endowed the human race "with memory, reason, and skill" (BCP 370). Prayers D and C taken together give substance to the creedal affirmation "We believe in one God, the Father, the Almighty, maker of heaven and earth, and of all that is, seen and unseen" (BCP: 358), and they remind us that creation extends far beyond this planet to "the vast expanse of interstellar space" (BCP: 370). They go on to affirm God's making us "in your own image" and "giving the whole world into our care." They also proclaim creation's revelatory power with the words "your mighty works reveal your wisdom and love" (BCP: 373).

Sanctus

At some appropriate point in this thanksgiving, the people "join the saints and angels" (BCP: 402) in the angelic hymn of the *Sanctus*, "giving voice to every creature under heaven" (BCP: 373). The eucharist is not simply the action of the particular congregation which happens to be assembled in a particular place, but of the whole Church, even of the whole creation, which joins with the celebrating congregation in singing the heavenly hymn of Isaiah 6 and Revelation 4. In addition to the angels and archangels who form the heavenly chorus in most eucharistic prayers, Prayer C mentions the participation of "prophets, apostles, and martyrs, and . . . those in every generation who have looked to [God] in hope" (BCP: 370). Prayer D adds the image of human beings joining the hymn as representatives of the whole of the voiceless creation, which is thereby enabled to praise and glorify God. The *Sanctus* and its introduction witness that the worship of God is a cosmic act in which the congregation is permitted to join, through Jesus Christ, in the power of the Holy Spirit.

Formal outlines usually place the *Sanctus* between the giving of "*thanks to God the Father for his work in creation and his revelation of himself to his people*" (BCP: 402) and the praise of "*God for the salvation of the world through Jesus Christ our Lord*" (BCP: 403). This placement, however, holds strictly true only for Forms 1 and 2 (BCP: 402, 404) in the Prayer Book and for some classic West Syrian texts.[26]

Thanksgiving for Redemption

The essence of the thanksgiving for redemption is, of course, the thanksgiving for the atoning life and death of Jesus Christ, which forms the core of this section in all eucharistic prayers:

> . . . thou, of thy tender mercy, didst give thine only
> Son Jesus Christ to suffer death upon the cross for our
> redemption; who made there, by his one oblation of
> himself once offered, a full, perfect, and sufficient sacri-
> fice, oblation, and satisfaction, for the sins of the whole
> world. . . . (BCP: 334)

Cranmer's careful, balanced language preserved in
Eucharistic Prayer I is the classic Anglican statement of
the sacrifice of the cross. By his atoning death Christ
offered the only sacrifice that can or should be offered
"for the sins of the whole world." It is "full, perfect,
and sufficient." In the eucharistic controversies of the
16th century, each of these words bore substantial
weight. The eucharist was to be considered in no sense
a completing of Christ's offering, a new oblation, or a
"satisfactory" sacrifice for sins not atoned for by
Christ's death. The "one oblation of himself once
offered" is unique, unrepeatable, and has done all that
can or need be done "for our redemption." From none
of this language do we wish to retreat. Eucharistic
Prayer A paints the same picture in visual image rather
than technical theological language:

> He stretched out his arms upon the cross, and offered
> himself, in obedience to your will, a perfect sacrifice for
> the whole world. (BCP: 362)

As mentioned above, only Eucharistic Prayer I
focuses narrowly on the atonement; the other prayers
are more inclusive in their thanksgiving. Eucharistic
Prayer B, which is based loosely on the third century
Apostolic Tradition of Hippolytus, begins with the call of
Israel and God's "Word spoken through the prophets,"
before turning to "the Word made flesh, Jesus, your
Son" (BCP: 368). The prayer recognizes that the
redemptive work of God in the Old Testament is a part
of the history of redemption for which we give thanks in
the eucharist. The entire process can, in fact, be

summed up in two sentences from Prayer D: "When our disobedience took us far from you, you did not abandon us to the power of death. In your mercy you came to our help, so that in seeking you we might find you" (BCP: 373). God's response to human sin has been redemptive love.

The redeeming work of Christ is not confined to his death. The fullest single account of that work is in Eucharistic Prayer D, but the proper prefaces provide a fuller expression still, speaking of Christ's incarnation, temptation, crucifixion, resurrection, ascension, giving of the Holy Spirit, and coming again, as well as the apostolic preaching and the witness of the saints. Prayer D says, "Incarnate by the Holy Spirit, born of the Virgin Mary, he lived as one of us, yet without sin" (BCP: 374). The Incarnation preface elaborates by saying that Jesus Christ, "by the mighty power of the Holy Spirit, was made perfect Man of the flesh of the Virgin Mary his mother, so that we might be delivered from the bondage of sin, and receive power to become [God's] children" (BCP: 378). By the grace of Christ's sinlessness in the face of temptation, the lenten preface tells us, "we are able to triumph over every evil, and to live no longer for ourselves alone, but for him who died for us and rose again" (BCP: 379). The Incarnation is the ground of our redemption and adoption as the children of God. Christ's sinless life and his death are a part of his atoning work. Like the creed, then, the eucharistic prayers bear witness to the Gospel testimony to the virgin birth, or more properly the virginal conception of Christ, but they do not make it the foundation of any further doctrinal elaboration. They do not say that certain things follow because Christ was born of a virgin. They are content to proclaim the scriptural story, assuring us that Jesus is not only "perfect Man of the flesh of the Virgin Mary" (BCP: 378) but also "co-eternal Son," of "one and equal glory" with the Father and Holy Spirit, "one

God, one Lord, in Trinity of Persons and in Unity of Being" (BCP: 380).

A single sentence in Prayer B recounts Christ's preaching, as the focus moves from the Incarnation to the death on the cross and its consequences:

> To the poor he proclaimed the good news of salvation; to prisoners, freedom; to the sorrowful, joy. To fulfill your purpose he gave himself up to death; and rising from the grave, destroyed death, and made the whole creation new. (BCP: 374)

The preaching of Christ the liberator, the focus of contemporary liberation theology, leads directly to his death, in fulfillment of God's purpose: not only the redemption and liberation of humankind, but the renewal of all creation. The mighty acts of God in Christ do not end with the crucifixion; they go on through the death-destroying resurrection, the ascension, and the sending of the Holy Spirit, Christ's "own first gift for those who believe" (BCP: 374).

Adding to the recital of the redemption event, the Ascension preface gives thanks that Christ has gone "to prepare a place for us; that where he is we might also be, and reign with him in glory" (BCP: 379). The image of the ascension is the same as that of the *sursum corda.* It is not that heaven is "up" but that the risen life is "higher," in the normal metaphorical use of the word, than the life of this world. That we are raised to reign with Christ in glory is the theological content here proclaimed.

The sending of the Holy Spirit is "to complete [Christ's] work in the world, and to bring to fulfillment the sanctification of all" (BCP: 374), and it finds its concrete expression in the pentecostal outpouring upon the disciples as described in the preface for Pentecost:

> . . . to teach [the disciples] and to lead them into all truth; uniting peoples of many tongues in the confession

of one faith, and giving to your Church the power to serve you as a royal priesthood, and to preach the Gospel to all nations. (BCP: 380)

To this, the preface for apostles and ordinations adds Christ's promise to his followers "to be with them always, even to the end of the ages" (BCP: 381) so that

> . . . when [Christ] shall come again in power and great triumph to judge the world, we may without shame or fear rejoice to behold his appearing. (BCP: 378)

The rehearsal of the mighty acts of God in Christ in the eucharistic prayers can be summed up in the concluding words of this section of Prayer B:

> In him, you have delivered us from evil, and made us worthy to stand before you. In him, you have brought us out of error into truth, out of sin into righteousness, out of death into life. (BCP: 368)

This is what God has done for us, God's fallen creation, and the Great Thanksgiving begins by giving thanks for creation and redemption through Jesus Christ.

The Institution Narrative

In the West Syrian structure which we are following, the thanksgiving reaches its climax and conclusion in giving thanks for the institution of the eucharist. The institution narrative concludes the more general thanksgiving by recalling the particular mighty act that is the focus of the service: the gift of Christ's body and blood to be our spiritual food and drink. In the Roman-Alexandrian structure followed by Eucharistic Prayer C, Form I, and by the Church of England, a prayer for the sanctification of the gifts, usually including an invocation of the Holy Spirit (an *epiclesis*), separates the institution narrative from the thanksgiving.

The Words of Institution have often been interpreted as "Words of Consecration." Certainly they
were so understood in pre-Reformation England.
Luther, attacking the Roman canon, called them
"words of life and salvation" included in the canon,
"just as in times past the ark of the Lord was placed in
the temple of idols next to Dagon."[27] In both his Latin
and German masses Luther omitted "the entire canon,"
leaving the Words of Institution to accomplish the consecration alone. St. Ambrose of Milan, writing in the
4th century, had commented:

> When the moment comes for bringing the most holy
> sacrament into being, the priest does not use his own
> words any longer: he uses the words of Christ. There-
> fore, it is Christ's word that brings this sacrament into
> being. What is this word of Christ? It is the word by
> which all things were made. . . . Before the consecra-
> tion it was not the body of Christ, but after the consecra-
> tion I tell you that it is now the body of Christ. He spoke
> and it was made, he commanded, and it was created. (*De
> Sacramentis* 4.14-16)[28]

Contemporary scholarship distinguishes between the
creative word of Christ spoken once for all at the Last
Supper, which does indeed bring the sacrament into
being, and the repetition of those words by the priest in
the eucharistic prayer.[29] Scholars hold that the *whole* of
the eucharistic prayer, not just the repetition of any
particular words, whether the Words of Institution or
the *epiclesis* of the Holy Spirit, effects consecration. In
other words, consecration is by thanksgiving rather
than by formula. The narrative itself says, ". . . when
he had given thanks to you, he broke it [the bread] and
gave it to his disciples, and said. . . ." (BCP: 362)
Thus, as they are recorded in the tradition, the words of
Jesus at the Last Supper are words of administration
accompanying the giving, not the words of thanksgiving
by which he consecrated the bread and wine. These

latter words were presumably some variant of the traditional Jewish forms.[30] Jeremias, in *The Eucharistic Words of Jesus*, refers to the "words of interpretation," and Dix, although he does not use the term, sees them as fulfilling that function.[31]

Except for the rubrics in each eucharistic prayer that direct the priest to hold the bread and cup while reciting the Words of Institution, there is nothing in the Prayer Book to suggest that these words are consecratory. However, we do not approach the liturgies of the *Book of Common Prayer* apart from the tradition of eucharistic practice, and if in our experience the words are accompanied by elevations and the ringing of sanctus bells, it is difficult not to approach the text without believing that these words are more than the final paragraphs of the thanksgiving for redemption.

Actually, since Eucharistic Prayer I, the traditional American "Prayer of Consecration," contains a specific petition for the consecration of the gifts later in the prayer at the *epiclesis* (BCP: 342), many Episcopalians have always had problems with the treatment of the Words of Institution as consecratory, and they have argued, with Cyril of Jerusalem:

> We call upon the merciful God to send the Holy Spirit on our offerings, so that he may make the bread Christ's body, and the wine Christ's blood; for clearly whatever the Holy Spirit touches is sanctified and transmuted. (*Mystagogical Catecheses* 5.7)[32]

If, however, it is praise and thanksgiving and not formulae which are consecratory, this position has many of the same weaknesses as does the view which considers the Words of Institution as consecratory. It does not take seriously the totality of the prayer as the Church's response to Christ's institution, but seeks to identify a "moment of consecration."[33] The particular difficulties involved in this search are well summarized

by John McKenna, a Roman Catholic priest, as a part of
the conclusions in a substantial study published by the
Alcuin Club:

> An attempt, however, to fix theologically an exact
> "moment of consecration," while perhaps reflecting a
> normal human tendency, hardly seems acceptable. To
> attempt such a precision seems to be, in effect, to
> attempt to pinpoint God's sovereign action. And this
> would be to run the risk of making God, or at least his
> free activity, an objectifiable "thing" to be gazed at,
> examined, etc. It is one thing, for instance, to say that
> the institution narrative expresses the necessary inten-
> tion of the Church to do what Christ commanded and
> her faith that he will realize his promises here and now
> and, thus, that the institution narrative has a consecra-
> tory value. It is quite another thing to pinpoint the
> exact moment when God joins his action to this inten-
> tion and faith of the Church.[34]

"Do This for My Anamnesis"

The Words of Institution over both the bread and the
cup are followed by the command "Do this for the
remembrance of me." Gregory Dix pointed out that
"Do this" cannot be the most important part of the
command, for it is attached to the one thing that Jesus
can be certain the disciples will do again.[35] Whenever
observant Jews come together to eat a formal meal,
there will be a solemn blessing of the bread at the beginning of the meal and a thanksgiving over a cup of wine
at its close. It was these ritual acts which Jesus adapted
to his new meaning at the Last Supper. He performed
traditional Jewish rituals which he and his disciples had
performed many times before, and which he could be
certain, insofar as any future event is certain, they
would perform many times in the future.

The important words, then, must be "for the remembrance of me." The Words of Institution are indeed "words of interpretation," for it is the new meaning given by the Lord's words over the bread and cup which are significant, so that whenever the disciples break the bread and bless the cup it will be the *remembrance* of Jesus' death and resurrection.

In Chapter Four on the Great Vigil of Easter, we have already seen the close relationship between the Paschal Mystery and the Jewish Passover. Whether we accept the Synoptic or the Johannine chronology, it was in the context of the feast of Passover that the great events of the passion and resurrection occurred. In one of the oldest parts of the Passover ritual, the head of the household proclaims:

> In every generation let each [person] look on himself as if he came forth from Egypt. . . . It was not only our [ancestors] that the Holy One, blessed be he, redeemed, but us as well did he redeem along with them. . . .
>
> Therefore, we are bound to thank, praise, laud, glorify, exalt, and adore him who performed all these miracles for our [ancestors] and for us. He brought us forth from slavery to freedom, from darkness to joy, from mourning to holiday, from darkness to light, and from bondage to redemption.[36]

This is the context in which the disciples celebrated the feast of Passover. It was *zikkaron*, the memorial of God's mighty acts of redemption, made present to the participants when they celebrated the feast, retold the story, and ate the paschal lamb and unleavened bread. When Jesus sat at table with his disciples at the Last Supper, all the meaning of the feast, both the redemption which God accomplished through Moses in the Exodus and the new and greater redemption that Christ himself was accomplishing, became focused in the meal. Thus, for us, the sharing of the broken bread and the cup of blessing become the remembrance, or *anamnesis,* of the Paschal Mystery and the means of our participation in it.

We who share in the paschal meal of the new covenant celebrate the real Passover from death to life, not only in the dying and rising of Jesus, but in our own dying and rising with him. Whenever we eat the bread and drink the cup we make present the whole saving action of Jesus Christ. It is not that Jesus comes down from heaven to be present on our altars in response to the repetition of a sacred formula by the priest, but that when we gather to celebrate the sacrificial meal of the new covenant, Christ, the true Paschal Lamb, is with us, and the whole complex of events which bring about the salvation of the world are renewed in and for us. The eucharist is for Christians the means to establish and maintain our union with Christ in the power of his one sacrifice once offered until his coming again—during that entire period of his heavenly priesthood in which we are in this world.

It has become customary in the last century to call this renewal of the mighty acts of God in Christ which bring about our salvation *anamnesis.* This is the Greek word for *remembrance* or *memorial,* just as *zikkaron* is the Hebrew word. We do this because the meaning of the English word has been eroded. *Memorial* or *remembrance* in English often mean only a psychological act of thinking about things past, a sort of nostalgia. *Anamnesis* carries the full weight of the biblical concept.[37] Through *anamnesis* we become participants in the events, not as history, but as present realities in our lives, where the timelessness of eternity overcomes the centuries and proclaims, "You are risen with Christ." This teaching is well reflected in and summarized by the Lima document:

5. The eucharist is the memorial of the crucified and risen Christ, i.e., the living and effective sign of his sacrifice, accomplished once and for all on the cross and still operative on behalf of all humankind. The biblical idea of memorial as applied to the eucharist refers to this present efficacy of God's work when it is celebrated by God's people in a liturgy.

6. Christ himself with all that he has accomplished for us and for all creation (in his incarnation, servanthood, ministry, teaching, suffering, sacrifice, resurrection, ascension and sending of the Spirit) is present in this *anamnesis*, granting us communion with himself. The eucharist is also the foretaste of his *parousia* and of the final kingdom. (WCC 1982: 11)

Anamnesis-Oblation

Anamnesis is also the technical name for the next element of the eucharistic prayer: we make remembrance of what Christ has done; we recapitulate all of the mighty acts for which we have given thanks; and we re-present them to the Father with the eucharistic gifts. Sometimes this element of the eucharistic prayer is also called the *oblation*:

> Wherefore, O Lord and heavenly Father, we thy people do celebrate and make, with these thy holy gifts which we now offer unto thee, the memorial thy Son hath commanded us to make; having in remembrance his blessed passion and precious death, his mighty resurrection and glorious ascension; and looking for his coming again with power and great glory. (BCP: 342)

A congregational acclamation recalling the saving acts of God in Christ is often a part of the *anamnesis*:

> We remember his death,
> We proclaim his resurrection,
> We await his coming in glory; (BCP: 368)

or:

Christ has died.
Christ has risen.
Christ will come again. (BCP: 363)

The *anamnesis* is central to the structure of the eucharistic prayer. It moves the focus from the celebration of what God has done in the past and will do in the future to the present action:

> We celebrate the memorial of our redemption, O Father, in this sacrifice of praise and thanksgiving. Recalling his death, resurrection, and ascension, we offer you these gifts. (BCP: 363)

It is because of all of those things for which we make *anamnesis* that we are able to "offer our sacrifice of praise and thanksgiving to you, O Lord of all; presenting to you, from your creation, this bread and this wine" (BCP: 369). The Scottish liturgy of 1764, on which the eucharistic prayer of the first American Prayer Book (our Eucharistic Prayer I) was based, printed the words "which we now offer unto thee" in capital letters, and it was the tradition of Scottish Episcopalians to elevate the bread and wine while these words were being said, as a sign of the eucharistic offering.[38] It is at this point in the eucharistic prayer, rather than at the offertory, that we properly speak of offering to God our sacrifice of praise and thanksgiving, the eucharistic gifts of bread and wine. Our offerings are of value only because they are a part of the *anamnesis*, the remembrance of Christ's perfect offering. They are not attempts to perform a good work in the sight of God, but only the signs of our obedience to the command of Christ and the signs of our participation in his action as members of the body of which he is the head.

The eucharistic prayer is the *anaphora* (the offering), and the *anamnesis* is the structural center and pivot of the prayer: ". . . we now celebrate the memorial of our redemption," says Eucharistic Prayer A. Remembering what Christ has done, we offer what he has commanded: ". . . offering to you [God], from the gifts you have given us, this bread and this cup, we praise you and we bless you" (BCP: 374).

Epiclesis-Invocation

Bread and wine are offered to God in Christ's name so that they may become what Christ has declared them to be, his Body and Blood and our food and drink for the new life we now live in him. The *epiclesis*, or invocation of the Holy Spirit, prays that the Holy Spirit "may descend upon us, and upon these gifts" (BCP: 375) to complete the work of sanctification:

> Sanctify them by your Holy Spirit to be for your people the Body and Blood of your Son, the holy food and drink of new and unending life in him. Sanctify us also that we may faithfully receive this holy Sacrament, and serve you in unity, constancy, and peace. . . . (BCP: 363)

The Holy Spirit is invoked both upon us and upon the eucharistic gifts. The invocation upon the gifts is described as "consecratory," since it asks that they be consecrated, or sanctified, "to be the Body and Blood of Jesus Christ our Lord" (BCP: 371). But the sanctification of the gifts is not for its own sake, but so "that we, receiving them according to thy Son our Savior Jesus Christ's holy institution, in remembrance of his death and passion, may be partakers of his most blessed Body and Blood" (BCP: 335). Consecration is for the sake of communion: they are "holy gifts for [God's] holy people, the bread of life and the cup of salvation" (BCP: 375), "the holy food and drink of unending life in [Christ]" (BCP: 363), "the Sacrament of the Body of Christ and his Blood of the new Covenant" (BCP: 369).

The Spirit is also invoked upon "us," the people of God assembled to make eucharist. In the classic West Syrian manner, Eucharistic Prayer D includes "us" with the gifts as objects of the same verb. Other prayers treat the dual objects of sanctification sequentially. Prayer B says:

> Unite us to your Son in his sacrifice, that we may be acceptable through him, being sanctified by the Holy Spirit. (BCP: 369)

The petition of Prayer D prays:

> Grant that all who share this bread and cup may become one body and one spirit, a living sacrifice in Christ, to the praise of your Name. (BCP: 375)

The unity of the Church is traditionally considered to be the essence of the eucharist, in accordance with our Lord's prayer of John 17:21. The eucharist is the sacrament of unity and is both the sign and the cause of the unity of the Church. Therefore, the *epiclesis* seeks after unity and peace for the sanctification of the Church. As Eucharistic Prayer B reminds us, it is through our union with Christ in his sacrifice that this will be accomplished. Generally, a prayer for worthy reception of the sacrament is included either in the *epiclesis* or as a separate paragraph later in the prayer.

Eucharistic Prayer C and Form 1 follow a different structural outline and place the *epiclesis* over the gifts prior to the Words of Institution. Neither prayer strictly follows the Roman-Alexandrian outline by including a proper *epiclesis* over the communicants at this point, but both include a prayer for the communicants. Form 1 prays, "Gather us . . . into one body in your Son Jesus Christ. Make us a living sacrifice of praise" (BCP: 403), while Eucharistic Prayer C includes a substantial prayer addressed to the Father, which includes the petitions:

Open our eyes to see your hand at work in the world about us. Deliver us from the presumption of coming to this Table for solace only, and not for strength; for pardon only, and not for renewal. Let the grace of this Holy Communion make us one body, one spirit in Christ, that we may worthily serve the world in his name. (BCP: 372)

Although these are not strictly *epicleses*, they fulfill the same function as the *epiclesis* over the people by praying for their unity. Prayer C also includes a petition for pardon, one of the fruits of participation in the eucharist, but asks that we go beyond the mere reception of benefits to be Christ's agents for continuing his mission in the world. Although such a "missionary" statement is not usually included in the eucharistic prayer at this point, the continuance of Christ's mission is an important role of the Church, and a role for which prayer is frequently offered.

"With Thy Word and Holy Spirit"

The *epiclesis* in all the eucharistic prayers in the Prayer Book invokes the Holy Spirit, but in two of the prayers it also invokes the Word. Eucharistic Prayer I, the prayer derived from the Scottish liturgy, prays, "vouchsafe to bless and sanctify, with thy Word and Holy Spirit, these thy gifts and creatures of bread and wine" (BCP: 335). Eucharistic Prayer II has simplified the language and eliminated the possibility that the *epiclesis* might be taken in a receptionist sense by returning to the language of 1549 and the Scottish liturgy, "that they may be unto us the Body and Blood of thy dearly-beloved Son Jesus Christ," but it retains the phrase "with thy Word and Holy Spirit" (BCP: 342). Interestingly, the Scottish liturgy, from which the phrase derives, began "word" with a small letter. According to Massey Shepherd:

> After its first edition, the American Prayer Book capitalized "Word" as well as "Holy Spirit," to prevent any misunderstanding that the "Word" referred to the Words of Institution rather than Christ the Word Himself.[39]

It is not the repetition of the Words of Institution by the priest but the words and acts of the Logos and the operation of the Holy Spirit which are effective. The action in the eucharist is the action of the Holy Trinity. The effective prayer of the Word through whom all things were made is addressed to the Father, who "sends down" the Spirit by whose power it is fulfilled. The inclusion of the Word in the eucharistic *epiclesis* is unique to Anglican Prayer Books and to the 4th-century *anaphora* of Sarapion of Thmuis,[40] but its Trinitarian eucharistic theology is traditional. The latter is reflected in the balanced words of the Lima document:

> It is the Father who is the primary origin and final fulfillment of the eucharistic event. The incarnate Son of God by and in whom it is accomplished is its living centre. The Holy Spirit is the immeasurable strength of love which makes it possible and continues to make it effective. The bond between the eucharistic celebration and the mystery of the Triune God reveals the role of the Holy Spirit as that of the one who makes the historical words of Jesus present and alive. Being assured by Jesus' promise in the words of institution that it will be answered, the Church prays to the Father for the gift of the Holy Spirit in order that the eucharistic event may be a reality: the real presence of the crucified and risen Christ giving his life for all humanity.
>
> It is in virtue of the living word of Christ and by the power of the Holy Spirit that the bread and wine become the sacramental signs of Christ's body and blood. (WCC 1982: 13)

Once more, we need to guard against the temptation to consider the *epiclesis* as a "moment of consecration." When human beings pray, it is necessary to express sequentially things which do not occur in a temporal sequence. The entire eucharistic action is epicletic, just as it is also anamnetic. The priestly activity of the Word is unceasing, as is the response of the Father in sending down the Spirit to fulfill that promise. We, on the other hand, are limited by time and space, and our liturgical action unfolds as a series of consecutive moments. The action of Father, Word and Spirit does not occur at some particular point in the prayer, but as the promised response to the eucharistic offering. Little can be gained by attempting to pin down the free, creative and redemptive activity of the Triune God.

Intercessions

Eucharistic Prayer D, alone among those in the Prayer Book, follows the West Syrian and Scottish tradition by including intercessions within the eucharistic prayer. Structurally, intercessions are an expansion of the *epiclesis* upon the congregation to include within the eucharistic action others for whom they pray. The eucharistic prayers of most other traditions include intercessions, but Anglicans have generally avoided them as a repetition of the prayers of the people. The Nonjurors included intercessions within their eucharistic prayer because they found them in their West Syrian models, but the American Prayer Book has never followed its Scottish source in this. Nonjuring theology also considered intercession to be more efficacious when it was offered after the consecration. Bishop Thomas Brett, an 18th-century Nonjuror bishop and liturgical scholar, wrote:

The Reason of the Thing also pleads for putting the
Prayer for all Estates and Conditions of Men after the
Consecreation, for as it is one general End of Sacrifice,
and of this Eucharistick Sacrifice in particular, to render
our Prayers more effectual . . . it is certainly most
proper, that the Sacrifice or Oblation should first be
offered, and that Prayer should be made whilst it lies
upon the altar, and is already dedicated to God.[41]

Certainly this argument has always exercised a powerful influence on Christian devotion, if not on Christian theology, and the special efficacy of prayer before
the Blessed Sacrament "whilst it lies upon the altar" is
not a belief confined to the Nonjurors. Nevertheless, an
unwillingness to lend support to this view is at least
partially responsible for the reluctance of most
Anglican Prayer Books to include intercessions within
the eucharistic prayer, in spite of the overwhelming
tradition for so doing. The prayer's ecumenical origin
and its fidelity to its ancient source are responsible for
the inclusion of the intercessions, at least optionally, in
Eucharistic Prayer D.[42]

It is not necessary to accept Brett's theology of the
greater efficacy of intercessions within the eucharistic
prayer to see their value. First, their inclusion places
the Episcopal Church in agreement with the great Catholic eucharistic traditions of East and West. Second,
intercessions provide an additional point of contact with
our liturgical roots in the Scottish Episcopal Church.
Finally, they provide a more formal opportunity than
do the prayers of the people to include corporate intentions in the eucharistic celebration. At the prayers of
the people all of the intercessions and concerns of the
congregation have a place. Within the eucharistic
prayer it is both traditional and appropriate to mention
the names of those with whom the particular celebration is especially concerned: the bride and groom at a
wedding, the deceased at a funeral, catechumens during

Lent, those baptized at the Great Vigil, ordinands at their ordination, and so forth.

The intercessions conclude with a prayer "that we may find our inheritance with [the Blessed Virgin Mary, with patriarchs, prophets, apostles, and martyrs, (with _____) and] all the saints," and that we might join with them in the eternal praise of God (BCP: 375). The blank line permits the insertion of the name of the saint whose festival is being kept, the patron saint of the parish, or both. The petition, like the final lines of the preface, reminds us that the eucharist is a part of the worship of the whole Church in heaven and on earth, as well as being a petition that we may have a share in that unending praise.

Eucharistic Prayers A and B, which do not include intercessions at this point, nevertheless contain a parallel petition at the end of the *epiclesis*. In Prayer A, that petition states: "bring us with all your saints into the joy of your eternal kingdom" (BCP: 363), while Prayer B prays at greater length:

> In the fullness of time, put all things in subjection under your Christ, and bring us to that heavenly country where, with [_____ and] all your saints, we may enter the everlasting heritage of your sons and daughters. (BCP: 369)

The Prayer of Oblation

Eucharistic Prayers I and II, following the *epiclesis*, offer what Anglicans have generally called the Prayer of Oblation. It is actually an extension of the *anamnesis* to include the oblation of "our selves, our souls and bodies, to be a reasonable, holy, and living sacrifice unto thee" (BCP: 336). It calls the action "our sacrifice of praise and thanksgiving" and asks that "by the merits and death of thy Son Jesus Christ, and through faith in his blood, we, and all thy whole Church, may obtain remission of our sins, and all other benefits of his passion" (BCP: 335).

This self-offering is an important aspect of the eucharist. Although such self-offering may be inferred from what is done at the offertory and the offering of the eucharistic gifts, since this action may be seen as symbolically including the self-offering of the worshipers, the tradition represented by Eucharistic Prayer I wishes to be unambiguous in asserting that self-oblation is a part of that "sacrifice of praise and thanksgiving" which is the eucharist. We offer the eucharist "although we are unworthy" and not by our own merits, but "by the merits and death" of Christ and through faith in his redeeming blood. The fruit of eucharistic offering is "remission of our sins, and all other benefits of Christ's passion." Even if we feel that remission of sins is overemphasized and wish to mention the other benefits of the passion more specifically, the remission of sins is certainly an important fruit of worthy participation in the eucharist.

The prayer asks that the benefits of Christ's passion might be bestowed upon the whole Church: that all who shall be worthy "partakers of this Holy Communion" may be united with Christ and be filled with every grace and blessing "that [Christ] may dwell in us, and we in him" (BCP: 336). This request parallels the petition for the eschatological unity of the Church which is found in the other eucharistic prayers. The request concludes by asking God to accept this sacrifice as "our bounden duty and service." Although we are unworthy to offer, yet we have no choice but to do so, through Jesus Christ.

Doxology and Lord's Prayer

The final element of all the eucharistic prayers is the closing doxology, which offers the prayer of the Church to the Father, through the Son, in the unity of the Holy Spirit. The fixed wording of the doxology leads to the final "Amen," the assent of the people of God in whose name the chief celebrant has given thanks. The doxology with its "Amen" is the climax and conclusion of the *anaphora*. Although we are unwilling and unable to establish or mark a "moment of consecration" in the prayer, the bursting forth of the final doxology clearly marks the completion of the Great Thanksgiving and the fulfillment of the promise of Christ, who is present in the power of his saving death and resurrection. Thus, the doxology and "Amen" are often joyfully sung in celebration of this mystery.

The Lord's Prayer forms the natural climax of our participation in Christ's self-offering. Its corporate recitation binds us together at a focal point in the celebration and expresses our unity with one another in Christ, in whom "we are bold to say, Our Father" (BCP: 336). The petition "Give us today our daily bread" (BCP: 364) has been seen from early times as preparation for the reception of communion and was apparently the original reason for including the Lord's Prayer between the eucharistic prayer and communion.

Fraction

The breaking of bread is primarily a utilitarian act. Bread is broken in order to be shared. In Jewish tradition the bread over which the blessing has been said is immediately broken and shared. In the scriptural accounts of the Last Supper Jesus follows this tradition. In the Emmaus story (Luke 24:13-35) Jesus was revealed to the disciples "in the breaking of the bread," and "the breaking of the bread" appears in Acts 2:42, 46 to be the name for the celebration of the eucharist. Christians have seen in the breaking of the bread a symbol of the breaking of the Lord's body on the cross and of their own need to be broken in order both to share in the life in Christ and to share that life with others.

Concelebrating priests join with the chief celebrant in the breaking of the bread (BCP: 354) as a sign of their participation in the eucharistic offering. Additional chalices, if any are needed, are filled at this time in preparation for communion (BCP: 407) so that the one bread and one cup may stand on the altar during the Great Thanksgiving as signs of the unity of the Church in receiving the eucharistic gifts.

> The bread which we break is a sharing of the Body of
>   Christ.
> *We being many are one bread, one body,*
> *for we all share in the one bread.* (BOS: 15)

The bread is broken in silence (BCP: 364), but an anthem called *confractorium* in the *Book of Occasional Services* (BOS: 15) may follow the initial fraction. The anthem "Christ our Passover is sacrificed for us; *Therefore let us keep the feast*" is printed in the texts of both Rite One (BCP: 337) and Rite Two (BCP: 364). The *Agnus Dei* is an alternative or additional anthem. *The Book of Occasional Services* includes fifteen *confractoria* for optional use (BOS: 15-19).

Both "Christ our Passover" and "Lamb of God" use the image of Christ as the paschal lamb. Throughout the eucharist we encounter both Paschal and sacrificial language. We have already discussed the eucharist as the Christian Passover, the *transitus,* or passing over from death to life with Christ. We have seen how it gathers up all the meaning of the Jewish Passover into itself and proclaims the new Exodus in the death and resurrection of Christ. We recognize that we celebrate the Paschal Feast by eating and drinking the food of the reign of God: the broken bread and the cup poured out which are the Body of the true Paschal Lamb and the blood of the new covenant. We must now turn our attention to the eucharist as the Christian sacrifice.

The Eucharistic Sacrifice

The New Testament describes the death of Christ in sacrificial terms. The Passover itself—the *Pesach*—was a sacrifice. Its most significant parts were the marking of the doorposts with the blood of the lamb and the eating of the lamb's flesh. The community participated in the sacrifice by eating the paschal lamb and the unleavened bread with which the lamb came to be most closely associated. Whatever else the eucharistic sacrifice means, its basic meaning is certainly that when we eat and drink the bread and wine of the eucharist in accordance with Christ's command and promise, we participate in Christ's sacrifice.

Another reference to the eucharist as sacrifice is found in the Epistle to the Hebrews. It identifies Christ with the high priest in the performance of the solemn rites of purification of Yom Kippur, the yearly Day of Atonement. The purpose of these rites was the removal of sin. Yom Kippur was a national day of penitence on which the high priest—not instead of the people, but as their leader and on their behalf—performed ancient rites to remove the sins of Israel so that they might be able to offer the sacrifices of the great Feast of Tabernacles which follows Yom Kippur. For Christians, Christ offers this sin offering, or "sacrifice for sins." But unlike the yearly Hebrew sacrifices, Christ's is offered once for all: "For by a single offering he has perfected for all time those who are sanctified" (Hebrews 10:12-14).

As the Epistle to the Hebrews accurately points out, the rites of Yom Kippur could not really take away sin, but only symbolize its removal, because the rites had to be repeated every year (Hebrews 9:9-10; 10:1-11). In the rites, the high priest took the blood of a bullock and a goat and purified the priests, the people, and the Temple itself with it. At the climax of the rite, amid clouds of incense and wearing special linen vestments, the high priest entered the Holy of Holies—the place where God's presence was most immediately experienced—and prayed to the Lord God of Israel (see Leviticus 16).

This is what Christ did in reality, not in symbol only. He did not purify us with the blood of sacrificial animals, but with his own blood. He did not enter the Holy of Holies in Jerusalem, but the true sanctuary, the throne of God in heaven, where he ever lives to make intercession for us (Hebrews 9:11-26). The rite of purification, the "sacrifice for sins," has been performed once and for all. The true sanctuary stands open, and Christ has taken the place of honor which is his by right.

In the rites of purification in the Old Testament, the bodies of the victims (bullock and goat) were neither offered on the altar nor eaten but hauled away and burned "outside the camp." The sacrifice of Christ, however, is offered to God at the heavenly altar itself, and the whole people of God are commanded, "Take and eat" (Hebrews 13:10-16). In this, the sacrifice of Christ resembles the Jewish sacrifice called *zebach todah*, the sacrifice of thanksgiving, in which the victim was offered on the altar and the worshipers feasted on its flesh. It is not accidental that *thusia eucharistika*, the Greek translation of *zebach todah*, can also be translated as "eucharistic sacrifice."

Christ is the perfect victim. By becoming human, he identifies himself perfectly with humankind. He is one of us—the perfect human being, the new Adam, the new *anthropos*. He lives a perfect human life among us and of his own will freely lays down his life as a sacrifice, a gift to the Father. As victim, Christ is slain on the cross. As priest, Christ himself performs the purification with his own blood, carries his prayer into heaven itself through his resurrection and ascension, and makes atonement for us. Christ's body is not burned but carried into heaven so that it may become the means of our union with God; and in the eucharist, Christ has provided us the means to make present those mighty acts and to eat and drink at his table in his kingdom, where they come from east and west to dine with Abraham and Isaac and Jacob.

Much more can be—and, in fact, has been—said about the eucharistic sacrifice.[43] Our treatment of "sacrifice" has been derived from the liturgy's use of the New Testament passages which are read during Holy Week and Easter, and from the language of the eucharist itself. The catechism replies to the question "Why is the Eucharist called a sacrifice?" by saying:

> Because the Eucharist, the Church's sacrifice of praise and thanksgiving, is the way by which the sacrifice of Christ is made present, and in which he unites us to his one offering of himself. (BCP: 859)

Communion

The breaking of the bread (the fraction) is the prelude to the reception of communion. Eating the bread and drinking the wine over which thanks have been given is the effective sign of our participation in Christ's sacrifice: eating his Body and drinking his Blood. The name Holy Communion is applied not only to the act of receiving but to the entire service and to its second half, the liturgy of the sacrament. For it is in receiving communion that we are most closely united with Christ in the saving acts of his dying and rising. Once for all in baptism, and week by week in the eucharist, Christians are sacramentally united with the crucified and risen Lord.

Rite Two has pruned all prayers from this part of the liturgy in order to emphasize the centrality of the eucharistic prayer and the fourfold action of the eucharist itself. Rite One has retained a classic 16th-century prayer in preparation for communion, the Prayer of Humble Access (BCP: 337). Many liturgies contain similar prayers that express the unworthiness of the priest or, as in this case, of the communicants, to approach the Lord's table. Such prayers are the almost inevitable devotional accompaniment to reflecting on participation in the eucharist:

> We are not worthy. . . . But thou . . . have mercy. . . . Grant us therefore, gracious Lord, so to eat the flesh of thy dear Son Jesus Christ, and to drink his blood, that we may evermore dwell in him, and he in us. (BCP: 337)

The Prayer of Humble Access applies to the individual communicant what has been proclaimed in the Great Thanksgiving.

It is true that the prayer says nothing new and that it obscures the clean lines of the liturgical structure. However, it is also true that the prayer meets the overwhelming devotional needs of countless communicants by focusing their spiritual dispositions at the moment they are coming forward to receive communion.

The Prayer of Humble Access has often been quoted as evidence that the Anglican Church believes in the Real Presence. Our discussion of *anamnesis* in the Great Thanksgiving should make it clear that the Episcopal Church speaks of the presence of Christ in the power of his saving death and resurrection in the eucharistic gifts. This presence is "real." It is the work of the Father through the power of the Holy Spirit in fulfillment of the promise of Christ. It is not simply a subjective experience of the worshipers, although it is only by faith that the Real Presence of Christ can be perceived.

The Anglican Church has traditionally been unwilling to go further in describing how and in what manner Christ is present. It has been content to say that the presence is promised by God, who is faithful to the promise. Christ's presence is objectively and spiritually real, not merely a psychological experience. Rather, it is a sacramental presence, different from the manner in which physical objects are present, yet nonetheless *real*.

Communion follows the ancient invitation, "The Gifts of God for the People of God" (BCP: 364). The people come forward to receive. Priests and deacons, and, if necessary, lay persons administer the consecrated gifts (BCP: 408), "The Body of Christ, the bread of heaven," and "The Blood of Christ, the cup of salvation" (BCP: 365).

A simple postcommunion thanksgiving concludes the service, which ends with a dismissal. Dismissal (*missa* in Latin) has also given its name to the entire service, the "mass." The note of dismissal is sounded first in the postcommunion prayers.

> . . . that we may continue in that holy fellowship, and do all such good works as thou hast prepared for us to walk in. . . . (BCP: 339)

> Send us now into the world in peace, and grant us strength and courage to love and serve you with gladness and singleness of heart. . . . (BCP: 365)

> . . . send us out to do the work you have given us to do, to love and serve you as faithful witnesses of Christ our Lord. (BCP: 366)

The Church which has gathered to make eucharist is sent out to be the Body of Christ in the world, to bear witness to Jesus and the resurrection. In the apt words of Louis Bouyer:

> The importance of the liturgical celebration itself implies a correlative importance in what we do after the

liturgical celebration, in daily living. The Mystery that is always present and always active in the liturgy can only show its presence and manifest its activity through the whole life of Christians, through that Cross and resurrection which are their permanent "witness" to the world.[44]

The dismissal asserts the relationship between liturgy and Christian living. It is a call to mission, not simply in the narrow sense of preaching religion, but in the broader sense of witnessing to the power of the risen Christ in daily living—a call to live the baptismal and eucharistic life in the world.

The bishop, or the priest, dismisses the people with a blessing (BCP: 366). In one sense the blessing is redundant for those who have just received the blessings of the Body and Blood of Christ, and Rite Two permits its omission. The actual dismissal is pronounced by the deacon, the minister most concerned with the Church's ministry in the world (BCP: 543) and whose proper liturgy is to assist others in taking their parts in the Lord's service. The liturgical eucharist ends with the people's response, "Thanks be to God," as they "go forth into the world, rejoicing in the power of the Spirit . . . to love and serve the Lord" (BCP: 366).

An Order for
Celebrating the Holy Eucharist

In addition to Rite One and Rite Two, the Prayer Book includes An Order for Celebrating the Holy Eucharist (BCP: 400-5), frequently but unofficially called Rite Three. This is not a liturgy but an *ordo* or *agenda* for a celebration. It is intended for informal celebrations on occasions other than the Sunday eucharist (BCP: 400) and includes no fixed texts. The theological importance of the Order for Celebrating is precisely that it does not contain text. It lists the elements which the

Episcopal Church requires for a celebration of the eucharist:

> The People and Priest
> Gather in the Lord's Name
> Proclaim and Respond to the Word of God
> Pray for the World and the Church
> Exchange the Peace
> Prepare the Table
> Make Eucharist
> Break the Bread
> Share the Gifts of God (BCP: 400f)

This list is an outline of the traditional order of service. It does not mean that every item on it is necessary for the validity of the eucharist, but that these are the integral components of the rite, without which it should not be celebrated. The service will always include both Word and Sacrament, common prayers, the peace, and the "four-fold shape" identified by Dix.[45] Great freedom is given as to the manner in which the service is conducted and to what the words are used. The inclusion of a Gospel reading is required, as is the use of one of the eucharistic prayers assigned to Rites One and Two, or of one of two Forms containing the text of the opening dialogue, the introduction to the Sanctus, the institution narrative, *anamnesis, epiclesis,* and the final doxology. Other parts of the eucharistic prayer may be prepared by the celebrant community, but the provision of fixed wording for the institution narrative, *anamnesis,* and *epiclesis* assures that all celebrations, no matter how informal, will conform to the tradition of the Church.

This Order underscores the nature of the eucharist as an action. It permits freedom in choice of words, except in the central sections of the Great Thanksgiving, but insists that certain actions be performed if the celebration is to be a service of the Episcopal Church.

Special Circumstances

A number of special circumstances which have theological implications are provided for in the Prayer Book.
First, it provides for supplementary consecration "if the
consecrated Bread or Wine does not suffice for the
number of communicants" (BCP: 408). Supplementary
consecration poses a difficult theological-liturgical
problem.[46] If the priest follows the second method suggested by the Prayer Book (consecrating both kinds by
saying the eucharistic prayer from the end of the Sanctus through the Invocation), there has in fact been a
second celebration of the eucharist within the first.
This may be unobjectionable if we see the eucharist
simply as a ritual for consecrating bread and wine for
communion; but if we consider the broader aspects of
the eucharist, as we have been doing, then this procedure is open to serious question. The Prayer Book's
second provision strongly suggests, of course, that *all*
the major sections of the eucharistic prayer are necessary for consecration, rather than one particular
"moment" or formula.

The Prayer Book's first method of supplementary
consecration directs the celebrant "to return to the
Holy Table, and consecrate more of either or both, by
saying. . . ." (BCP: 408) What follows is a brief *epiclesis*
joined to the Words of Institution, asking "that it [bread
or wine], also, may be the Sacrament of the precious
Body (Blood) of thy (your) Son. . . ." There is no suggestion that this short form is sufficient as a eucharistic
prayer but only that, in the context of the celebration of
the eucharist, when the eucharistic prayer has already
been proclaimed, this form is sufficient to extend consecration to *additional* bread or wine, so that all present
may receive communion.

A second special circumstance provided by the
Prayer Book is the administration of communion from

the reserved Sacrament to the sick or to "others who for weighty cause could not be present at the celebration" (BCP: 408f). A special form of service is included for this purpose (BCP: 396-9), and the reservation of the Sacrament for the communion of the sick and the administration of communion by a deacon when no priest is available are expressly permitted.

Taking of the Sacrament to those who could not be present at the eucharist is a way of extending participation in the celebration to other members of the body. The practice has been traditional among Christians since at least the second century. It is also possible to celebrate the eucharist for shut-ins (BCP: 396), but taking communion to the sick from the parish eucharist is a way of including them in the *parish* celebration and thereby affirming their membership not only in the Body of Christ but also in the particular local congregation which is celebrating the eucharist.

Finally, disciplinary rubrics prescribe the exclusion from eucharistic communion, or excommunication, of those whose notoriously evil lives would tend to destroy the eucharistic community if they were permitted to participate without repentance and amendment of life (BCP: 409). However infrequently the priest, with the requisite notification of the bishop, uses these provisions, they witness that the Church must give account of its stewardship, that the eucharistic life must be lived in a moral manner, and that "whenever [we] fall into sin, [we must] repent and return to the Lord" (BCP: 304).

Chapter Seven:
The Pastoral Offices

Pastoral Offices is the title of a section of the *Book of Common Prayer* (BCP: 411-507) containing rites for particular occasions in the lives of individual Christians. The eucharist, the daily offices, and Christian initiation are integrated into the celebration of the liturgical year. The pastoral offices, on the other hand, are geared to the pattern of individual life, and are printed in more or less choronological order. The Prayer Book includes confirmation in this section as a convenience for occasions when it is celebrated apart from baptism (BCP: 413-9), but we have already considered confirmation along with baptism in Chapter Four and will not deal with it again.

A Form of Commitment to Christian Service (BCP: 420-1) provides an opportunity for a person at a critical moment in his or her life to make or renew personal commitment to a particular form of Christian service in the world. This might be done, for example, at graduation, when changing vocations, when entering a course of study, or upon retirement. It includes an opportunity for the person to make an individual statement of intention and to renew the baptismal promises. This commitment might be combined with the reaffirmation of the baptismal covenant before the bishop (BCP: 419), but more often it is made at the Sunday eucharist in the presence of the congregation and the parish priest. Use of this form is entirely optional, but it provides an appropriate way for the congregation to join liturgically in celebrating a significant moment in the life of an individual member.

Christian Marriage

The opening rubric of *Concerning the Service* reads: "Christian marriage is a solemn and public covenant between a man and a woman in the presence of God" (BCP: 422). "The bond and covenant of marriage," we are told, "was established by God in creation . . . " (BCP: 423). Marriage is, therefore, a natural state of men and women, not a concession to human weakness. "It signifies to us the mystery of the union between Christ and his Church . . . " (BCP: 423). The author of Ephesians—the Scripture to which the Prayer Book refers—presumes that his readers' familiarity with the marital union will provide them with a basis for understanding "the mystery of the union between Christ and his Church." The Prayer Book describes the purposes of this covenanted union in the opening address of the service.

> The union of husband and wife in heart, body, and mind is intended by God for their mutual joy; for help and comfort given one another in prosperity and adversity; and, when it is God's will, for the procreation of children and their nurture in the knowledge and love of the Lord. (BCP: 423)

These three purposes of marriage are derived immediately from the English Prayer Book of 1662 and ultimately from *The King's Book* of 1543. They have been "common coin in the West since the time of Augustine."[1] The explicit sexual references of the earlier rite have been removed or softened. The English *Alternative Service Book 1980* has dealt with them more straightforwardly, recasting and expanding the highly compressed structure of the original to make the meaning clear.

The American version is compact and expresses the
concepts with sufficient theological clarity, while the
English version is probably easier for the usual congregation at a wedding to understand:

> It is God's purpose that, as husband and wife give them-
> selves to each other in love throughout their lives, they
> shall be united in that love as Christ is united with his
> Church. Marriage is given, that husband and wife may
> comfort each other, living faithfully together in need
> and in plenty, in sorrow and in joy. It is given, that with
> delight and tenderness they may know each other in
> love, and, through the joy of their bodily union, may
> strengthen the union of their hearts and lives. It is
> given, that they may have children and be blessed in
> caring for them and bringing them up in accordance
> with God's will, to his praise and glory. (ASB,
> 1980: 288)

Therefore, marriage is a covenanted relationship
between a man and a woman, not a ceremony performed by a priest. The role of the presiding priest or
bishop is to witness the vows of the couple, pronounce
the nuptial blessing and preside at the eucharist (BCP:
422). The prayers of the people of God, participation in
the eucharist, and the nuptial blessing are the distinc-
tively Christian rites connected with marriage. Since
"the bond and covenant of marriage was established by
God in creation" (BCP: 423), real marriages can and do
take place without any Christian rites being celebrated.
The Episcopal Church recognizes these marriages and
provides The Blessing of a Civil Marriage (BCP: 433f)
for those who wish to add the distinctive Christian rite
to a marriage already contracted.

Marriage, unlike most religious rites, is also a concern
of the state. In the United States the minister acts on
behalf of the civil government as a witness to the marriage vows and is charged by civil law to deliver a legal

record of the marriage to the appropriate state authorities. This is not true in many other countries, where church weddings have no civil validity and where all legal marriages must be performed by officers of the state. The "church wedding" follows the civil ceremony and is a celebration and blessing of the marriage already legally contracted.

The Celebration and Blessing of a Marriage

The Celebration and Blessing of a Marriage is a true liturgy. It involves the congregation and the normal liturgical ministries: the bishop or a priest to preside, a deacon to read the Gospel and lead the prayers for the couple, lay persons to read the lessons (BCP: 422). If the celebration of the eucharist is to follow, the newly married couple normally bring forward the eucharistic gifts (BCP: 431-432). The context of this celebration is the eucharistic Ministry of the Word. The address to the congregation already mentioned immediately follows the entrance of the ministers and the wedding party.

At the conclusion of the address, the members of the congregation are charged, "If any of you can show just cause why they [the couple] may not lawfully be married, speak now; or else for ever hold your peace" (BCP: 424). The charge to reveal impediments to the proposed marriage is also made in the banns, which may be published at three Sunday services prior to the wedding (BCP: 437). Part of the concern is legal, but the public nature of the marriage covenant is also involved. These declarations make clear that this relationship is being entered into publicly and that the assembled people of God know of no reason why it should be forbidden. A similar charge is given to the couple (BCP: 424).

Declaration of Consent

The history of the marriage rite[2] has produced an apparent duplication in the Anglican tradition between the declaration of consent (BCP: 424) and the actual vows (BCP: 427). In the Prayer Book they are separated by the Ministry of the Word. The declaration of consent has the formal purpose of ascertaining that the couple are entering into the marriage covenant freely and of their own will. In practice, it sets forth what is expected of each partner. The questions addressed to both partners are identical: Will you "live together in the covenant of marriage," love, honor, comfort, keep, and "forsaking all others, be faithful . . . as long as you both shall live?" (BCP: 424). The response, "I will," signifies the consent of each partner to enter into this lifelong relationship. The celebrant then asks "all of you witnessing these promises" to "do all in your power to uphold these two persons in their marriage" (BCP: 425), thereby recognizing both the liturgical nature of the rite, which involves the supporting prayers of the congregation, and the importance of the support of the community by its actions and attitudes for the success of a marriage.

"Giving the Bride Away"

A "presentation" or "giving in marriage" may follow (BCP: 437). Hatchett correctly comments, "The form is a survival from a period when women were thought of as property."[3] The force of ritual custom is so strong, particularly in rites as intimately connected with the structure of human life as marriages and burials, however, that many brides wish to be "given away" by their fathers; and optional alternatives permit the presentation of the woman or of both partners by one or both parents or by other presenters, or the complete omission of the ceremony. The most positive interpretation possible would have the two families presenting their children to each other that they might become a new family.

The persistence of this ceremony of "giving away the bride" in the face of raised feminine consciousness is a classic example of the resistance of ritual to change. Many such ritual customs have survived the total abandonment of the "theology" by which they were once explained and have found a new and acceptable rationale for their continuance. It is in fact a commonplace among historians of religion that the reason given for the performance of a rite is seldom the reason for which it was adopted.

The Marriage

The Marriage (BCP: 427f) follows the Ministry of the Word, for which a large selection of readings are given. "*A homily or other response to the Readings*" is optional (BCP: 426). The marriage vows are modernized forms of those traditional in English-language marriage rites. Unlike earlier versions, this version makes no distinction of roles between the partners.[4] The vows are made "in the Name of God," and conclude with "This is my solemn vow." Each person promises:

> . . . to have and to hold from this day forward, for better for worse, for richer for poorer, in sickness and in health, to love and to cherish, until we are parted by death. (BCP: 427)

Nothing that has not already been undertaken in the declaration of consent is promised here. However, this time the couple speak the words themselves, and the words "from this day forward" indicate that the covenant is now in effect. The exchange of vows is ritualized by the couple's holding hands and exchanging rings. The rings are described as "*signs* of the vows by which this man and this woman have bound themselves to each other," and individually as symbols of the vows (BCP: 427). The Prayer Book presumes that two rings will be exchanged, although one ring or "some other suitable symbol of the vows," may be used (BCP: 437). The public exchange of these vows and the attendant symbolic actions by the couple constitute their entrance into the marriage covenant, and the celebrant formally declares this, pronouncing "that they are husband and wife, in the Name of the Father, and of the Son, and of the Holy Spirit" (BCP: 428). To this the celebrant adds, "Those whom God has joined together let no one put asunder" (see Mark 10:9).

The Prayer Book calls this entire section "The Marriage," but the wording of the declaration makes it clear that it is the actions of the couple, not the priest's pronouncing them married, which are the effective, or sacramental, signs of the marriage.

The Prayers and Blessing

"*The Deacon or other person appointed*" leads the intercessions, just as he or she would do at a celebration of the eucharist (BCP: 429). To each prayer the congregation respond *Amen.* The focus of the intercessions is, of course, the newly married couple: ". . . this man and this woman whom you make one flesh in Holy Matrimony"; but they also include the entire "world you have made, and for which your Son gave his life" (BCP: 429).

The gifts asked for the couple include wisdom and devotion that they may fulfill their covenant in their common life. A significant gift requested is grace "to recognize and acknowledge their fault, and to seek each other's forgiveness and yours" when they have hurt each other. More corporate and communitarian aspects appear in the petition that the couple's life together may be "a sign of Christ's love to this sinful and broken world, that unity may overcome estrangement, forgiveness heal guilt, and joy conquer despair" and "that they may reach out in love and concern for others."

Prayer is made for "all married persons who have witnessed these vows," that they "may find their lives strengthened and their loyalties confirmed" (BCP: 430). This prayer signals a renewal of all married couples present. This renewal happens not because of the example of the newly married couple but by the already-married couples' participation in the rite, with the repetition of the marriage vows. The power of ritual to evoke the past is recognized and made the ground of this prayer. The intercessions conclude with prayer for the unity of all the children of God, living and dead, and their transformation through grace so that God's will "may be done on earth as it is in heaven" (BCP: 430). The Lord's Prayer is the model for all Christian prayer, and this use of one of its principal petitions is a strong conclusion, especially when the eucharist is not celebrated and the recitation of the Lord's Prayer immediately precedes the intercessions (BCP: 428).

The nuptial blessing follows the prayers. It is the specific liturgy of the priest or bishop, who adds the Church's blessing to the marriage "that [the bride and groom] may faithfully live together in this life, and in the age to come have life everlasting" (BCP: 431).

The newly married couple greet each other with the kiss of peace, "*after which greetings may be exchanged throughout the congregation*" (BCP: 431). This is the traditional kiss between bride and groom; it has remained a part of wedding customs even when separated from its context in the peace. The exchange between husband and wife is often seen as a "sealing" of the marriage covenant and a ceremonial beginning of their fulfillment of the promise to "love, honor, and cherish each other." In this context, the exchange of the peace is a rite of inclusion that marks both the liturgical community's acceptance of the couple in their new status as husband and wife and the community's own redefinition of itself.

The peace either concludes the rite or serves as a bridge to the celebration of the nuptial eucharist. Like the peace, the nuptial eucharist is a rite of inclusion. The Christian couple begin their new life together by participating in the eucharist, bringing the eucharistic gifts to the altar, and receiving communion. This is both a form of blessing their new life and a recognition of the central place of their membership in the Christian eucharistic community in that life. The eucharistic preface introduces another biblical image of marriage:

> Because in the love of wife and husband, you have given us an image of the heavenly Jerusalem, adorned as a bride for her bridegroom, your Son Jesus Christ our Lord; who loves her and gave himelf for her, that he might make the whole creation new. (BCP: 381)

The new Jerusalem as the bride of Christ, the renewal of creation, and the marriage of the Lamb (Revelation 21) provide striking visual iamges to accompany the more common reference to Ephesians 5:22-33. They also strongly suggest the identification of the eucharist with the "marriage supper of the Lamb" (see Revelation 19:9) and hence its appropriateness as a part of The Celebration and Blessing of a Marriage.

Related Services

The Blessing of a Civil Marriage (BCP: 433f) meets the needs of those couples who wish to receive the nuptial blessing on their already-existing marriage. This ceremony is sometimes popularly but erroneously described as "being remarried in church." The rite clearly recognizes the existence and validity of the civil marriage. The opening address says, "You have come here today to seek the blessing of God and of his Church upon your marriage," and the couple are asked to promise, "with the help of God, to fulfill the obligations which Christian Marriage demands." The promises, based on the declaration of consent in the marriage rite, say unambiguously, "N., you have taken N. to be your wife (husband). . . ." Only after affirming the existence of the civil marriage does the Prayer Book ask the couple to promise to love, honor, keep, "and forsaking all others, to be faithful to [each other] as long as [they] both shall live" (BCP: 433). Even if lifelong fidelity is not among the expectations of contemporary society in civil marriage, it is here set down as an obligation of Christian marriage.

The rings, which have already been exchanged, are blessed without being removed (BCP: 434). Matthew 19:5 ("Those whom God has joined together. . . ") is pronounced over the couple, and the service continues with the nuptial blessing and eucharist.

The already-existing marriage is recognized. The couple promise to fulfill the obligations of Christian marriage, and the distinctive Christian elements, the nuptial blessing and eucharist, are added. The service is of great pastoral and practical value, but its chief theological significance is in its identification of those elements which distinguish Christian marriage from civil marriage, since both are necessarily intermixed in the marriage service itself.

An Order for Marriage

An Order for Marriage (BCP: 435f), like An Order for Eucharist, is the outline of a service. Only the text of the vows is fixed. The Order permits those couples who

desire to write their own wedding service great freedom
to do so, yet it requires it to conform to the standards set
by the Church. The use of this form makes it possible to
express in the rite marriage customs of other traditions,
whether old traditions of families or ethnic groups or
new traditions which the couple and their contemporar-
ies are developing. The following nine elements make
up the Order. Obviously, all nine are not essential to
the validity of a marriage, but they are necessary to the
proper ordering of a Christian marriage rite.

> 1. "The teaching of the Church concerning Holy Matri-
> mony" is briefly stated. It is set forth in the opening
> address of the marriage service (BCP: 423); its language,
> but not its content, can be freely changed.
> 2. The consent of both man and woman must be publicly
> given.
> 3. Readings, "one of which is always from Holy Scrip-
> ture," may be included. This permits the inclusion of
> other material, or the omission of the readings alto-
> gether. However, if the eucharist is to be celebrated, the
> Gospel must always be included.
> 4. The vows are exchanged.
> 5. "The Celebrant declares the union of the man and
> woman as husband and wife in the Name of the Father,
> and of the Son, and of the Holy Spirit." The declaration
> of the marriage is a requirement of civil law in most
> places, but the Church requires that it be done in the
> name of the Trinity.
> 6. Prayers are offered for the couple, the Christian com-
> munity, and the world.
> 7. A priest or bishop pronounces a solemn nuptial bless-
> ing, although not necessariy in the form from the Prayer
> Book service.
> 8. The couple exchange the peace.
> 9. The nuptial eucharist may follow, according to any of
> the authorized forms.

This Order is far from being a license to ignore the
tradition of the Church. In fact, it permits the use of

prayers from the 1928 Prayer Book or some other traditional rite. It sets the bounds on legitimate freedom within the tradition of the Church. Theologically, the value of this Order is that it separates those elements which the Church believes should be included in the celebration of a marriage from the language in which they are expressed. Some of that language is traditional, but much of it is newly composed. The language and ceremonial are subject to change, but the theological content expressed by the words and the liturgical actions is not.

The Reconciliation of a Penitent

"The ministry of reconciliation" has its roots in the Gospel and in the reconciling ministry of Jesus Christ. It "has been committed by Christ to his Church" (BCP: 446). This is explicitly stated by St. Paul in 2 Corinthians 5:18-19. Matthew 16:19, Matthew 18:15-18, and John 20:22-23 are the principal Gospel passages that underlie the statement. Matthew 18 sets "binding" and "loosing" squarely in the context of the way in which the New Testament Church deals with sin and its prevalence and power even within the community of believers. Dealing effectively with sin by the authority and command of Christ is part and parcel of the life of the Church and not a special sacerdotal power to be exercised by priests apart from the body of believers. John 20 attributes the command to forgive sins to the risen Christ. It follows his greeting of peace and is a part of the *shalom* which is his gift to his people. It is also tied to the gift of the Holy Spirit, who acts in the Chruch to accomplish the sanctification of God's people. Reconciliation is a divine act in which the Church participates.

[It] is exercised through the care each Christian has for others, through the common prayer of Christians assembled for public worship, and through the priesthood of the Church and its ministers declaring absolution. (BCP: 446)

Living the baptismal and eucharistic life is itself a ministry of reconciliation. The ministry of the laity includes carrying on "Christ's work of reconciliation in the world" (BCP: 855). This involves not only forgiving others as we would be forgiven, but working as representatives of Christ and his Church to establish mercy and justice in our society.

"Forgive us our sins" is of course a petition of the Lord's Prayer, and the common prayers of the Church contain many such prayers—for example, the general confessions in the eucharist and daily offices, the proper liturgy for Ash Wednesday (BCP: 264-9), various prayers and collects, and the petitions for pardon in the prayers of the people, such as "for ourselves; for the forgiveness of our sins, and for the grace of the Holy Spirit to amend our lives, we pray to you, O Lord" (BCP: 391).

Baptism is described in the Nicene Creed as "for the forgiveness of sins" (BCP: 359), and the eucharistic "sacrifice of praise and thanksgiving" is especially offered that "we, and all thy whole Church, may obtain remission of our sins, and all other benefits of [Christ's] passion" (BCP: 335). It is only in the light of the Paschal Mystery of the death and resurrection of Christ that forgiveness of sins takes place. As the sacraments of participation in that mystery, baptism and eucharist are the primary sacraments of reconciliation.

God reconciles us to himself and to one another through both common prayer and sacrament; and it is within the context of the common prayer and sacramental life of the Church that we approach "the priesthood

of the Church and its ministers declaring absolution"
(BCP: 446).

In Chapter Six we discussed the priestly absolution
following the general confession in public services. The
Exhortation from the Penitential Order at the Eucharist, after describing self-examination in preparation for
communion, continues:

> And if, in your preparation, you need help and counsel,
> then go and open your grief to a discreet and under-
> standing priest, and confess your sins, that you may
> receive the benefit of absolution, and spiritual counsel
> and advice; to the removal of scruple and doubt, the
> assurance of pardon, and the strengthening of your
> faith. (BCP: 317)

The Reconciliation of a Penitent provides for this
private and personal, or *auricular,* confession. It is available "for all who desire it . . . anytime and anywhere"
(BCP: 446). The "seal of the confessional" binds those
who hear the confession not to reveal or discuss its contents with either the penitent or anyone else.

> The content of a confession is not normally a matter of
> subsequent discussion. The secrecy of a confession is
> morally absolute for the confessor, and must under no
> circumstances be broken. (BCP: 446)

The above directive makes two different points. First,
it states that the content of a confession is not *normally* a
matter of subsequent discussion. This allows for the
possibility that the penitent might wish to discuss matters raised during the confession with the confessor at
another time. The penitent might, for example, wish
further advice, or assistance in obtaining help. Second,
it clearly states that the confessor must *under no circumstances* break the seal of secrecy. Moral theologians may
disagree about the exact meaning of the term "morally
absolute," but there is no doubt as to the meaning of the
rubric: the confessor is forbidden to violate the secrecy

of the confession, no matter what the circumstances. To do so would not only canonically violate the rubrics of the *Book of Common Prayer*; it would constitute a moral wrong.

The Rite of Reconciliation

The two forms provided for reconciliation are specifically declared to be equivalent (BCP: 446). It is therefore legitimate to consider them together and to interpret one in the light of the other. Form One (BCP: 447f) is simple, direct, and based on traditional Western forms that have been widely used by Episcopalians throughout the years. Form Two (BCP: 449-52) is influenced by Eastern Orthodox forms, and it sets sin and forgiveness within the framework of the baptismal life in Christ.

> Through the water of baptism you clothed me with the shining garment of [Christ's] righteousness, and established me among your children in your kingdom. But I have squandered the inheritance of your saints, and have wandered far in a land that is waste. . . . I turn to you in sorrow and repentance. Receive me again into the arms of your mercy, and restore me to the blessed company of your faithful people; through him in whom you have redeemed the world, your Son our Savior Jesus Christ. (BCP: 450)

Reconciliation restores the sin-damaged relationship with Christ that was established in baptism. For although the baptismal bond cannot be broken (BCP: 298), we can and do squander our baptismal inheritance. We live as if we were not united to Christ. The baptismal relationship is denied by sin, but within the unbreakable baptismal bond reconciliation and restoration to the baptismal life in Christ are both possible and necessary. The imagery of the rite is that of the parable of the prodigal son (Luke 15:11-32). It speaks of the father's unmerited gift, his overflowing love, and his willingness to forgive. To receive the gift we have only to admit that we have wandered away and return. The English word "repentance" translates the Greek *meta-noia*, which has the root meaning of changing one's mind. The equivalent Hebrew root *shvb* has the literal meaning of turning around, which corresponds exactly with the action of the prodigal in the parable.

The father's immediate and overwhelming response to the prodigal's confession, "Father, I have sinned against heaven and before you; I am no longer worthy to be called your son," is to receive him into the arms of his mercy and to celebrate his return with a joyful feast. The words of the father are reflected in the final blessing of Form Two: "Now there is rejoicing in heaven; for you were lost, and are found; you were dead, and are now alive in Christ Jesus our Lord" (BCP: 451). Reconciliation restores the penitent to active membership in the Christian community. That restoration, in turn, renews the community. Reconciliation celebrates the the sinner's conversion, the turning again to Christ, and the renewal of the baptismal covenant. Reconciliation is the work of God, the "heavenly Father, [who] formed [the penitent] from the dust in [God's] image and likeness, and redeemed [the penitent] from sin and death by the cross of [God's] Son Jesus Christ" (BCP: 450).

At the beginning of the rite the priest prays that God will enlighten the heart and open the lips of the penitent to make a true and humble confession (BCP: 447, 449). The penitent confesses "all serious sins troubling the conscience" and gives "evidence of due contrition" (BCP: 446). The priest "gives such counsel and encouragement as are needed and pronounces absolution" (BCP: 446). The confession is made "to Almighty God, to his Church, and to [the confessor]" (BCP: 447), or "in the presence of Christ, and of . . . his minister"

(BCP: 450). The priest hears the confession as the minister of Christ, to whom it is properly made, but also as the representative of the Church, the community involved in and injured by the sins of its members.

The Confession of Sin

A formal definition of sin is given in the catechism: "Sin is the seeking of our own will instead of the will of God, thus distorting our relationship with God, with other people, and with all creation" (BCP: 848). From its definition we see that sin is not a series of wrong acts but a sort of disease of the will. The actions we call sins are the symptoms of the disease, the effects of seeking our own will rather than the will of God.[5] We commit sins "in thought, word, and deed, in things done and left undone," and we commit them "by [our] own fault." In the confession the penitent names the ways in which he or she has committed sins, begs "forgiveness of God and his Church" and asks the confessor for "counsel, direction, and absolution" (BCP: 447).

We do not confess things that are not our own fault. Such things either are not sins or are the sins of other people. The goal of the confessor's counsel and direction is not to remove the symptoms of sin but to root out the disease—the cancer—of sin itself from the soul by the power of the redeeming love of Christ. Reconciliation is not a program for self-improvement but an opening of the soul to salvation and redemption through the Paschal Mystery. This opening to salvation might also be described as taking place through the Blood of the Cross, or by grace through faith.

A portion of Psalm 51, the great penitential psalm, and the proclamation of the Gospel of salvation in the "comfortable words" (BCP: 449-50) begin Form Two. This structure prevents us from thinking that it is *our*

repentance which initiates reconciliation. From beginning to end reconciliation is the action of God, to whose
call to repentance we respond. Form Two is also specific about seeking "evidence of due contrition." After
offering "words of comfort and counsel," the priest asks
the penitent, "Will you turn again to Christ as your
Lord?" and "Do you, then, forgive those who have
sinned against you?" (BCP: 450f). In Form One the
penitent formally states, "I am truly sorry. I pray God
to have mercy on me. I firmly intend amendment of
life" (BCP: 447).

"Before giving absolution, the priest may assign to
the penitent a psalm, prayer, or hymn to be said, or
something to be done, as a sign of penitence and act of
thanksgiving" (BCP: 446). This is commonly called a
"penance," and the entire rite has frequently been
called penance. The Prayer Book is unambiguous in
calling the penance "a sign of penitence and act of
thanksgiving." It is not intended to be a condition of
absolution or an act of satisfaction. There is nothing a
human being can do to atone for sin or make satisfaction for it. Christ has made "by his one oblation of
himself once offered, a full, perfect and sufficient . . . satisfaction, for the sins of the whole world"
(BCP: 334). There is literally nothing left to do. We can
only accept, with penitence and thanksgiving, the
unmerited gift of which the penance is a sign.

Priestly Absolution

There are two alternative forms of absolution, either of
which may be used with either form of reconciliation.
One is from the English Prayer Book and has been
widely used by Episcopalians for many years:

> Our Lord Jesus Christ, who has left power to his Church
> to absolve all sinners who truly repent and believe in

him, of his great mercy forgive you all your offenses;
and by his authority committed to me, I absolve you
from all your sins: In the Name of the Father, and of the
Son, and of the Holy Spirit. (BCP: 448)

This form begins with the assertion that it is the
power and authority of Jesus Christ through which the
penitent and believing sinner is absolved. This authority has been committed by him to the Church and to the
priest as the minister of Christ and the Church. The
priest does not claim to forgive sins. This is done by the
Father, the Son, and the Holy Spirit.

The other form is even more explicit that it is Jesus
Christ, through the power of his atoning sacrifice, who
absolves. The priest is merely the minister through
whom Christ acts, "by the grace of the Holy Spirit." It
also adds the assurance that absolution restores the penitent's broken relationship to the Church, an important
aspect of reconciliation not otherwise explicitly
mentioned.

Our Lord Jesus Christ, who offered himself to be sacrificed for us to the Father, and who conferred power on
his Church to forgive sins, absolve you through my ministry by the grace of the Holy Spirit, and restore you to
the perfect peace of the Church. (BCP: 448)

The rite ends with the declaration "the Lord has put
away all your sins" (BCP: 451). In Form One the confessor asks the penitent to "pray for me, a sinner" (BCP:
449), recognizing that the confessor, too, is a sinner in
need of God's forgiveness.

Lay Confessors

The Prayer Book recognizes that another Christian
who is not a priest may be asked to hear a confession,

and requires such a person to make it clear to the penitent that absolution will not be pronounced. Instead, a "declaration of forgiveness" is used (see BCP: 446):

> Our Lord Jesus Christ, who offered himself to be sacrificed for us to the Father, forgives your sins by the grace of the Holy Spirit. (BCP: 448, 452)

This declaration is rooted in the assurance that God "pardons and absolves all those who truly repent, and with sincere hearts believe his holy Gospel" (BCP: 269). The sincere penitent receives God's forgiveness, whether through the sacramental ministry of the ordained priest or not. Christians are often called upon to hear the confessions of other Christians. Parents hear the confessions of their children. Friends hear the confessions of friends. Those seeking spiritual guidance and counsel have always sought out holy men and women, whether ordained or lay, to be their guides. The Prayer Book recognizes this as a part of the Church's tradition and provides a prayer for lay confessors to use. They cannot and do not pronounce priestly absolution, but their ministry, like the priest's, is a continuation of the Lord's ministry of reconciliation which he has committed to his Church.

The Sacramental Theology of Reconciliation

The reconciliation of penitents is not a sacrament of the Gospel in the sense that baptism and the eucharist are. The Gospel's primary call to repentance is always a call to be baptized, and the New Testament does not portray Christ as instituting a rite to deal with post-baptismal sin, nor does the apostolic Church appear to have acted as if it possessed such a rite. However, the gospels record the commission to forgive sin in Christ's name as central to the mission of the apostles. Separation from the Church is, in a sense, the visible sign of separation from God of which sin is the cause. Reconciliation and restoration to "the perfect peace of the Church" is the earthly sign by which we receive the inward and spiritual grace of reconciliation with God. Like the sacraments of the Gospel, reconciliation is founded upon the Paschal Mystery and the promise of Christ. And like the sacraments, reconciliation is found within the visible community of the Church.

In the celebration of the rite, the penitent is not simply the recipient of the sacramental action. In a real sense, the priest and penitent concelebrate the rite, renewing and restoring the baptismal covenant within which both stand. The priest does not simply pronounce absolution while the penitent accepts restoration and forgiveness. The penitent repents and confesses to the Church that he or she has sinned. The Church prays for the penitent sinner and through the ministry of the priest pronounces absolution. The acts of the penitent, as much as those of the priest, are a part of the mystery of reconciliation. Together, priest and penitent have concelebrated the sacrament within the community of the universal or catholic Church.[6]

The sacramental sign in the Prayer Book is the laying of the priest's hand upon the head of the penitent (BCP: 451), but unlike the great sacraments of the Gospel, the sign is not of dominical authority.[7] Throughout its history the Church has established many rites and means of fulfilling its dominical commission to forgive, and will presumably continue to do so.[8] The rites for the reconciliation of a penitent in the *Book of Common Prayer* are those authorized by the Episcopal Church. But the truth to which they give expression does not change. God forgives our sins by the power of the cross and resurrection. In baptism we die to sin and are raised to newness of life. In the rites of reconciliation that baptismal experience is renewed. Our sins are bound by the love and power of the crucified One and loosed by our restoration to the resurrection life in Christ.

Ministration to the Sick and Dying

If we are looking for changes in theology in the *Book of Common Prayer* 1979, we will do well to look at the Ministration to the Sick. It replaces the Visitation of the Sick, the least used and least usable service in the 1928 Prayer Book. Earlier forms based on medieval models accurately reflected the state of medical science in the 16th century and did not seriously consider the possibility that the sick person might recover. They tended to pray for grace to accept sickness patiently and die well. The anointing of the sick came to be popularly called "last rites," and it was administered only to those in danger of death. The rites also tended to treat sickness as a punishment for sin.

The 1928 Prayer Book began the reaction against these views and introduced many useful prayers for healing, but it did not omit the earlier prayers nor change the format of the service. The theological thrust of the Ministration to the Sick in the *Book of Common Prayer* 1979 is precisely *healing*. It is grounded in our Lord's own healing ministry and that which the apostles exercised in his name, which, the Prayer Book assumes, the Church continues. A separate section, Ministration at the Time of Death, guards against the opposite error of not dealing with the fact of death and with the certainty that some sick people will not recover. Still, the change in theology in the Ministration to the Sick is real and substantial. This change had already begun to be reflected in the alternatives introduced in 1928.[9] Thus, the rites of the 1979 Prayer Book are, in this case, the fruit rather than the cause of

theological development, although they may themselves become the cause of further growth and development in the theology and practice of the healing
ministry.

Ministry of the Word

The rite (BCP: 453-7) provides a framework within
which various ministries may be offered to the sick person, without expecting that all will necessarily be used at
the same time. First of all, in the Ministry of the Word,
the rite appoints Scripture passages which may be read
to the sick person by anyone with the time and ability to
read (BCP: 453f). Their theme is the love and healing
power of God. The celebrant may comment briefly on
any of the readings, and appropriate prayers may be
offered (BCP: 454). A number of prayers for the sick
(BCP: 458-60) are provided at the end of the service, as
well as prayers for use by the sick person (BCP: 461).
The following is typical of the theological stance of the
prayers:

> May God the Father bless you, God the Son heal you,
> God the Holy Spirit give you strength. May God the
> holy and undivided Trinity guard your body, save your
> soul, and bring you safely to his heavenly country; where
> he lives and reigns for ever and ever. (BCP: 460)

Health and strength are the gifts of God, who "by the
might of [God's] command drive[s] away from our bodies all sickness and all infirmity" (BCP: 458), and it is
presumed that they are God's will for us. A prayer for
the sanctification of illness retains the positive elements
of the older prayers by asking "that the sense of *his*
weakness may add strength to *his* faith and seriousness
to *his* repentance" and that the sick person may live with
God "in everlasting life" (BCP: 460).

A prayer for doctors and nurses speaks of "their ministries" and of God's call "to the study and practice of the arts of healing, and to the prevention of disease and pain" (BCP: 460). The healing ministry of the Church is not opposed to the practice of medicine, but as is stated in Ecclesiasticus 38, the first lesson for St. Luke's Day (BCP: 924), prayer to the Lord and the ministry of the physician work together, "for healing comes from the Most High" (Ecclesiasticus 38:2).

Confession of Sin

If the sick person wishes to make a confession, the form for The Reconciliation of Penitents follows the Bible readings and prayers, or the general confession may be used (BCP: 464). A priest pronounces absolution, while a deacon or lay person prays for forgiveness of the sick person (BCP: 455). Forgiveness of sin is an integral part of the healing process. Matthew 9:2-8 and James 5:14-16, both included among the appointed scriptural readings for the Ministration to the Sick, connect the forgiveness of sins with the ministry of healing. Human beings are complex creatures of body, mind and spirit, and healing must include the entire person. The sick person needs an opportunity to deal with the sense of sin and separation which often accompanies sickness.

Laying on of Hands and Anointing

Secondly, the rite of Ministration to the Sick offers the Church's principal healing ministries: the laying on of hands and anointing of the sick (BCP: 455-7). According to the catechism, unction is one of the "other sacramental rites evolved in the Church under the guidance of the Holy Spirit" (BCP: 860). It is defined as "the rite of anointing the sick with oil, or the laying on of hands, by which God's grace is given for the healing of spirit, mind, and body" (BCP: 861). The readings appointed "when Anointing is to follow" (James 5:14-16 and Mark 6:7, 12-13) are the New Testament precedents for the anointing of the sick. The blessing of the oil expresses the intention of the Church to continue this ministry:

> . . . as your holy apostles anointed many that were sick and healed them, so may those who in faith and repentance receive this holy unction be made whole; through Jesus Christ our Lord. (BCP: 455)

An optional addition to the form for anointing, derived from the 1549 Prayer Book, underscores the sacramental nature of the rite:

> As you are outwardly anointed with this holy oil, so may our heavenly Father grant you the inward anointing of the Holy Spirit. Of his great mercy, may he forgive you your sins, release you from suffering, and restore you to wholeness and strength. May he deliver you from all evil, preserve you in all goodness, and bring you to everlasting life. (BCP: 456)

The outward and visible anointing is the effective sign of the inward unction of the Holy Spirit, who forgives sin, delivers from suffering, and restores to wholeness. Viewing the anointing of the sick in sacramental terms, however, produces a serious problem: if the effect of the sacrament is intended to be bodily healing, then it is notoriously undependable. Sacraments are, by definition, based upon the sure promises of God, and a sacrament which may or may not work is theological nonsense. Thomas J. Talley has suggested that the object of the sacrament of anointing has been confused with the charismatic gift of healing:

> The object of the rite of anointing can be understood as renewal of the baptismal anointing by which each of us is *christos* so that the suffering and separation of sickness become identified as participation in the *pascha Christi*.

> By such anointing, *anamnesis* is made of the passage of
> Christ through death to life and of the patient's conse-
> cration to that mystery. By such anointing, further, the
> suffering of the illness is oriented to a reopened future,
> a sense of movement in Christ through the present pas-
> sage toward the kingdom. . . . The meaning of every
> illness is dying, and every healing is resurrection. The
> sacrament is more than a struggle against illness. It is a
> sign of the conquest of death.[10]

The strength of Talley's theological suggestion is
that it places the sacrament of healing in the context of
the Paschal Mystery. Like reconciliation, unction is a
restoration and renewal of the baptismal state. It unites
the sick person with Jesus in his suffering and death, and
thereby also in his resurrection. The anointing of the
sick is the sacrament of resurrection and life in Christ.
It renews the relationship of the sick person to Christ
and to the Church which continues to exercise Christ's
healing ministry. Like all true sacramental signs, the
anointing is a sign of new life, of the resurrection life in
Christ.[11]

One of the forms to be used for the laying on of hands
states its purpose this way:

> . . . beseeching our Lord Jesus Christ to sustain you
> with his presence, to drive away all sickness of body and
> spirit, and to give you that victory of life and peace
> which will enable you to serve him both now and ever-
> more. (BCP: 456)

Union with Christ in his victory over death is, as we
have seen, a primary purpose of the healing ministry.
This form clearly anticipates bodily healing. Its alternative says only, ". . . beseeching him to uphold you and
fill you with his grace, that you may know the healing
power of his love" (BCP: 456). But whether we die now
or later, the message of the Gospel is that Christ has
overcome death and in him we do and shall live.

The sacrament of healing renews that relationship with life in the face of sickness and suffering.

The anointing and laying on of hands are described as alternatives in the catechism (BCP: 861), but in the liturgy itself the laying on of hands by the priest appears as the primary rite, with anointing as an optional supplementary action (BCP: 456). This may simply reflect pastoral practice in which the laying on of hands is a normal accompaniment of the priest's visit to the sick, while the anointing is reserved for more solemn occasions. The intention expressed in the catechism is that the two rites have the same sacramental purpose. Either or both may be used "*at a public celebration of the Eucharist*" (BCP: 453), and *The Book of Occasional Services* arranges the material for use as A Public Service of Healing (BOS: 147-54), for which it supplies a Litany of Healing to be used in place of the prayers of the people, a collect and postcommunion prayer, and an extensive table of suggested lessons and psalms.

In practice it is difficult, if not impossible, to anoint without laying on hands. The rubric in the Public Service of Healing describes the ordinary procedure, "The Celebrant then lays hands on each person (and, having dipped a thumb in the oil of the sick, makes the sign of the cross on their foreheads)" (BOS: 151). The Prayer Book implies that they will be successive acts, each accompanied by its own formula of administration (BCP: 455f).

The oil for the anointing must be blessed by a bishop or priest, but, in case of necessity, the anointing may be performed by a deacon or lay person (BCP: 456). This marks a partial return to the practice of the early Church which encouraged lay people to use holy oil blessed by the priest or bishop to anoint the sick at home.[12] The Prayer Book restricts the laying on of hands to the priest (BCP: 455), but *The Book of Occasional Services* permits "*lay persons with a gift of healing*" to join the celebrant in laying on hands" (BOS: 151). This seems to be an attempt to associate the sacramental ministry of the priest with the charismatic gift of healing so that both may be brought into play in the healing service, since all healing is the gift of God.

Holy Communion of the Sick

Thirdly, and finally, the rite offers the sick person Holy Communion. This may take the form of a bedside celebration of the eucharist or communion from the reserved sacrament (BCP: 457). The celebration of the eucharist with the sick person is particularly desirable *"when persons are unable to be present"* [at the public celebrations] *for extended periods"* (BCP: 396). Such celebrations in nursing homes or with the households of shut-ins can be a powerful ministry witnessing to the Church's concern for those unable to attend the parish eucharist and binding them to the Church in its chief act of worship. It is seldom convenient to celebrate the eucharist when people are acutely ill or unable to give their attention to the service. Communion with elements reserved from the parish eucharist, on the other hand, will not only be more convenient in many circumstances but permits the sick to join in the particular parish celebration from which they are unavoidably absent, and thus binds them to the eucharistic life of the congregation.

Communion in One Kind

If the sick person cannot receive either the consecrated Bread or the Wine, it is suitable to administer the Sacrament in one kind only. (BCP: 457)

Communion in one kind became normal for lay people in the Late Middle Ages, and the restoration of the

chalice to the laity was one of the significant gains of the
Reformation. Communion in one kind lacks the completeness of the sacrament's sign value. Jesus instituted
the sacrament under both kinds, and communion
should be so administered in fulfillment of his command. It is difficult, nevertheless, to sustain the theological argument that receiving communion in both
kinds bestows different or greater benefits than receiving in one kind. Christ cannot be "more present" in
larger quantities of the elements, or more in one element than the other. The Prayer Book does not authorize *general* communion in one kind, but it does allow a
sick person to receive communion under one kind if he
or she is unable to receive one or the other eucharistic
element. For example, the person unable to eat the
consecrated Bread may receive the Wine only; and the
person unable to drink consecrated Wine may receive
the Bread only.

Communion in both kinds by intinction "in a manner
approved by the bishop" is permitted, even at regular
celebrations in church (BCP: 407f). Although this form
of reception also diminishes the sign value of reception
in both kinds, it is an historically acceptable method of
communicating large numbers of people and of inhib-
iting the spread of contagious disease. Communion in
one kind or by intinction is frequently used for the
communion of the sick from the reserved sacrament,
since it does not require the carrying of Wine to the sick
person, and since one of these methods has been customary from the early years of the Church. Even when
transporting the consecrated Wine is not a problem, it is
often difficult for a person unable to sit up to drink
from a cup.

Finally, the Prayer Book assures the sick person that
"if a person desires to receive the Sacrament" but is
unable to do so, "all the benefits of Communion are

received" (BCP: 457). This is traditionally called "spiritual communion." It provides real evidence that the sacrament is not considered magic. Those who desire to communicate truly receive all the benefits, whether they receive in both kinds at the parish eucharist, or by intinction, or in one kind from the reserved sacrament, or only in their hearts by faith. This is not to reduce the benefits of communion to mere psychological aids to devotion, but to recognize that God does not limit divine activity to those who are able to participate fully in the sacraments. God accepts the will for the deed when we cannot do what we would. It is the principle which the psalmist recognized in saying that God would accept prayer "as incense" and the lifting up of hands "as the evening sacrifice" (Psalm 141:2).

Ministration
at the Time of Death

All of the rites included in Ministration to the Sick may, of course, be received by a dying person. Confession, unction, and communion have traditionally been considered to be appropriate sacramental rites with which to strengthen the dying person for the final journey, and they are presumably included in *"the ministrations of the Church"* which the *"Minister of the Congregation"* is to provide for the person approaching death (BCP: 462). In addition, the Prayer Book contains prayers for the dying, a Litany at the Time of Death (BCP: 462-4) which may also be used on appropriate occasions prior to the funeral (BCP: 465, 467), and prayers of commendation.

The commendation bids the dying Christian to depart from this world in the name of the Trinity and prays, "May your rest be this day in peace, and your dwelling place in the Paradise of God" (BCP: 464). The commendatory prayer asks Christ to acknowledge "a

sheep of your own fold, a lamb of your own flock, a
sinner of your own redeeming" and prays: "Receive *him*
into the arms of your mercy, into the blessed rest of
everlasting peace, and into the glorious company of the
saints in light" (BCP: 465).

The heart of the litany lies in the series of petitions:

> That it may please you to deliver the soul of your servant
> from the power of evil, and from eternal death.
>
> That it may please you mercifully to pardon all *his* sins.
>
> That it may please you to grant *him* a place of refresh-
> ment and everlasting blessedness.
>
> That it may please you to give *him* joy and gladness in
> your kingdom, with your saints in light. (BCP: 463)

The concluding collect prays:

> Deliver your servant, N., O Sovereign Lord Christ,
> from all evil, and set *him* free from every bond; that *he*
> may rest with all your saints in the eternal habitations.
> (BCP: 464)

The Church prays for deliverance, redemption, pardon, rest, blessedness, and refreshment in paradise with
the saints for the dying Christian. The "promise of life
everlasting, given in the resurrection" of Jesus Christ—
found in *A Prayer for a Person Near Death* (BCP: 462)—
lies at the center of all prayers for the dying.

These are all *liminal* prayers, celebrated as the dying
Christian passes over with Christ from death to life.
They reflect both a separation from the Church on
earth and the assurance of incorporation into the
Church Triumphant. They have the ambiguity of rites
of transition. They do not yet celebrate the victory, but
they hold its promise before our eyes and those of the
dying believer:

> May *his* soul and the souls of all the departed, through
> the mercy of God, rest in peace. (BCP: 465)

Before the Funeral

"It is appropriate that the family and friends come together for prayers prior to the funeral" (BCP: 465). The Prayer Book calls this "a Vigil," but the direct English translation, "wake," is the more common name. In many places these vigils or wakes are regularly held the night before the funeral at the place where the body of the deceased is laid out, whether at a home, a funeral parlor, or the church. Prayers from the burial service or the Litany at the Time of Death may be used, for both are appropriate in this liminal period.

An alternative litany with the response *"Into your hands, O Lord, we commend our brother (sister) N."* may be also used (BCP: 465). In addition to the usual prayers for rest and light, it asks, "Wash *him* in the holy font of everlasting life, and clothe *him* in his heavenly wedding garment." Washing and clothing are baptismal images, and the "wedding garment" reminds us both of the parable of the wedding garment (Matthew 22:11-12) and of our eschatological participation in the marriage supper of the Lamb (Revelation 19:9), the *goal* of the baptismal life.

The litany prays that the departed Christian may hear Christ's words of invitation, "Come, you blessed of my Father," the words addressed to the righteous in Matthew 25:24, and may come to gaze upon God face to face (Revelation 22:4). The beatific vision of God is the traditional expression of the blessedness of the saved, and the litany goes on to ask that the deceased person may "taste the blessedness of perfect rest" and be surrounded by saints and angels. Its concluding prayer includes the petition "Let *his* heart and soul ring out in joy to you, O Lord, the living God and the God of those who live" (BCP: 466). The grief of loss begins to give way to expressions of joy that the one who has died has entered into "the courts of [God's] heavenly dwelling place."

The Burial of the Dead

The proper place for the burial service of baptized Christians is the church. The local church gathers to celebrate the death of one of its members. The eucharistic Word liturgy provides the context for the burial rites, and the celebration of the eucharist is a normative part of Christian funerals.[13] A priest, as the liturgical leader of the local church, is the normal celebrant, but when a priest is unavailable, "a deacon or lay reader may preside" (BCP: 468) and the eucharist be either omitted, or conducted after the burial when a priest is available. Usually the corpse is brought to the church and lies before the altar in a closed coffin covered by a funeral pall during the service, but the committal and burial may be held first and the service conducted in the church without the presence of the body. When the body is brought into the church, it is customary for the celebrant to meet it at the church door and go into the church before it (BCP: 468, 490).

"*A member of the congregation bearing the Paschal Candle may lead the procession into the church*" (BCP: 467). The Paschal Candle symbolizes the resurrection, the dominant theme of the burial service. "*The liturgy for the dead is an Easter liturgy. It finds all its meaning in the resurrection. Because Jesus was raised from the dead, we, too, shall be raised.*" For this reason, the Prayer Book says that the liturgy "*is characterized by joy,*" but that joy is mixed with grief: "*So, while we rejoice that one we loved has entered into the nearer presence of our Lord, we sorrow in sympathy with those who mourn*" (BCP: 507). The best liturgical expression of this mixture of feelings is the Russian *contakion* for the departed, which forms a part of the commendation and includes the line "All of us go down to the dust;

yet even at the grave we make our song: Alleluia, alleluia, alleluia" (BCP: 499).

The burial service, like the eucharist, is presented in three forms in the *Book of Common Prayer*. Rite One (BCP: 469-89) is in traditional language and makes extensive use of material from earlier versions of the Prayer Book. Rite Two (BCP: 490-505) is in contemporary language and incorporates much new material. The structure of the two services, however, is identical. An Order for Burial (BCP: 506) is an *ordo* or *agenda* for the service for those occasions when, *"for pastoral considerations, neither of the burial rites from* [the Prayer] *Book is deemed appropriate." The Book of Occasional Services* (BOS: 156-9) contains suggestions for psalms, lessons, prayers, and a form of committal to be used with that *ordo* for the Burial of One Who Does Not Profess the Christian Faith, an occasion on which the Order for Burial is often used.

The Service in the Church

Anthems from the Scripture are sung or said at the beginning of the service either while the body is borne into the church or, if the body is already present, during the entrance of the ministers, or are at least said by the celebrant "standing in the accustomed place" (BCP: 468, 490). The first anthem, "I am the resurrection and the life," sets the Easter theme for the liturgy (BCP: 469). Rite Two permits a number of alternatives, including a medieval antiphon which has begun the service at the grave since 1549 and is still included there in Rite One. The anthem uses a form of the Trisagion as a response (BCP: 490-1).

Rite Two permits the celebrant to address the congregation after the anthem, *"acknowledging briefly the purpose of their gathering, and bidding their prayers for the deceased and the bereaved"* (BCP: 492). This is excellent pastoral advice when there are many people present who are unfamiliar with the burial rites and customs of the Episcopal Church. It also makes clear that praying for the deceased and the bereaved is an important aspect of the congregation's role at a funeral.

The collect of Rite One (BCP: 470) prays to the God "whose mercies cannot be numbered" for "entrance into the land of light and joy, in the fellowship of thy saints." Rite Two includes two additional alternative collects. The first well expresses the Paschal nature of the rite:

> O God, who by the glorious resurrection of your Son Jesus Christ destroyed death, and brought life and immortality to light: Grant that your servant N., being raised with him, may know the strength of his presence, and rejoice in his eternal glory. (BCP: 493)

The second alternative does not pray directly for the departed but gives thanks to God "for giving *him* to us, *his* family and friends." It asks consolation for those who mourn, and that we may see in death the gate of eternal life and have the confidence to "continue our course on earth, until, by [God's] call, we are reunited with those who have gone before" (BCP: 493). It was newly composed for this Prayer Book and differs from the more traditional collects in focusing not on the departed but on the effect of that person's death on the living. An optional additional prayer for the mourners, which may follow the collect, has the same force. These are certainly significant secondary themes, but the commendation of the departed Christian to God with the prayer of the Church is the more traditional primary focus.

Scripture Lessons
at the Burial

A wide selection of Scripture readings emphasize different aspects of biblical teaching concerning the dead. Among them are Isaiah 25:6-9 ("[God] will swallow up death for ever, and the Lord God will wipe away tears from all faces."); Wisdom 3:1-5, 9 ("The souls of the righteous are in the hand of God, and no torment will ever touch them. In the eyes of the foolish they seem to have died. . . , but they are at peace."); Romans 8:14-19, 34-35, 37-39 ("The sufferings of this present time are not worth comparing to the glory that is to be revealed to us. . . . For I am sure that neither death nor life . . . nor anything else in all creation, will be able to separate us from the love of God in Christ Jesus our Lord."); 1 Corinthians 15:20-26, 35-38, 42-44, 53-58 ("As in Adam all die, so also in Christ shall all be made alive."); 1 John 3:1-2 ("We know that . . . we shall be like him."); Revelation 7:9-17 ("They are before the throne of God, and serve him day and night within his temple, and he who sits upon the throne will shelter them with his presence."); and Revelation 21:2-7 ("Death shall be no more, neither shall there be mourning nor crying nor pain.").

The appointed Gospel selections (BCP: 480, 495) are all from the fourth Gospel. John 5:24-27 not only tells us that whoever believes has passed from death to eternal life but proclaims: "The hour is coming, and now is, when the dead will hear the voice of the Son of God, and those who hear will live." Similarly, John 6:37-40 says, "This is the will of my Father, that everyone who sees the Son and believes in him should have eternal life, and I will raise him up at the last day." John 10:11-16 is the familiar story of the Good Shepherd. John 11:21-27 is the beginning of the story of the raising of Lazarus and contains the affirmation with which the burial service begins, "I am the resurrection and the life; he who believes in me, though he die, yet shall he live, and whoever lives and believes in me shall never die." Finally, John 14:1-6, in which Jesus says, "I am the way, and the truth, and the life," also says, "In my Father's house are many rooms," and "I go and prepare a place for you."

These, and the other readings and psalms appointed, although they will not all be read at any one funeral, provide the scriptural basis for the teaching about death and resurrection in the burial service. The death of the Christian is always to be seen in the light of the resurrection of Christ, "the first fruits of those who have fallen asleep" (1 Corinthians 15:20). We do not know what the resurrection life for us will be like, "but we know that when he appears, we shall be like him" (1 John 3:2). What is promised is not "immortality of the soul," although the word "immortality" as a part of the hope of the dead appears in Wisdom 3, but resurrection in Jesus, for the unending service of God in God's presence (Revelation 7:15). Joy, rest, peace, and the vision of God are the images continually used to describe this state in which nothing can ever separate us from the love of God in Christ Jesus (see Romans 8:39).

Many attempts have been made by poets, philosophers and theologians to describe what is basically indescribable. Even the descriptions in the Scripture are obviously highly figurative, but they provide the substance of our prayer for the departed, and the way we pray for the dead is the primary constitutive factor in determining our belief about the resurrection. Easter celebrates the Paschal Mystery. The Burial of the Dead celebrates our participation in it. Therefore the Burial of the Dead is intimately linked with baptism, the sacrament of death and resurrection; and the eucharist, itself a celebration of the Paschal Mystery, is an appropriate part of the celebration. The Apostles' Creed, the baptismal affirmation of faith, may also be used in the service: "In the assurance of eternal life given at Baptism, let us proclaim our faith and say, I believe in God. . . " (BCP: 496).

The Prayers of the People

The prayers of the people in the two rites are quite different in content. That in Rite One (BCP: 480f) is a series of petitions to which the people respond "Amen." The address of the opening petition picks up the phrase from the All Saints' Day collect: "God, who hast knit together thine elect in one communion and fellowship in the mystical body of thy Son Christ our Lord" (BCP: 194). It reminds us that it is our unity with the risen Christ in the communion of saints that makes possible prayer for the departed as well as for the living.

The prayers ask for light and peace for the "whole Church in paradise and on earth," and then "that all who have been baptized into Christ's death and resurrection may die to sin and rise to newness of life" and that we may pass with Christ "through the grave and gate of death" to our own joyful resurrection (BCP: 480).

We pray for the guidance of the Holy Spirit for all "who are still in our pilgrimage," for cleansing from sin, for peace in which to serve God, for consolation for those who mourn, and for help for ourselves "in the midst of things we cannot understand, to believe and trust in the communion of saints, the forgiveness of sins, and the resurrection to life everlasting" (BCP: 481).

We also pray that we may have grace to entrust the departed Christian to God's never-failing love, and that God will "receive *him* into the arms of [God's] mercy, and remember *him*" favorably, that "increasing in knowledge and love of [God], *he* may go from strength to strength in the life of perfect service in [God's] heavenly kingdom" (BCP: 481). This final phrase is taken from a collect (BCP: 488) that originally appeared in the burial office of the 1928 Prayer Book. It does not ask for peace and light, but for growth in knowledge and love of God. Behind the prayer lies the recognition that no one is ready at the time of death to enter into life in the nearer presence of God without substantial growth precisely in love, knowledge and service; and the prayer also recognizes that God will provide what is necessary for us to enter that state. This growth will presumably take place between death and resurrection, but Scripture does not provide enough information to do more than speculate on how this growth will happen. In fact, such speculation has frequently produced a developed doctrine of "the intermediate state," or even of purgatory, but there is little scriptural basis to ground such developments. The liturgy is vague, because we walk without knowledge but with firm faith in Christ's love and promises.

The conclusion of the prayers asks that we, with the saints and "with all who have died in the hope of the resurrection," may share "eternal and everlasting glory" and "the crown of life" promised to those who share Christ's victory (BCP: 481). This set of petitions are, then, general prayers for the whole Church, but they make special mention of the deceased person.

The prayers of the people in Rite Two (BCP: 497) are more personal. We mention the departed by name as we pray "to our Lord Jesus Christ who said, 'I am the Resurrection and I am the Life.'" Jesus is directly addressed: ". . . you consoled Martha and Mary in their distress. . . . You wept at the grave of Lazarus, your friend; comfort us who mourn. You raised the dead to life. . . . You promised paradise to the thief who repented; bring our brother (sister) to the joys of heaven" and to eternal life.

If applicable, the prayers specifically mention that the dead person "was washed in Baptism and anointed with the Holy Spirit," and "nourished with [Christ's] Body and Blood." In turn, these statements are made the grounds for asking fellowship with the saints and "a place at the table in [Christ's] heavenly kingdom."

The first of two alternative concluding collects commends to Christ "our brother (sister) N., who was reborn by water and the Spirit in Holy Baptism," and then widens the scope of the prayers to include ourselves:

> Grant that *his* death may recall to us your victory over death, and be an occasion for us to renew our trust in your Father's love. Give us, we pray, the faith to follow where you have led the way; and where you live and reign with the Father and the Holy Spirit, to the ages of ages. (BCP: 498)

The second alternative collect offers the traditional prayers for "all those whom we love but see no longer":

> Grant to them eternal rest. Let light perpetual shine upon them. May *his* soul and the souls of all the departed, through the mercy of God, rest in peace. (BCP: 498)

This set of prayers of the people is more personal than the form in Rite One, because the prayers address Christ directly and focus specifically on the person being buried. The Rite One version is easily adaptable for use at the Commemoration of All Faithful Departed on November 2 (BCP: 29). Indeed it seems more suitable for a general memorial service than for a funeral. It is more difficult, but by no means impossible, to adapt the Rite Two form to a general memorial service. Its specificity is both a weakness and a strength.

When the eucharist is being celebrated, the proper preface commemorates the resurrection victory of Christ and offers us this assurance:

> For to your faithful people, O Lord, life is changed, not
> ended; and when our mortal body lies in death, there is
> prepared for us a dwelling place eternal in the heavens.
> (BCP: 382)

The postcommunion prayer (BCP: 498) picks up other
familiar themes. It reminds us that the eucharist is "a
foretaste of [God's] heavenly banquet . . . a comfort
in affliction, and a pledge of our inheritance in that
kingdom where there is no death, neither sorrow nor
crying, but the fullness of joy with all [God's] saints."

The Commendation

At the close of the service, whether or not the eucharist
is celebrated, the commendation is said over the body.
It is the Church's leave-taking of its departed member.
It consists of an anthem and a prayer, while the celebrant and other ministers stand "*at the body*" (BCP: 482,
499). Although another "*suitable anthem, or a hymn*" may
be substituted, the anthem is the Russian *contakion* from
which we quoted above. Its thematic refrain is

> Give rest, O Christ, to your servant(s) with your saints,
> *where sorrow and pain are no more,*
> *neither sighing, but life everlasting.* (BCP: 499)

The prayer is the same commendatory prayer used at
the time of death (BCP: 469). Structurally, the funeral
liturgy is a "rite of separation" marking the separation
of the departed from the Church Militant. It proclaims
the assurance and hope that the departed will pass with
Christ through the liminal area the liturgy calls "the
grave and gate of death" (BCP: 480) to be incorporated
—in a manner of which we have no knowledge—into
the Church Triumphant. The sorrow of separation, the
uncertainty of liminality, and the joy and triumph of
incorporation into Christ enthroned in glory are inter-
twined in all aspects of this liturgy.

The commendation is often accompanied by ritual acts, such as walking around the coffin and sprinkling the body with holy water in remembrance of baptism. While the body is carried out of the church, ideally to the grave, a hymn, canticle, or anthem is sung (BCP: 499-500). The *Benedictus, Nunc dimittis,* or *Pascha nostrum* (the Easter canticle) is suggested. Among the anthems specifically provided for this occasion, the first and last are particularly significant. According to Hatchett,

> The first four of the five anthems were prepared as a unit by the Rev. Dr. Thomas J. Talley. The first is a text from the Byzantine rite which initiates the celebration of the Easter Eucharist, and which is sung as the body is carried to the grave during the Easter season.[14]

The text is "Christ is risen from the dead, trampling down death by death, and giving life to those in the tomb" (BCP: 483, 500). Along with the liturgy's opening anthem, "I am the resurrection" (BCP: 469, 491), this anthem serves to frame the entire service in the church within the resurrection theme. The last anthem, of medieval Gallican provenance, has many well-known musical settings and is a prayer for the departed:

> Into paradise may the angels lead thee; and at thy coming may the martyrs receive thee, and bring thee into the holy city Jerusalem. (BCP: 484)

The Committal

The committal service takes place at the grave, although it may be said in the church if it is more practical to do so (BCP: 468, 490). It begins with an anthem, the original purpose of which was to accompany the procession from the church to the grave. Either the

anthem "In the midst of life we are in death" given here
in Rite One (BCP: 484) but as an alternative to "I am
the Resurrection" in Rite Two (BCP: 492) or the
anthem "Everyone the Father gives to me will come to
me" (BCP: 501, 484) may be used. The second anthem
is a cento of appropriate Scripture verses. "In the midst
of life" is a medieval prayer to Christ the judge of the
living and the dead: "O worthy and eternal Judge, do
not let the pains of death turn us away from you at our
last hour" (BCP: 492). It asks the Lord "who knows the
secrets of our hearts" to pardon our sins. The respon-
sorial refrain in the Rite Two version is based on the
Trisagion:

> *Holy God, Holy and Mighty*
> *Holy and merciful Savior*
> *deliver us not into the bitterness of eternal death.*
>   (BCP: 492)

Such prayers for acquittal by the eternal Judge and
for deliverance from the pains of hell are, perhaps,
more at home in the medieval or Reformation liturgy
than in contemporary rites, but changing liturgical and
theological fashions do not abolish either judgment or
"the bitterness of eternal death." Christ's invitation,
"Come, O blessed of my Father; inherit the kingdom
prepared for you," which is found in the anthems at the
end of the service in the church (BCP: 483, 500), in the
first additional prayer of Rite One (BCP: 487), and in
the sixth additional prayer of Rite Two (BCP: 505), is
from the parable of the sheep and goats (Matthew
25:34). In the parable, Christ's invitation is balanced by
"Depart from me, you cursed, into the eternal fire prepared for the devil and his angels" (Matthew 25:43). It
is both traditional and appropriate to pray that those we
love will be numbered among the blessed rather than
the cursed. The liturgy does not speculate about hell or
the punishment of the damned; neither does it set forth

any doctrine of damnation nor require us to believe in the actual damnation of anyone. Rather, it prays that we all may be among the saved.

During the actual burial, the celebrant commends the person of the departed, not just the soul, to God and commits the body to the ground or other resting place "in sure and certain hope of the resurrection to eternal life through our Lord Jesus Christ" (BCP: 485, 501). Often the burial itself is only symbolic, a cross of sand being poured onto the coffin. However, the intention of the rite is that earth be cast upon the coffin to bury it while the committal is said, and the words lose much of their force if real burial is avoided.

The Lord's Prayer follows the committal, and other prayers are added. Immediately following the Lord's Prayer, Rite One includes a prayer for optional use which is not found in Rite Two (BCP: 486). The prayer asks that "those who rest in Jesus" may receive the blessings of God's love, "that the good work which [God began] in them may be made perfect unto the day of Jesus Christ." Here again, as in the Rite One prayers of the people, the Church prays that the departed may grow into perfection. Hatchett points out that this is typical of the prayers for the departed that entered the Prayer Book in the 1928 revision.[15] We better understand such insertion when we remember that this particular aspect of our concern for the departed was in the forefront of the consciousness of those who revised the Prayer Book in the years after World War I. The loss of so many American lives in the war provided the impetus for restoring prayers for the dead to the Book of Common Prayer, from which they had been absent since 1552. Thus, although light, peace, joy and refreshment are more typical of the things which Christians traditionally ask of God for their departed friends and relatives, growth and service have also been prominent, at least during this century.

The traditional versicles, beginning, "Rest eternal grant to *him*, O Lord," follow the prayers (BCP: 486, 502). Rite Two adds the Easter acclamation "Alleluia. Christ is risen" and a dismissal. Both rites conclude with Hebrews 13:20-21, which refers to "the God of peace, who brought again from the dead our Lord Jesus Christ, the great shepherd of the sheep, through the blood of the everlasting covenant" (BCP: 486, 503). By using this scriptural reference as a final blessing and dismissal of the people, both rites end on the Paschal theme with which they began.

Additional Prayers

A form for consecrating a grave (BCP: 487, 503) is appended to both services. It prays "that *he* whose body is buried here may dwell with Christ in paradise, and may come to [God's] heavenly kingdom."

Nine additional prayers are given in Rite One (BCP: 487-9) and eight in Rite Two (BCP: 503-5), of which five are versions of prayers in Rite One. The third prayer of Rite One (BCP: 488) is a prayer of commendation asking God to receive "thy servant N., our dear *brother*." Its content might be considered not unlike the other 1928-type prayers for the dead, but its wording is more traditional, and its imagery is especially graphic:

> Wash *him*, we pray thee, in the blood of that immaculate Lamb that was slain to take away the sins of the world; that, whatsoever defilements *he* may have contracted in the midst of this earthly life being purged and done away, *he* may be presented pure and without spot before thee.

This prayer clearly expresses our need at the time of death for purification "in the blood of the immaculate Lamb." Without it we may not enter into joy, peace, rest, and refreshment.

The sixth additional prayer in Rite One (BCP: 489)—
the second in Rite Two (BCP: 504)—based on a prayer
from Jeremy Taylor's *Holy Dying*, asks that we be made
aware "of the shortness and uncertainty of human life,"
that we may die:

> . . . having the testimony of a good conscience, in the
> communion of the Catholic Church, in the confidence
> of a certain faith, in the comfort of a religious and holy
> hope, in favor with you, our God, and in perfect charity
> with the world. (BCP: 504)

This is a classic statement by a great spiritual master of
the way in which Christians hope to come to their death.
Its use at a funeral serves the secondary purpose of
allowing the congregation to hear and be edified by this
instruction in how to approach their own deaths.

The seventh additional prayer in Rite One (BCP:
489)—the third in Rite Two (BCP: 504)—"O God, the
King of saints," was discussed in Chapter Two. It asks
that we may share in the "inheritance of the saints in
light" and enumerates three ways in which the saints,
known and unknown, assist us: by example, fellowship
and prayer. Hatchett quotes the 1938 doctrinal report
of the Church of England describing this collect as representing "a true balance of thought" in its expression
of our fellowship with the saints in prayer.[16] The collect
was also quoted from the Scottish Prayer Book by James
Pike and Norman Pittenger in *The Faith of the Church*, a
volume in the original Church's Teaching Series, where
it was described as drawing out "the fullest implications
of our faith in the communion of saints,"[17] and it was
included in the popular Forward Movement tract "For
Those Who Mourn."

The eighth prayer in Rite One (BCP: 489), which is
also the final prayer of the Good Friday liturgy (BCP:
282), is addressed to Jesus and pleads that he might set
his passion and death "between [his] judgment and our

souls, now and in the hour of our death." Its petitions
encompass the entire Church:

> Give mercy and peace to the living, pardon and rest to
> the dead, to thy holy Church peace and concord, and to
> us sinners everlasting life and glory.

Conclusion

The pastoral offices mark the significant moments in
the lives of individual Christians. They are set within
the baptismal and eucharistic context and grounded in
the Paschal Mystery of our participation in the dying
and rising of Jesus through his Body the Church. In
various ways, these offices renew our union to Christ in
the central mystery of our redemption. They are personal and individual, but they are also corporate. They
celebrate moments in the life of the local Church to
which the individual belongs, and the Church has a
place in their celebration. This corporate dimension
may be less obvious in the reconciliation of penitents,
but even there the Church is involved; for the priest
does not act on his own authority, but as a minister of
Christ and the Church to whose fellowship and peace
the penitent is restored.

A passage from *A Parish Program* of Associated Parishes which was quoted in Chapter One can also serve as
a summary and conclusion of this chapter:

> From the altar, God's redeeming and renewing power
> reaches out into every phase of life; to the altar every
> aspect of our existence is to be gathered up and offered
> to God through Christ in the fellowship of his Holy
> Spirit.[18]

Chapter Eight:
Ordination Rites

Even though only a small number of people are ordained, ordination rites are of great importance to the entire Church. The ordained ministry is "a gift from God for the nurture of his people and the proclamation of his Gospel everywhere" (BCP: 510). For example, the Chicago-Lambeth Quadrilateral of 1886 spoke of the historic episcopate, from which the Episcopal Church takes its name, as part of the sacred "deposit of Christian Faith and Order committed by Christ and his Apostles to his Church unto the end of the world, and therefore incapable of compromise or surrender by those who have been ordained to be its stewards and trustees for the common and equal benefit of all men" and also "as essential to the restoration of unity among the divided branches of Christendom" (BCP: 877). The Quadrilateral is printed in the Prayer Book among the Historical Documents of the Church because it is a major benchmark to which Episcopalians look as they pursue the ecumenical goal of "restoration of the organic unity of the Church" toward which the bishops embarked in Chicago in 1886. Its contemporary relevance is established by its continued use by Anglicans as a platform for ecumenical discussion. Its inclusion in this revision of the Prayer Book, where it had not previously appeared, testifies to its importance.

The pattern of ordination rites has been altered from that which had prevailed since Cranmer's Ordinal of 1550 in order to make plain that the essence of ordination is "solemn prayer and the laying on of episcopal hands" (BCP: 510). In Cranmer's rite the "solemn prayer" was separated from "the laying on of episcopal hands." The latter was accompanied by an imperative formula, the best-known example of which was that for the ordination of priests in the revised form which appeared in the English Prayer Book of 1662 and in all American Prayer Books until the present revision:

> Receive the Holy Ghost for the Office and Work of a Priest in the Church of God, now committed unto thee by the Imposition of our hands. Whose sins thou dost forgive, they are forgiven; and whose sins thou dost retain, they are retained. And be thou a faithful dispenser of the Word of God, and of his holy Sacraments; In the Name of the Father, and of the Son, and of the Holy Ghost. (BCP, 1928: 546)

A significant recent study of the Anglican Ordinal by Paul Bradshaw, a priest of the Church of England, comes to the following conclusions about Cranmer's ordination rite:

> If there is one point which stands out clearly from this survey of the history of the Anglican Ordinal, it is the unsatisfactory nature of the rite . . . particularly in the absence of an ordination prayer in close association with the imposition of hands. . . .
>
> In spite of the importance attached by many Anglicans to the imperative formulas at the imposition of hands in the Anglican rites, particularly that in the rite for the priesthood, their continued use can no longer be defended. They have no place in the primitive pattern of ordination, and they only serve to detract from the ordination prayers and induce erroneous ideas about ordination; they suggest, for example, that the grace of Order can be bestowed by command rather than sought in prayer.[1]

Since the condemnation of Anglican orders as "absolutely null and utterly void" by Pope Leo XIII in 1896,

Anglicans have been defensive about the Ordinal, seeking to defend the validity of its ordination rites from the
frontal attack of the papal bull rather than to critique
them by asking whether they were good rites as well as
valid ones, or how they could be improved. The ordination rites of the 1979 Prayer Book, as we have said,
abandon Cranmer's pattern for a pattern that accurately reflects the essential elements of ordination,
which Cranmer himself described in the Preface to the
Ordinal of 1550 as "Public Prayer with the Imposition
of Hands."

Another problem with the older version of the Ordinal is that it embodied a basically medieval and clerical-
ist view of the ministry which treated ordained ministers
as somehow radically different from lay people and set
clergy over against laity. It also treated the orders
themselves as a sort of ladder of promotion from deacon
to bishop, instead of seeing them as three different ministries to which people are called. None of these difficulties, however, is insuperable. Overcoming them is
often simply a matter of changing emphasis, not aban-
doning concepts. The new pattern of the ordination
rites of the 1979 *Book of Common Prayer* attempts to do
just that. It is important for the ministry of the entire
Church that ordination rites say clearly what they are
about and what they intend to do. The final paragraph
of Bradshaw's study concludes:

> The new pattern is to be welcomed, and the boldness of
> the American revision in attempting to deal with the
> language as well as the structure of the rites is to be
> commended. With certain alterations this Ordinal
> would seem to be the best of all the modern rites for
> providing the foundation of a new Anglican Ordinal to
> replace Cranmer's much-loved but liturgically unsatis-
> factory rite.[2]

The Preface
to the Ordination Rites

The Preface to the Ordinal has been a source of both pride and embarrassment for many years. Its strong statement of the intention of the Church to continue and reverently use the apostolic ministry was partially undercut by its assertion:

> It is evident unto all men, diligently reading Holy Scripture and ancient Authors, that from the Apostles' time there havé been these Orders of Ministers in Christ's Church,—Bishops, Priests and Deacons. (BCP, 1928: 529)

Although this has the ring of authority, it is obviously not "evident unto all men," as the existence of many non-episcopal churches in the world bears witness. It is also less than clear to biblical scholars that the pattern of the threefold ministry which we find so clearly expounded by Ignatius of Antioch at the end of the 1st century[3] was universal in the churches founded by the apostles. The more modest claim of the present revi sion is closer to what we understand to be the facts:

> The Holy Scriptures and ancient Christian writers make it clear that from the apostles' time, there have been different ministries within the Church. In particular, since the time of the New Testament, three distinct orders of ordained ministers have been characteristic of Christ's holy catholic Church. . . . It has been, and is, the intention and purpose of this Church to maintain and continue these orders. (BCP: 510)

The present revision does not retreat from asserting the importance of the threefold ministry, nor does it aban-don the intention of the Episcopal Church to continue it. However, the modification of the historical claims for this ministry makes the statement of the Preface more acceptable to contemporary scholarship, both

Catholic and Protestant. In fact, the Preface makes a new claim for the ordination rites which was not in the older versions:

> . . . the manner of ordaining in this Church is to be such as has been, and is, most generally recognized by Christian people as suitable for the conferring of the sacred orders of bishop, priest, and deacon. (BCP: 510)

This "manner" is, of course, set out at length in the services, but the Preface itself states that it involves the admission of "persons who are chosen and recognized by the Church as being called by God to the ordained ministry" to "sacred orders by solemn prayer and the laying on of episcopal hands." The "call" is from God. The role of the Church is choosing, recognizing and admitting. Two concepts of ministry which have often been placed in opposition are placed together: the minister as the person called by God, and the minister as the person chosen and ordained by the Church. Much contemporary theological discussion of ministry has revolved precisely around this question of the relationship of ministry as charism to ministry as office, which opens onto the larger question of the relationship of the Church as the community of faith to the Church as institution. This latter question is that raised archetypically by the conversion of St. Paul and the relationship of his apostleship to that of the Twelve. Are ministers charismatic leaders called forth by God from among the believing people, or are they the officers of the corporate body known as the Church? The answer given in the Preface is that ideally they are both: the corporate body is the Body of Christ, and its officers are members of Christ, called by God, and chosen, recognized and admitted to sacred orders by the Church as the Body of Christ, the people of God. The Preface gives no hints how to resolve classic "worst-case scenarios," such as the prophetic ministry of Amos and the official ministry of Amaziah, beyond the obvious implication that the Church should choose, recognize and ordain the persons called by God, and reject the applications of others.

The "three distinct orders" are described as "characteristic of Christ's holy catholic Church," not as "the exclusive property" of the Anglican Churches. The bishops "carry on the apostolic work of leading, supervising, and uniting the church." The presybters, or priests, are "associated with them . . . in the governance of the Church, in the carrying out of its missionary and pastoral work, and in the preaching of the Word of God and administering his holy Sacraments." The deacons have "a special responsibility . . . to minister in Christ's name to the poor, the sick, the suffering, and the helpless" and generally to assist bishops and priests in the work of ministry (BCP: 510).

The claims made for the threefold ministry may be tested to some degree by comparing them with the Lima document of the Faith and Order Commission of the World Council of Churches, *Baptism, Eucharist and Ministry*, which says of them:

> During the second and third centuries, a threefold pattern of bishop, presbyter and deacon became established as the pattern of ordained ministry throughout the Church.

> Although there is no single New Testament pattern, although the Spirit has many times led the Church to adapt its ministries to contextual needs, and although other forms of the ordained ministry have been blessed with the gifts of the Holy Spirit, nevertheless the threefold ministry of bishop, presbyter and deacon may serve today as an expression of the unity we seek and also as a means for achieving it. (WCC 1982: 24)

Lima describes ordination as "in the name of Christ by the invocation of the Spirit and the laying on of hands" (WCC 1982: 30), supporting the claim of the

Prayer Book rite to be "such as has been, and is, most generally recognized by Christian people as suitable" for ordination to the sacred ministry (BCP: 510). The lack of full mutual recognition of ordained ministries is a primary obstacle to Christian unity today. Movement toward this will involve, for Episcopalians, a renewed understanding of our own practice and an acceptance of the challenge of the Lima document:

> Churches which have preserved the episcopal succession are asked to recognize both the apostolic content of the ordained ministry which exists in other churches which have not maintained such succession and also the existence in those churches of a ministry of *episkopé* in various forms.

> Churches without the episcopal succession, and living in faithful continuity with apostolic faith and mission, have a ministry of Word and sacrament, as is evident from the belief, practice and life of those churches. These churches are asked to realize that the continuity with the Church of the apostles finds profound expression in the successive laying on of hands by bishops and that, though they may not lack the continuity of the apostolic tradition this sign will strengthen and deepen that continuity. They may need to recover the sign of episocpal succession. (WCC 1982: 32)

The Preface to the Ordination Rites, then, describes the threefold ministry of bishops, priests, and deacons as the characteristic ministry of the holy catholic Church and declares the intention of "this Church" to maintain and continue this ministry by providing rites of ordination for that purpose and by forbidding those not so ordained "with the laying on of hands by bishops who are themselves duly qualified to confer Holy Orders" to exercise these offices. It does this within an ecumenical context in which it hopes that other Christians will recognize this ministry as Christ's gift to the Church.

The structure of the three ordination services is the same. They are a part of the celebration of the eucharist. Ordinands are presented in white robes, without insignia of rank or order. The presentation of the candidates takes place after the Collect for Purity at the beginning of the service, and the laying on of hands takes place at the end of the Ministry of the Word. The term "The Consecration" is used for all three orders to mean the laying on of hands with prayer, and the term "ordination" is similarly used to mean the entire service. The ordination of bishops is printed first to avoid the suggestion of a succession of ministerial ranks leading from deacon to bishop.

The Ordination of a Bishop

"In accordance with ancient custom," bishops are ordained on Sundays or other feasts of our Lord, or on the festivals of apostles or evangelists (BCP: 511), suggesting their role of carrying on the apostolic ministry. The proper preface of the apostles and ordinations makes the same connection:

> Through the great shepherd of your flock, Jesus Christ our Lord; who after his resurrection sent forth his apostles to preach the Gospel and to teach all nations; and promised to be with them always, even to the end of the ages. (BCP: 381)

The ordinands are the ministers whom our Lord sends forth to preach the Gospel (as apostles and evangelists) and through whom he continues his presence and ministry to and in the world.

The ordination of a bishop is an activity of the entire Church. The Presiding Bishop of the Episcopal Church, or a bishop whom he designates to represent him, is chief consecrator. At least two other bishops, representing the episcopal order, take part as co-consecrators; and presbyters, deacons and laity of the new bishop's diocese take the liturgical roles appropriate to their order (BCP: 511). In all ordinations, whether to the episcopate or to any of the other orders, "Opportunity is always given to the people to communicate" (BCP: 536). The reception of communion by the people at the hands of the new bishop is the most powerful symbol of their active participation in the ordination rite, and the Prayer Book is careful to insist that it not be omitted for "practical" reasons.

Priests and lay persons representing "the clergy and people" of the diocese which has elected the new bishop present the candidate to the Presiding Bishop, who "presides from a chair placed close to the people, so that all may see and hear what is done," and the other bishops are seated to his left and right (BCP: 511). The representatives present the ordinand by asking the bishops "to lay [their] hands upon *him* and in the power of the Holy Sporit to consecrate *him* a bishop in the one, holy, catholic, and apostolic Church" (BCP: 513). After the testimonials of election are read, the Presiding Bishop invites the congregation to voice their approval of the ordination and their support of their new bishop and to join in silent prayer and in a litany for "the work to which we trust the Holy Spirit has called *him*" (BCP: 514). In this way the corporate nature of the Church and the role of all the orders, clerical and lay, in the episcopal election and ordination are signified. The bishop is the leader of the local Church, and it is the local Church which elects and presents the candidate to the assembled bishops (the representatives of the universal Church) for ordination and consecration.

The bishop-elect, like candidates for ordination to the other orders, pronounces and publicly signs the following declaration:

> I do believe the Holy Scriptures of the Old and New
> Testaments to be the Word of God, and to contain all
> things necessary to salvation; and I do solemnly engage
> to conform to the doctrine, discipline, and worship of
> the Episcopal Church. (BCP: 513)

The words of the declaration are explained in the catechism, which asks, "Why do we call the Holy Scriptures the Word of God?" and responds, "We call them the Word of God because God inspired their human authors and because God still speaks to us through the Bible" (BCP: 853). The Church is scripturally based, and the declaration sets forth a principle that the Bible *contains* all things necessary to salvation. This principle does not claim that it is necessary to believe everything in the Bible, but that the Bible is the basis of the faith of the Church and that we do not consider anything a necessary doctrine which is not derived therefrom. The principle's practical effect is that the Church can maintain an attitude of agnosticism toward non-scriptural doctrines, such as the assumption of the Virgin Mary, neither affirming nor denying them, but rather insisting that belief in them is not necessary to salvation, since they are not contained in the Holy Scriptures.

The promise of conformity to the "doctrine, discipline, and worship of the Episcopal Church" is of a different nature. It does not claim truth or excellence for these things, but only that a person who wishes to exercise ministry within the Episcopal Church conform to its faith and practice. These are expressed in the Scripture and creeds, in the *Book of Common Prayer,* and in the Constitution and Canons of the Episcopal Church. It is, of course, the belief of the Episcopal Church that its doctrine is founded upon the Scripture and expressed in the ecumenical creeds, and therefore to be believed. It is the express teaching of the Preface to the Prayer Book, adopted in October 1789, that "what cannot be clearly demonstrated to belong to Doctrine must be referred to Discipline; and therefore, by common consent and authority, may be altered. . . " (BCP: 9). This is self-evidently true in the case of rules of order and organizational structures, but it is also true of the customs and words of worship, which may be, and have been changed, "provided the substance of the Faith be kept entire" (BCP: 9). The worship of the Episcopal Church, to which all who are ordained in it promise to conform, is the *Book of Common Prayer* and other supplementary liturgical books, such as *Lesser Feasts and Fasts* or *The Book of Occasional Services,* authorized by the General Convention of the Church at that time.

The ordination rite's lessons from the Old Testament and the Epistle are read by lay persons (BCP: 515), even though a large number of bishops, priests and deacons may be participating in the service. Reading the Scripture in the liturgy is a lay ministry from which lay people are not displaced by supernumerary clerics. Again, this practice reaffirms the corporate nature of the Church as a body in which all orders, bishops, priest, deacons, and laity, have their ministries, rather than as an episcopal or clerical preserve.

The readings themselves may be taken from those of the Sunday or major feast on which the ordination is held, or chosen from a list of proper lessons. Isaiah 61:1-8, the passage read by Jesus in the synagogue at Nazareth, and Isaiah 42:1-9, a passage from the Servant Songs, both remind the ordinand of the mission of the one called by God to be a light to the nations, a minister of healing and freedom, one who proclaims the liberating rule of God. Hebrews 5:1-10 points out that high priests are "appointed to act on behalf of men in relation to God" and are themselves sinners who must deal gently with others. The reading also sets the example of

Christ as high priest before the bishop-elect. The figurative identification of bishops with the high priest of the Old Covenant is already found in the apostolic fathers.[4] 2 Timothy 3:1-7 names personal qualities to seek in "one who aspires to the office of bishop." 2 Corinthians 3:4-9 makes the claim that God "has qualified us as ministers of a new covenant."

The reading of the Gospel is assigned to a deacon, whose proper liturgy it is, but, recognizing the possibility that there may be no deacon actually present at the ordination, the rite permits a priest to read it (BCP: 516). The Prayer Book suggests three alternative readings. John 20:19-23 is the Johannine account of the post-resurrection commissioning of the apostles: "As the Father has sent me, even so I send you" and "Receive the Holy Spirit. If you forgive the sins of any, they are forgiven. . . ." It is one of the central passages concerning the authority of the apostolic ministry and is a significant choice for an episcopal ordination, suggesting that the one being ordained bishop receives the same commission. Luke 24:44-49a parallels John 19. The Lucan passage expounds what is written in the Scripture about the Lord's resurrection and charges the apostles to preach repentance and forgiveness of sins in Christ's name; the passage concludes: "You are witnesses of these things. And behold, I send the promise of my Father upon you." John 17:1-9, 18-21 is a portion of the high-priestly prayer of Jesus at the Last Supper; it prays for the apostles and includes them in Jesus' mission: "As thou didst send me into the world, so I have sent them into the world." The passage concludes with the prayer for the unity of those who believe "through the preaching of the apostles." All three passages proclaim the divine authority of the apostolic mission and invite the preacher to apply that mission and promise to the ordination taking place.

The Examination and Consecration

After the sermon and a hymn, the bishop-elect stands facing the bishops. The address of the Presiding Bishop, which begins the examination, contains the liturgy's major description of the episcopate (BCP: 517). A bishop "is called to be one with the apostles" in proclaiming the resurrection, interpreting the Gospel and bearing witness to the sovereignty of Christ the King, all of which is clearly implied in the appointed Gospel readings. The bishop is "to guard the faith, unity, and discipline of the Church; to celebrate and to provide for the the administration of the sacraments of the New Covenant; to ordain. . . "; to be a pastor and example for the people; and to share with the other bishops in the leadership of the worldwide Church. This description is again summarized later in the examination when the bishop-elect is called "a chief priest and pastor" (BCP: 518).

The episcopate is clearly a ministry of Word and Sacrament, not an administrative office. It is also, as its name indicates, a ministry of *episkopé*, or overseeing. The bishop is called not only to celebrate the sacraments but to provide for their celebration, and to ordain priests and deacons and join in ordaining other bishops to celebrate the sacraments. Not only is the bishop the chief priest and pastor of the local Church, but together with the other bishops he shares in the leadership of the catholic Church. A part of that leadership is maintaining, or guarding, the Church's faith, unity, and discipline so that the local Church does not lose its unity with the other local Churches, which together comprise the catholic, or universal, Church.[5]

In the questions which follow in the examination, the bishop-elect is asked to "encourage and support all baptized people in their gifts and ministries, nourish them with the riches of God's grace, pray for them without ceasing, and celebrate with them the sacraments of our redemption" (BCP: 518). The episcopate, like all ministries, is a call to serve the Body of Christ and its members. The bishop, "as chief priest and pastor," is the chief enabler of the ministry of the body. The episcopate is also a call to follow Christ in "be[ing] merciful to all, show[ing] compassion to the poor and strangers, and defend[ing] those who have no helper." Other aspects of *episkopé* are brought out in the following question:

> Will you share with your fellow bishops in the government of the whole Church; will you sustain your fellow presbyters and take counsel with them; will you guide and strengthen the deacons and all others who minister in the Church? (BCP: 518)

In the government of the whole Church, the bishop has a collegial relationship with other bishops. In the local Church the bishop is collegially related to "fellow presbyters," whom he is to sustain and with whom he is to take counsel. The presbyters are not described as subordinates but as colleagues and counselors with whom the bishop shares the presbyterate. The images are not hierarchical but collegial. The bishop is not the "ruler" of the local Church but its chief minister, who shares his ministry with fellow presbyters, with deacons whom he is "to guide and strengthen," and with lay people, whom he[6] is to support and encourage "in their gifts and ministries." The bishop has the ministry of overseeing and governance, but it is a ministry in association with other ministers for the building up of the Body of Christ and for enabling the ministry of the people of God.

The bishop-elect gives ritual expression to the role of "guardian of the Church's faith" by leading the congregation in confessing that faith through reciting the Nicene Creed (BCP: 519).

For the consecration, the bishop-elect kneels before the Presiding Bishop while a hymn invoking the Holy Spirit is sung (BCP: 520). Three versions of the traditional consecration hymn *Veni Creator Spiritus,* including John Cosin's well known "Come, Holy Ghost, our souls inspire," and two versions of *Veni Sancte Spiritus,* called the Golden Sequence, are included in *The Hymnal 1982.*

The Prayer of Consecration of a Bishop

The prayer which accompanies the laying on of hands, or Prayer of Consecration (BCP: 520f), is the oldest surviving Christian prayer for this purpose. It is taken from the *Apostolic Tradition* of Hippolytus, which dates from the beginning of the 3rd century. The new *Roman Pontifical* has adopted a different translation of the same prayer. This is an important ecumenical event, for both Episcopal and Roman Catholic churches have revived the same ancient prayer to use in their episcopal ordinations.[7] This use of this prayer indicates not only the belief of both Churches that they are ordaining to the same office, the one episcopate of the Holy Catholic Church of Jesus Christ, but also their belief that the office of bishop presently in the Church, in spite of change and development, is that episcopate to which the early Church also ordained. The use of this prayer is primarily an expression of continuity with the Church in which it was originally composed and used. If it does not necessarily say the things we think today are most significant about the office of bishop, it testifies magnificently to "the intention and purpose of this Church to maintain and continue" the historical episcopate (BCP: 510).

The prayer is addressed to the God and Father of our Lord Jesus Christ as "Father of mercies and God of all comfort" who knows "all things before they come to pass." God is not only the merciful creator of all that exists, the God who knew all before it existed; God is also the God who has acted in Jesus Christ for the salvation of the world. God has chosen a people, "the heirs of the covenant of Abraham," namely the new Israel of the Church, and throughout history has raised up in it prophets, priests and kings. Interestingly, prophets are not mentioned in the original Hippolytan prayer. They are an addition of the Prayer Book version, an addition which recognizes the divine authority of the prophetic ministry. The prophet, priest and king were the "anointed" servants of God in the Old Testament. The prayer also gives thanks that God has always accepted the ministry of those whom God calls (BCP: 520).

The prayer then invokes the Holy Spirit, asking God to give to the bishop-elect the Spirit bestowed on Jesus and on the apostles. It calls the office of bishop "the high priesthood" and speaks of the bishop as

> serving before [God] day and night in the ministry of reconciliation, declaring pardon in [God's] Name, offering the holy gifts, and wisely overseeing the life and work of the Church. (BCO: 521)

The Church sets this picture of the early Christian bishop before the contemporary members of that order. That it seems to us more descriptive of the ministry of the parish priest is an indication of the way the life of the Church has changed and developed. These are priestly ministries for which the bishop as chief priest and pastor is responsible throughout the local Church committed to his charge, even though the presbyters, now "generally known as priests" (BCP: 510), actually perform this ministry for most people, under the bishop's overseeing. It is, in fact, precisely because the presbyters generally performed these ministries that they, like the bishops, came to be called priests.

The laying on of hands takes place during the prayer's central section, which begins, "Therefore,

Father, make N. a bishop in your Church. . . " (BCP: 521). The hymn invoking the Holy Spirit, the silent prayer of the people, and the prayer spoken by the Presiding Bishop are brought together with the imposition of hands by the bishops, all of whom join the Presiding Bishop in this action. In this way, the relationship between the solemn prayer and *epiclesis* of the Spirit (or "form" of the sacrament) and the action of the episcopal imposition of hands upon the candidate (or "matter" of the sacrament) is made clear.

The Vesting
of the New Bishop

The new bishop, having been ordained and consecrated, is vested *"according to the order of bishops"* (BCP: 521). The Prayer Book does not explain what this vesture is. Presumably it is the same vesture worn by the consecrating bishops, to whose order the new bishop now belongs. The new bishop, who has worn an alb or rochet throughout the service, is (traditionally) vested in stole, dalmatic and chasuble to symbolize the bishop's role as chief priest and chief deacon (or minister) of the local Church. Frequently the dalmatic is omitted, or the bishop is vested in stole and cope. Alternatively, bishops are sometimes vested in the traditional episcopal choir habit of rochet and chimere. If the vestments are to be blessed, this takes place before the service, not during it, lest it interrupt the flow of the service and give undue prominence to the vestments which are described in a prayer for their blessing as *"tokens* of your servant's ministry and dignity" (BCP: 552).

After the vesting, a Bible is presented to the new bishop with the charge

Feed the flock of Christ committed to your charge, and
defend them in his truth, and be a faithful steward of
[God's] holy Word and Sacraments. (BCP: 521)

This presentation emphasizes once again the nature of
the episcopate as a pastoral ministry of overseeing the
flock of Christ, not as an administrative office. *"Other
symbols of office"* may also be presented (BCP: 521). A
"ring, staff, and mitre" are specifically mentioned as
suitable (BCP: 553). No mention is made of a pectoral
cross, but one is almost universally worn by Anglican
bishops and is normally included among the vestments,
so that it may be placed around the neck before the
mitre is put on.

The new bishop, vested according to that order and
wearing the insignia of office, is presented by the chief
consecrator to the clergy and people for *"their acclamation and applause."* Having first elected the candidate,
then affirmed their support at the presentation, they
are now given the opportunity to express their approval
of what has been done, and to exchange the peace at the
invitation of their new bishop (BCP: 522).

After the peace *"the new Bishop, if the Bishop of the
Diocese, may now be escorted to the episcopal chair."* *The Book
of Occasional Services* provides a form to be said by the
dean of the cathedral in seating the bishop in the episcopal chair (BOS: 226), which may be done upon another
occasion if the episcopal ordination does not take place
in the cathedral. The episcopal chair has often incor-
rectly been called a throne. It is rather the "chair," (the
seat of the person who presides), from which the word
"chairman" is derived. It is also like the "chair" which
we speak of professors holding, the symbol of the
authority of the teacher. The Greek name for the
"chair" is *cathedra,* from which the word "cathedral" (in
which the *cathedra* is located) is derived. The bishop is
not enthroned as a ruler of the local Church, although it

was often seen that way in the Middle Ages,but is seated in the chair to preside over the assembled Church and to teach them in the name of Jesus Christ.

The liturgy continues with the offertory. The family and friends of the newly ordained bring forward the gifts (BCP: 511). "*Deacons prepare the Table,*" and the newly ordained bishop is chief celebrant of the eucharist (BCP: 522). Some of the consecrating bishops and representative presbyters of the diocese stand at the altar, joining "as fellow ministers of the Sacrament" (BCP: 553). The new bishop begins to function as the chief priest of the local Church by presiding at its eucharist, assisted by the consecrating bishops, representing the whole Church and other local Churches, and by the presbyters, deacons, and lay people of the diocese. The new bishop continues so to function by administering communion to the people, with the assistance of other ministers, and by giving "the pontifical blessing" to the congregation (BCP: 523, 553).

The Ordination of a Priest

The service for the Ordination of a Priest is written in the singular. Provision is made in the additional directions (BCP: 553f) for adapting the service to the ordination of two or more, but the prayers and rubrics are written for the ordination of one person. Cranmer's Ordinal had assumed the continuation of the medieval custom in which groups of ordinands from throughout the diocese were presented *en masse,* usually by the archdeacon, and ordained together. This custom has survived in many places. The way the service is written in the Prayer Book today, however, favors the ordination of individual candidates, either in the church in which they will serve, or in the church which has canonically recommended them for ordination. The Prayer Book does not actually require this practice, and does permit the other custom to continue.

There is more involved in the Prayer Book's favoring the one practice over the other than the convenience of bishop, ordinand, and congregation. The ordination of a group of priests by the bishop at the cathedral is thoroughly consonant with the concept of the presbyter as a member of the bishop's council and an associate of the bishop. The ordination of the priest in the parish church emphasizes the role of the presbyter as pastor and priest of a particular congregation. Ministers are not ordained simply as officers of the universal Church, but to a specific local Church. A bishop is ordained to a specific diocese, a priest or deacon to a specific *cura animarum*, a parochial or other ministry. Those Churches which identify the local Church with the local congregation usually ordain ministers in the congregations which they will serve. The Episcopal Church formally identifies the local Church with the diocese. Ordinands are presented to the bishop "on behalf of the clergy and people of the Diocese of N." (BCP: 526). Priests are also normally ordained to be pastor or curate of a specific local congregation. The presidency of the bishop and the presentation on behalf of the diocese ritualize the relationship of the priest to the diocese as local Church. Ordination in the local congregation enhances the priest's identification with the people committed to his or her charge. At the practical level, priests ordained at the cathedral and sent to local congregations to be vicars or priests-in-charge may appear to members of the congregation to be "branch managers" sent out from "headquarters" to make sure the "local outlets" adhere to company policy. Congregations are much more likely to identify with a pastor in whose call and ordination they have had a share.

Wherever the ordination takes place, however, it is a significant event in the life of the local Church. It is

most fittingly performed for a single candidate, unless
there is a specific reason for ordaining a particular
group of people together. Theologians and devotional
writers have often drawn an analogy between ordination and marriage.[8] The simultaneous ordination of
several people is similar to a double wedding. It should
not take place simply because there is more than one
candidate at a given time, but because there are good
reasons why the events should not be separated.

The Prayer Book requires the participation of at least
two presbyters with the bishop in the ordination of a
priest (BCP: 524). Ordination is not simply an act of the
bishop. It is an act of the Church, represented by the
bishop, at least two presbyters, and the lay people. The
presbyters also represent their order, into which the
new priest is being ordained.

The structure of the rite parallels that for the ordination of a bishop, and many of the comments made about
that rite apply equally well to the ordination of a priest
or a deacon. As at those ordinations, the candidate,
vested in a plain white robe, is presented both by priests
and by lay people on behalf of the clergy and laity of the
diocese. The presenters testify to the qualifications of
the candidate for the ministry, and the candidate makes
the required declaration of conformity (BCP: 526).
The congregation is asked, first, if there are objections;
second, if it is their "will that N. be ordained a priest";
and, third, if they will uphold the ordinand in that ministry (BCP: 527). The Canons have provided in many
ways for the involvement of representative lay people
and clergy of the diocese and of the congregation of
which the ordinand has been a member in selecting and
examining the candidate for ordination. Members of
the diocesan standing committee and the commission
on ministry, and the rector and vestry of the candidate's
home parish have all formally voted to approve of the
ordination. That process is recognized and ritualized in

the formal statements of the presenters and in the questions to the congregation and their responses. The new priest is ideally to be the choice of the clergy and people. At the very least, they must have no objections.

The Ministry of the Word

Lay persons read the two lessons which precede the Gospel (BCP: 528), as at the ordination of a bishop or a deacon. The lessons themselves may be those of a Sunday or major feast but will generally be selected from among those appointed in the rite itself. Isaiah 6:1-8, the call of Isaiah, speaks God's call and our response. Numbers 11:16-17, 24-25 is the account of the selection of the seventy elders by Moses: "The Lord . . . took some of the spirit that was upon [Moses] and put it upon the seventy elders, and when the spirit rested upon them, they prophesied." The Christian presbyters have often been identified with the elders chosen by Moses. *The Apostolic Tradition* of Hippolytus, the source of the consecration prayer for bishops, mentions the selection of elders by Moses in the prayer of consecration of presbyters, identifying the spirit given to the elders with the Holy Spirit given to the presbyters of the Christian Church. The ministry of the presbyters is described in the Book of Numbers as a sharing in the ministry of Moses. By analogy, the Christian presbyters share by delegation in the ministry to which God has called the bishop, with whom they are associated in the exercise of that ministry.

Psalm 43 has had a long association with the entrance rite of the eucharist and with the preparation of the ministers for the eucharist. Its most obviously appropriate verse, and the one for which it was associated with the eucharist, is "That I may go to the altar of God, to the God of my joy and gladness," although the advice, "Put your trust in God; for I will yet give thanks to him, who is the help of my countenance and my God," is also certainly appropriate for one being ordained. As an alternate, Psalm 132:8-19 was apparently chosen for its references to priests. Both psalms provide more devotional "hooks" than theological insights. There is no intention of equating the priesthood of the new and old covenants, or the altar of the Temple with the Christian altar, but rather to apply the Old Testament images to their Christian counterparts. When this is done theologically with the intention of bringing out the Christian meaning of the text, it is called typological interpretation. In this instance, however, it is probably better described as poetic allusion.

1 Peter 5:1-4 is an exhortation to the presbyters from a fellow presbyter to tend the flock of Christ committed to their charge in a way that "when the chief Shepherd is manifested [they] will obtain the unfading crown of glory." Most of the English translations of the text use the word "elder," but the Prayer Book directs the substitution of the Greek "presbyter" (BCP: 528), identifying the priest now being ordained with the New Testament elders.

Ephesians 4:7, 11-16, a passage quoted in the prayer of consecration of the priest, reminds us of the unity of various ministries in the Body of Christ. It also reminds us that all gifts are given, not for the benefit of those who receive them, but "to equip the saints for the work of ministry, for building up the body of Christ" so that all may attain "the measure of the stature of the fullness of Christ." This reading provides a valuable corrective to the erroneous views that priesthood exhausts the meaning of ministry, absorbing all other ministries into what Boone Porter has described as "omnivorous priesthood,"[9] and that ordination is for the personal spiritual growth of the ordinand. In attempting to avoid a minimalizing view of ordination as mere authorization to perform a function within the congregation,

we have often absolutized it, so that priesthood became
a thing in itself, conferring status and spiritual benefit
on the priest. This has led men and women to seek
ordination to the priesthood because it met their own
spiritual needs, rather than because the Church needed
their gifts "to equip the Saints, for the work of ministry,
for building up the body of Christ."

Philippians 4:4-9 ("Rejoice in the Lord always.")
offers words of encouragement to Christians. The
words "in everything by prayer and supplication with
thanksgiving let your requests be made known to God"
are the most directly applicable to the ordination,
although the whole passage is appropriate advice to the
ordinand just as it is to all the people of God.

The Gospel is read by a deacon, if one is present
(BCP: 529). The participation of deacons in the ordination of a priest is not simply a ceremonial enrichment
but, like the participation of lay people, a sign of the
participation of the entire Church in the ordination.
The bishop presides; priests participate in the presentation of the ordinand, join in the laying on of hands, and
concelebrate with the new priest and the bishop; the
deacon reads the Gospel, prepares the altar at the offertory, and dismisses the people; lay people join in the
presentation, assent to the ordination, read the lessons,
pray for the candidate, join in the peace, bring up the
gifts at the offertory, and receive communion. All
orders have significant roles, and deacons, if possible,
should be present to assume the diaconal roles, which
must otherwise be filled by a priest.

Matthew 9:35-38 ("The harvest is plentiful, but the
laborers are few.") speaks of Jesus teaching, preaching,
and healing those who were "like sheep without a shepherd." The ordained are, by implication, the laborers
sent by the Lord of the harvest to participate in these
ministries. John 10:11-18 offers the model of Jesus as

the Good Shepherd to the priest, who is to be a shepherd and not a hireling, one who is prepared to follow Jesus in laying down his or her life for the sheep. John 6:35-38 ("I am the bread of life. . . "), a eucharistic passage from the Fourth Gospel, suggests the role of the priest in presiding at the eucharist and reminds us that just as Jesus came to do the will of the Father, priests are not sent to do their own will but that of Christ. Unlike the Gospel selections for the ordination of a bishop, none of these three passages speaks directly about the work of the ministry.

The Examination and Consecration

The examination of the ordinand takes place following the sermon and Nicene Creed (BCP: 529ff). The address of the bishop first describes the ministry of all the baptized "to make Christ known as Savior and Lord, and to share in the renewing of his world" (BCP: 531). The special ministry to which the ordinand is called is the work of pastor, priest and teacher, a work shared with "[the ordinand's] bishop and fellow presbyters," with whom the new priest is to take a share in the councils of the Church. The work of the priest is described this way:

> You are to love and serve the people among whom you work. . . . You are to preach, to declare God's forgiveness to penitent sinners, to pronounce God's blessing, to share in the administration of Holy Baptism and in the celebration of the mysteries of Christ's Body and Blood, and to perform the other ministrations entrusted to you. (BCP: 531)

In the questions, the candidate is asked to "respect and be guided by the pastoral leadership and direction of your bishop," and to work with the people and "your fellow ministers to build up the family of God" (BCP:

532). The ministry described is that of Word and Sacrament: to preach, bless, absolve, baptize, and celebrate the eucharist. The priest is called to serve specific people under the pastoral direction and leadership of a bishop and in association with fellow presbyters.

At the consecration, the priests who are present stand to the right and left of the bishop and join in the laying on of hands. This action symbolizes their association with the bishop in the ministry of Word and Sacrament, their role as their bishop's council, and their acceptance of the new presbyter into their number. This, at least, is the way in which Episcopalians have traditionally viewed this action, and it is certainly the way in which the Episcopal Church understands it. The rite itself, however, is also open to a "Presbyterian" interpretation in which the bishop ordains jointly with those whom the ordination of a bishop calls his "fellow presbyters" (BCP: 518). This rite has been so interpreted, at various times, both by those within the episcopal Churches and by those who wished to find a basis for including ordination by bishops within a basically presbyterian system. This theological position has never actually been excluded by Anglicanism as long as the practice of episcopal presidency of presbyterial ordinations was maintained, and it may well prove a valuable opening in ecumenical conversions with Churches which presently lack the historical episcopate.

The Prayer of Consecration of a Priest

The prayer of consecration gives thanks for God's "calling us to be a holy people in the kingdom of [God's] Son Jesus our Lord" (BCP: 533). It names the various ministerial gifts from Ephesians 4 and asks:

. . . give your Holy Spirit to N.; fill *him* with grace and power, and make *him* a priest in your Church. (BCP: 533)

These words are said while the bishop and priests lay their hands on the candidate's head. When more than one person is ordained, this paragraph is repeated for each candidate while hands are imposed (BCP: 533f). The prayer goes on to describe the priesthood, making specific what it is that is being asked, praying that the new priest may

> offer spiritual sacrifices acceptable to you; boldly proclaim the gospel of salvation; and rightly administer the sacraments of the New Covenant. (BCP: 534)

God is asked to make the priest "a faithful pastor, a patient teacher, and a wise councilor." The word *councilor* means a member of a council, one who advises the bishop, not one who gives pastoral counseling.

The New Priest

"The new priest is now vested according to the order of priests" (BCP: 534). The additional directions mention a "stole worn about the neck, or other insignia of the office of priest" (BCP: 553). The new priest will be already wearing an alb or surplice (BCP: 524). Traditionally the stole and chasuble are placed over the alb at this time, so that the new priest is vested for the celebration of the eucharist. Alternatively the stole may be placed around the priest's neck and worn over the surplice. A Bible is given "as a sign of the authority . . . to preach the Word of God and to administer his holy Sacraments" (BCP: 534). "Afterwards, other instruments of office may be given" (BCP: 553). In the Ordinal of 1550, following the pre-Reformation custom, a chalice and paten were given as signs of the priest's sacramental

ministry, and they are frequently still given as the traditional "instruments of office." If they are given, it is appropriate to use them in the following eucharistic celebration.

The bishop greets the new priest, and the priest extends the greeting of the Peace to the congregation (BCP: 534). The deacons prepare the Table at the offertory, and the new priest stands with the bishop and other presbyters at the altar, joining in the celebration of the eucharist and in the breaking of the bread (BCP: 535). It is important that priests other than the newly ordained stand with them and the bishop at the altar during the Great Thanksgiving to represent the order or "college" of presbyters to which the newly ordained are now joined. In this way, the new priest exercises his or her liturgical ministry, concelebrating the eucharist with the bishop and the diocesan presbyters. Each new priest is to break the consecrated Bread and receive communion (BCP: 554). The new priest is invited by the bishop to give the final blessing (BCP: 535).

The rite exhibits both in word and in liturgical action the nature of the Church as a eucharistic community and the nature of the priesthood within that community and in relationship to the ministries of bishop, deacon, and lay people. It is important, therefore, that lay persons and deacons fulfill the functions assigned to them in the ordination rite and that these roles not be usurped by other priests, thereby obscuring the variety of ministries in the Church and promoting the erroneous identification of the priesthood with "real ministry."

The Ordination of a Deacon

The ordination of deacons in Cranmer's Ordinal was the least satisfactory of the three ordination rites. There was no proper "solemn prayer" or *epiclesis* of the

Holy Spirit. Its reference to the diaconate as "this inferior office" and its prayer that the new deacons "may be found worthy to be called unto the higher ministries in thy Church" (BCP, 1928: 535), although of venerable antiquity, made the rite most unsuitable for the ordination of "permanent" or "perpetual" deacons and perpetuated the idea that the diaconate was not a true order but only an apprenticeship for "the higher ministries." The rite of the *Book of Common Prayer* 1979 remedies these defects. Since the structure of the rite is parallel to that of the ordination of priests and bishops, the comments below refer only to those things peculiar to the ordination of a deacon.

"*A Priest and a Lay Person*" present the ordinands (BCP: 538). The rite makes no provision for the inclusion of deacons among the presenters, although a deacon might serve as one of the optional "additional presenters." The diaconal ministry is not collegial in the same way as the episcopate and presbyterate, but deacons are servants of the Church and assistants to the bishop and priest.

The appointed Old Testament lessons deal with vocation. Jeremiah 1:4-9 tells how the Lord called the prophet before he was formed in the womb, and how God puts the Lord's own words in the prophet's mouth. By analogy, the deacon is to exercise a prophetic ministry, speaking God's Word against the established order. Ecclesiasticus 39:1-8 lays out a program for one "who devotes himself to the study of the law of the Most High." It is sage advice for a minister, but both choices are more inspirational than theological.

2 Corinthians 4:1-6 speaks of "having this ministry by the mercy of God" and reminds all who minister in Christ's name that "what we preach is not ourselves, but Jesus Christ as Lord, with ourselves as your servants for Jesus' sake." The diaconate is particularly the ministry of service, following the example of Christ, "who is the

likeness of God." Ministerial office is not for the bestowal of status upon the minister, but for service to the Body of Christ. The passage concludes by affirming that God "has shone in our hearts to give the light of the knowledge of the glory of God in the face of Christ."

1 Timothy 3:8-13 actually gives the qualifications for deacon in the late New Testament period. Those who fill that office today should, presumably, have the same qualities. The statement "they must hold the mystery of faith with a clear conscience" has frequently been seen as having liturgical implications and referring to the deacon's role in holding the chalice. The phrase is also used in the invitation to the people's acclamation in Eucharistic Prayer A, "Therefore we proclaim the mystery of faith" (BCP: 363), where it unmistakably refers to the Paschal Mystery, which is a more likely interpretation of its meaning in the pastoral epistles. It is this central mystery of the faith which the deacon is to hold as the grounding of ministry. New Testament scholars do not agree whether the "women" mentioned in the lesson are the wives of male deacons or are themselves deacons, although Phoebe, called a *diakonos* in Romans 16:1, is clearly herself a deacon. Certainly the early Church knew deacons of both sexes, and the inclusion of this passage, which goes back to Cranmer's Ordinal of 1550, serves to raise the possibility of ordaining women to the diaconate. In 1550, Cranmer's concern may well have been to affirm clerical marriage, as verse 12 of the passage clearly does. The passage concludes, "Those who serve well as deacons gain a good standing for themselves and also great confidence in the faith which is in Christ Jesus."

Acts of the Apostles 6:2-7, the ordination of the Seven, also dates from the 1550 Ordinal. Massey Shepherd commented on this passage:

Though the account does not specifically call the Seven "deacons," the Church has always interpreted this narrative as the institution of the Diaconate, because of the similarity of functions for which the Seven were ordained and those duties always entrusted to the Order of Deacons.[10]

Stephen and Philip, the only ones of the Seven whom Acts mentions again, are portrayed as preaching and evangelizing, not as exercising the ministry described in this passage. Whatever the ministry of the Seven may have actually been, Luke certainly intends the reader of Acts to identify them with the diaconate, and the Church has regularly done so. Serving tables, both to serve the worshiping community and to feed the hungry, has always been prominent among the diaconal ministries. St. Stephen has been the traditional patron of deacons.

Since the consecration of the deacon does not take place until after the Nicene Creed, an already-ordained deacon reads the Gospel (BCP: 541). In Cranmer's Ordinal deacons were ordained before the Gospel, which was then read by the new deacon (BCP, 1928: 534). Following the pattern of the ordination of the bishop and priest for the ordination of a deacon precludes that possibility in the new ordination rite, but it does provide an opportunity for another deacon to have a share in the ordination.

Luke 12:35-38 is an exhortation to watchfulness: "Blessed are those servants whom the master finds awake when he comes." This presents an eschatological theme, the favorable judgment of God upon those who are faithful to their ministry. Once again the diaconate is presented as a ministry of service, this time service to the Lord, who will reward the faithful servant. Luke 22:24-27 concludes with the saying of Jesus "I am among you as one who serves." The Greek verb *diakonein* has the same root as *diakonos,* and the final

phrase could be translated "as a deacon." It ties the
diaconate directly to the ministry of Jesus. The deacon
is one who shares our Lord's ministry of service.

The bishop's address at the examination describes
the diaconate as "a special ministry of servanthood
directly under [the] bishop" (BCP: 543). It then goes on
to describe the work of the deacon:

> You are to make Christ and his redemptive love known,
> by your word and example, to those among whom you
> live, and work, and worship. You are to interpret to the
> Church the needs, concerns, and hopes of the world.
> You are to assist the bishop and priests in public worship
> and in the ministration of God's Word and Sacra-
> ments. . . . At all times, your life and teaching are to
> show Christ's people that in serving the helpless they are
> serving Christ himself. (BCP: 543)

Being a witness to Christ in the world and an interpreter of the world's needs to the Church is a ministry
for a person living in the world, for a person with some
experience of the world, not for an apprentice cleric.
The diaconate is a ministry in its own right, one different from the priesthood, and one which is quite essentially ministry to people. Liturgically the deacon assists
the bishop and priests, but liturgical ministry for the
deacon is symbolic of ministry in the world. It is, for
example, as the interpreter to the Church of the needs
and concerns of the world that the deacon leads the
prayers of the people. In the questions of the examination, the ordinand is asked, "Will you look for Christ in
all others, being ready to help and serve those in need?"
(BCP: 544). Since "it is also a special responsibility of
deacons to minister in Christ's name to the poor, the
sick, the suffering, and the helpless" (BCP: 510), it is
this ministry which is singled out for mention in the
examination. In the final question the candidate is
asked, "Will you in all things seek not your glory but the

glory of the Lord Christ?" (BCP: 544). This question could well be asked in all ordinations. It picks up the theme of 2 Corinthians 4:5-6, one of the choices for the Epistle, and names the only acceptable motive for accepting ordination.

The Prayer of Consecration identifies the diaconate with the ministry of Jesus, "who took on himself the form of a servant," and prays:

> As your Son came not to be served but to serve, may this deacon share in Christ's service, and come to the unending glory of him who, with you and the Holy Spirit, lives and reigns, one God, for ever and ever. (BCP: 545)

The bishop alone lays on hands during the central section of the prayer, a custom we can trace back to *The Apostolic Tradition* of Hippolytus, who explains it in this way:

> When a deacon is ordained, let the bishop alone lay on hands, for the reason that he is not ordained for the priesthood, but for serving the bishop, to do those things which are commanded him. For he is not a member of the council of the clergy, but attends to responsibilities and makes known what is necessary to the bishop; not receiving the common spirit of the presbyter, of which the presbyters are sharers, but that which is entrusted [to him] under the power of the bishop.[11]

We may detect in this passage some antipathy between the presbyter Hippolytus and the powerful Roman deacons, one of whom had apparently just been elected bishop. Nevertheless, the custom Hippolytus describes has been a constant feature of ordinations to the diaconate, and it does reflect the deacon's "special ministry of servanthood directly under [the] bishop" (BCP: 543), over against the ministry of the presbyter as a councilor (BCP: 534). Bishops share the government of the Church with their "fellow bishops" and speak of priests as "fellow presbyters" (BCP: 518). Priests are to share with their "bishop and fellow presbyters" in the councils of the Church (BCP: 531) and to work with their "fellow ministers to build up the family of God" (BCP: 532). There is no mention of "fellow deacons" in the ordination of deacons. The omission should, perhaps, be remedied, but it is consistent with the view of the diaconate presented throughout the ordination rites.

"The stole worn over the left shoulder" (BCP: 554), worn over the alb or surplice, is the traditional vesture of the order of deacons. The dalmatic, the traditional diaconal vestment, worn with the alb and either over or under the deacon's stole, is the only "other insignia of the office of deacon" (BCP: 554) in common use. The stole may be worn in either the Western fashion, tied or joined under the right arm with the ends hanging down, or in the Byzantine manner, with the center of the stole under the right arm and crossing both ends over the left shoulder with the ends hanging from the front and back of that shoulder.

The deacon receives a Bible "as a sign of [his or her] authority to proclaim God's Word and to assist in the ministration of his holy Sacraments" (BCP: 545). Traditionally, deacons have received a Book of the Gospels, symbolizing their role as reader of the Gospel in the eucharistic liturgy, and Cranmer's Ordinal directed the deacon to be given a New Testament (BCP, 1928: 534) for the same purpose. The role of the deacon is here described as proclaiming God's Word, not simply reading the Gospel; this apparently recognizes the traditional role of the deacon as a preacher, for which earlier Ordinals required the deacon to have a special license from the bishop (BCP, 1928: 534), a provision which had been largely ignored for many years. The deacon's liturgical assistance is similarly not identifed merely with reading the Gospel, but as assisting in the ministration of the sacraments, a role for which the Prayer Book makes extensive provision.

At the offertory, the new deacon prepares the bread, pours the wine and water into the chalice, and places the vessels on the altar (BCP: 546), thereby functioning as a deacon at the eucharist, acting as a waiter or servant at the Lord's Table. The new deacon continues to fulfill the liturgical functions of the diaconate by assisting in the administration of communion (BCP: 554) and saying the dismissal (BCP: 547). The deacon may also "remove the vessels from the Altar, consume the remaining Elements, and cleanse the vessels in some convenient place" (BCP: 555). This is a normal liturgical function of a deacon assisting at the eucharist, which may be filled at the ordination liturgy by the newly ordained deacon or another deacon, such as the one who read the Gospel. The additional directions suggest that the deacons may "carry the Sacrament and minister Holy Communion to those communicants who, because of sickness or other grave cause, could not be present at the ordination" (BCP: 555). In this way, the new deacon would be plunged immediately into the ministry to the sick and suffering, which is his or her special responsibility.

The Theology of the Ordination Rites

The ordination rites and other episcopal services provide the material not only for a theology of the ministry but for a theology of the Church. In the prayers of consecration for the different orders and in the address of the bishop at the examination, the Episcopal Church's understanding of the ministry is most fully spelled out. Likewise, the celebration of the rites themselves exhibits the pattern of the liturgical life of the

Church. The rites demonstrate that the bishop presides over the local Church, both in its worship and in its governance, preaching the Word of God, ministering the sacraments, and acting as the chief priest of the people of God. Associated with the bishop are the priests, or presbyters, who collectively serve the bishop as councilors and who stand together with him at the altar as concelebrants at the Lord's Table. In the same way, they stand with the bishop and join in laying hands on other presbyters who may be ordained to their number. Individually, they represent the bishop as the pastor and priest of individual local congregations, where they preach the Word and minister the sacraments under the general direction of the bishop. Priests are called to their office by God and are chosen by their fellow clergy and lay people, who all have a share in their ordination and induction into specific pastoral charges. The deacons are ministers *par excellence,* following Christ in serving those in need and making the needs of the world known to the Church. This ministry is characterized by the deacons' liturgical duties: reading the Gospel, leading the prayers of the people, setting the Table, ministering communion, and dismissing the people. For their part, the people are not passive recipients of ministry but are themselves ministers of Christ and the Church: bearing witness to the Lord in the world and taking their share in the life, worship, and governance of the Church (BCP: 855). This ministry is ritualized by the people's roles in the ordination services: presenting and accepting the candidates, reading the lessons, and participating in the prayers, the peace, and the celebration of the eucharist and reception of communion. The interdependence of the orders is manifested in the interrelationship of the various liturgical roles.

   The relation of the local Church to the whole catholic Church is most clearly shown in the ordination of a bishop by the participation of the bishops of other dioceses in the ordination—both in the imposition of hands and in the celebration of the eucharist—as well as by the actual canonical requirement that the Standing Committees of other dioceses approve of the candidate, evidences of which are read at the service (BCP: 513). The view that the bishops share with the fellow bishops the government of the whole Church (BCP: 518) is distinctive of the episcopal polity from which we take the name the Episcopal Church. The Presiding Bishop presides over a "college" of bishops who oversee, in association with presbyters and lay people, the Episcopal Church, and no principle of union beyond the unity of the bishops and their local Churches with each other in the Body of Christ is seen as holding the Catholic Church together. It is this polity and ecclesiology which the ordination rites express and reflect.

Other Episcopal Services

In addition to the ordination rites, the Prayer Book contains two other Episcopal Services—exclusive of confirmation, which is included both as a part of the baptismal service (BCP: 298-314) and among the Pastoral Offices (BCP: 412-19). The first is called the Celebration of a New Ministry; the second is the Dedication and Consecration of a Church.

The Celebration of a New Ministry (BCP: 557-65) is intended for the institution and induction of the rector of a parish, but it may be adapted for use at the inauguration of other ministries (BCP: 558). It is set within the context of a celebration of the eucharist at which the bishop is the chief celebrant and the priest being inducted and the other priests serving that congregation are concelebrants. A deacon being inducted reads the Gospel and fulfills other diaconal liturgical functions.

The institution is the bishop's authorization and empowerment of the new minister to execute the particular ministry. In the case of rectors of parishes, deans of cathedrals, "and others having similar tenure of office" (BCP: 564), an official Letter of Institution signed and sealed by the bishop is read (BCP: 557). For other ministries, the bishop states briefly "the nature of the person's office and the authority being conferred" (BCP: 565). The institution takes the form of the presentation of symbols of office to the new minister by the bishop, representatives of the congregation and diocesan clergy (BCP: 561f). The bishop presents water as a symbol of his presidency at Christian initiation and his authorization of the priest to "(help the bishop) baptize in obedience to our Lord" (BCP: 561). The clergy present a copy of the Constitution and Canons of the Church, signifying the priest's "share in the councils of this diocese" (BCP: 562). The Churchwardens present a new rector or vicar with the keys to the church as a sign of the rector's control of the church property, but with the admonition ". . . let the doors of this place be open to all people" (BCP: 562). Representatives of the congregation present a Bible and bread and wine. Other symbols include a stole, a book of prayers, and olive oil.

No new theological statements are made in this service, but it expresses publicly the relationship of the priest both to the local congregation and to the diocese, and it inaugurates a new ministry with the common celebration of the eucharist by priest and people, under the presidency of the bishop, and with the assistance of representative diocesan clergy. A comparable service for the Recognition and Investiture of a Diocesan Bishop who has been previously ordained and consecrated is in *The Book of Occasional Services* (BOS: 216-23).

The second Episcopal Service is The Dedication and Consecration of a Church (BCP: 566-79). The primary

meaning of "church" in Christian theology has always
been the people of God, not the building, which was
called *domus ecclesiae*, "the house of the church." It was
only after the conversion of Constantine that Christians
began to consecrate church buildings and to think of
them as holy places, as houses of God. "The Most High
does not dwell in houses made with hands" (Acts 7:48).
A Litany of Thanksgiving for a Church, which may be
used on the anniversary of the consecration, or on other
suitable occasions, specifically reminds us of this: "Eternal God, the heaven of heavens cannot contain you,
much less the walls of temples made with hands" (BCP:
578).

Christ himself has always been the Temple in Christian theology (see John 2:21; Revelation 21:22), and
Christians joined to him are also called the temple of
God (1 Corinthians 3:16). 1 Peter 2:1-9, one of the
selections for Bible readings at the consecration,
includes the lines:

> Come to him, to that living stone, rejected by men but in
> God's sight chosen and precious; and like living stones
> be yourselves built into a spiritual house, to be a holy
> priesthood, to offer spiritual sacrifices acceptable to
> God through Jesus Christ.

The same passage forms the basis of the proper eucharistic preface:

> Through Jesus Christ our great High Priest, in whom
> we are built up as living stones of a holy temple, that we
> might offer before you a sacrifice of praise and prayer
> which is holy and pleasing in your sight. (BCP: 381)

Nothing in the Consecration service suggests that the
church building is a dwelling place for God. It is a house
of prayer and praise, a place set apart for the Ministry of
the Word and sacrament (BCP: 567). Calling upon
God, the Prayer for the Consecration of the Church
describes the church as

> . . . [a] place to which we come to praise your Name,
> to ask your forgiveness, to know your healing power, to
> hear your Word, and to be nourished by the Body and
> Blood of your Son. (BCP: 568)

Although the prayer also refers to the church as "a
temple of [God's] presence and a house of prayer," this
reference must be understood in the light of 1 Kings
8:30, a part of one of the appointed Old Testament
readings: "When we pray toward this place, yea, hear
thou in heaven thy dwelling place."

The service itself follows the traditional Christian
pattern of dedicating things to sacred uses by using
them for that purpose. The bishop leads the congregation into the church and marks a cross on the threshold
with the pastoral staff (BCP: 568). The Prayer for the
Consecration of the Church is then said by the bishop, a
warden, and the rector. The font is dedicated and filled
with water and, if possible, is used immediately for baptism (BCP: 569f). The lectern and pulpit are then dedicated, and the Liturgy of the Word follows (BCP:
570ff). Other pastoral offices may follow the sermon
(BCP: 576). The altar is "set apart" and vested, and the
eucharist is offered (BCP: 573f, 576). The prayer for
the setting apart of the altar says, in part:

> Sanctify this Table dedicated to you [God]. Let it be to
> us a sign of the heavenly Altar where your saints and
> angels praise you for ever. Accept here the continual
> recalling of the sacrifice of your Son. Grant that all who
> eat and drink at this holy Table may be fed and
> refreshed by his flesh and blood, be forgiven for their
> sins, united with one another, and strengthened for
> your service. (BCP: 574)

The earthly altar in the church is to be a sign of the
heavenly altar where the eternal High Priest ever lives
to make intercession for us. The eucharist celebrated
here is the recalling, the *anamnesis*, of Christ's sacrifice,

and the benefits of participation are refreshment, for-giveness, union, and strength. Thus, this prayer pro-vides a good brief summary of the content of the eucharist.

Chapter Nine:
The Theology of
the Prayer Book

In addition to its liturgical contents, the *Book of Common Prayer* contains a number of items of an overtly theological nature—that is, of propositional, or secondary, theology. Most importantly, it contains the Nicene and Apostles' Creeds, which are integral parts of the liturgical services.

The Apostles' Creed is the liturgical statement of the baptismal faith made by candidates at the time of their baptism, renewed at confirmation and annually at the Great Vigil of Easter, and whenever baptism is publicly celebrated or baptismal vows renewed.

The Nicene Creed, the ecumenical symbol of the faith, adopted by the 4th-century Councils of Nicea and Constantinople and still recognized as the necessary foundation of ecumenical discussion of the apostolic faith, sits rather more loosely in the eucharistic liturgy. It is not a necessary part of the eucharist. It was a late addition to the liturgy and is used only on Sundays and Major Feasts. It is, however, required on those occasions, and at the very least it expresses the commitment of the Episcopal Church today to continuity with the catholic and apostolic Church of the 4th century. Furthermore, its recitation at the Sunday and Holy Day eucharistic celebrations shares with the Creed's statements the liturgy's ability to impress itself on the devotional consciousness of the people, and therefore to be accepted by them as a part of the *lex orandi*, the faith of the Church at worship. As a liturgical symbol, therefore, the Creed is theologically significant, quite apart from its acceptance by the ecumenical councils and its formal adoption by the Church as a necessary standard of belief.

A section of the Prayer Book entitled Historical Documents of the Church (BCP: 864-78) contains a number of historically significant statements of secondary theology.[1] The Definition of the Union of the Divine and Human Nature in the Person of Christ of the 5th-century Council of Chalcedon is an ecumenical dogmatic definition: our Lord Jesus Christ is "at once complete in Godhead and complete in manhood" (BCP: 864). *Quicunque Vult,* or The Creed of Saint Athanasius, a Western statement of Trinitarian and Christological belief, is a part of Morning Prayer in the English Prayer Book and is one of "The Three Creeds" of Article VIII of the Articles of Religion. It has never been in the American Prayer Book until now, and its inclusion there testifies to its historic importance for Anglicanism and to the intention of the Episcopal Church not to depart from the doctrine of the Church of England. Objections to it in the eighteenth century centered on the technical language of its doctrine of the Trinity and the forthright damnatory language of its opening and closing lines:

> Whosoever will be saved, before all things it is necessary that he hold the Catholic Faith. Which Faith except everyone do keep whole and undefiled, without doubt he shall perish everlastingly.

> This is the Catholic Faith, which except a man believe faithfully, he cannot be saved. (BCP: 864f)

It is certainly the intention of the Episcopal Church to support "the Catholic Faith" as defined in the ecumenical creeds and expressed in the liturgy, and the *Quicunque Vult* is another expression of that faith. It would not seem permissible, however, to use the Athanasian Creed to "prove" that the Episcopal Church taught a particular doctrine, unless that doctrine was also clearly found elsewhere.

The most extensive document in this section is the Articles of Religion, printed in the form adopted by the General Convention in 1801, with notes to indicate differences from the original form adopted in England in 1571 (BCP: 867-76). The Articles have held a privileged place in Anglican doctrinal history since the 16th century. Clergy of the Church of England are required to "subscribe" to the Articles by the canons of 1604, and the Articles have been printed, in their revised form, with the American Prayer Book since their adoption. Massey Shepherd has well described their status:

> It should be borne in mind that the Articles do not profess to be, anymore than the Creeds, a full and complete statement of the doctrine of Anglicanism, but like all such standards they deal only with those points that were in dispute at the time of formulation.[2]

This excellent statement is, of course, of more general application than simply to the Articles of Religion. All these documents of secondary theology—even the ecumenical creeds—are products of a particular time and place and reflect that history. Nicea and Constantinople were concerned with Trinitarian doctrine, against the Arian heresy, and the Nicene Creed devotes the majority of its attention to that question. Chalcedon was concerned with Christology in the face of the Nestorian and Monophysite controversies, and although we would not wish to deny the truths to which the Councils witnessed, we must admit that to a great extent their concerns are different from ours. It is the use of the Nicene and Apostles' Creed in the liturgy that keeps the creeds before us as ecumenical doctrinal standards. The

Thirty-Nine Articles, as they are usually called, are specifically directed against the errors of the medieval Latin Church, on one hand, and those of the Anabaptists on the other. Their moderation is, in a sense, typical of Anglicanism. Shepherd goes on to say of them:

> They are Protestant to the extent that they do not claim any doctrines as necessary to salvation except those which may be proved and established by the Holy Scriptures, but they are also Catholic in the sense that they do not reject the developed traditions of the undivided Church of the early centuries that are in accord with the mind of Scripture.[3]

Seeking to establish a *via media* between Roman Catholicism and sectarian Protestantism is not only the typical stance of the Thirty-Nine Articles but of the Episcopal Church itself. Dr. Shepherd, whose comments we have cited, was a distinguished member of the Standing Liturgical Commission of the Episcopal Church throughout the revision process which produced the 1979 Prayer Book. The moderation he expresses here is enshrined in the Prayer Book as a whole. I am not suggesting that Dr. Shepherd is responsible for this, although his personal influence on the revision was considerable, but that he is a true spokesman for the tradition of the Anglican Church in this regard. What he said about the Articles as they appeared in the 1928 Prayer Book is even more relevant as we consider them in the *Book of Common Prayer* 1979:

> It is important to remember that the doctrine of the Anglican communion is enshrined in the Prayer Book as a whole. The Articles should be interpreted in the light of the teaching of the entire Prayer Book. They are not a norm by which the rest of the Prayer Book must of necessity be judged and explained.[4]

The Chicago-Lambeth Quadrilateral is even less of a definitive doctrinal statement than the Thirty-Nine Articles are. Rather, it is a platform for ecumenical action, and one we have already had occasion to quote in Chapter Eight. It was originally adopted by the bishops of the American Episcopal Church in 1886 and restated by the bishops of the entire Anglican Communion two years later. It has formed the basis of every ecumenical action of the Anglican Churches ever since. For our purposes, the most relevant sections of the Quadrilateral are the following:

We . . . do hereby solemnly declare. . . :

Our earnest desire that the Savior's prayer, "That we all may be one," may, in its deepest and truest sense, be speedily fulfilled;

That we believe that all who have been baptized with water, in the name of the Father, and of the Son, and of the Holy Ghost, are members of the Holy Catholic Church;

That in all things of human ordering or human choice, relating to modes of worship and discipline, or to traditional customs, this Church is ready in the spirit of love and humility to forgo all preferences of her own. . . .

But furthermore, we do hereby affirm that Christian unity . . . can be restored only by the return of all communions to the principles of unity exemplified by the undivided Catholic Church during the first ages of its existence; which principles we believe to be the substantial deposit of Christian Faith and Order committed by Christ and his Apostles to the Church unto the end of the world, and therefore incapable of compromise or surrender by those who have been ordained to be its stewards and trustees for the common and equal benefit of all. . . . (BCP: 876f)

The four points which give the name Quadrilateral to the document follow in the text and are inherent parts of that faith which the bishops see as the foundation of Christian unity.

Anglican ecumenical theology has become more sophisticated since 1886, but it has not changed its basic stance. It is firmly grounded on the four points of the Quadrilateral, and it was in that context that the Episcopal Church took part in the founding of the Faith and Order Movement. The original wording of the four points at Chicago was:

> 1. The Holy Scriptures of the Old and New Testaments as the revealed word of God.
> 2. The Nicene Creed as the sufficient statement of the Christian Faith.
> 3. The two Sacraments—Baptism and the Supper of the Lord—ministered with unfailing use of Christ's words of institution and of the elements ordained by Him.
> 4. The Historic Episcopate, locally adapted in the methods of its administration to the varying needs of the nations and peoples called of God into the unity of His Church. (BCP: 877)

The Quadrilateral has been continuously reaffirmed by the Episcopal Church and the other Churches of the Anglican Communion as they engage in ecumenical discussion. It is by no means intended to be a complete doctrinal statement, but it does deal with the points most at issue in contemporary ecumenical discussion. The Faith and Order commission of the World Council of Churches is seeking to bring separated Christians together today on the basis of agreements on baptism, eucharist, ministry, and the contemporary profession of the apostolic faith. Certainly the statements of the Quadrilateral are derived from the faith and practice expressed in the Prayer Book as a whole.

An Outline of the Faith

A second body of theological material in the Prayer Book is An Outline of the Faith, commonly called the Catechism (BCP: 844-62). This is described as "an outline for instruction" and "a commentary on the creeds" as well as "a brief summary of the Church's teaching for an inquiring stranger who picks up a Prayer Book." It "is not meant to be a complete statement of belief and practice" (BCP: 844).

The catechism is set in a question-and-answer format and deals with doctrine under a number of systematic headings: Human Nature, God the Father, The Old Covenant, The Ten Commandments, Sin and Redemption, God the Son, The New Covenant, The Creeds, The Holy Spirit, The Holy Scriptures, The Church, The Ministry, Prayer and Worship, The Sacraments, Holy Baptism, The Holy Eucharist, Other Sacramental Rites, and The Christian Hope. Since the catechism is propositional secondary theology, it is not our intention to examine the catechism as such but to use its headings —systematic headings officially accepted by the Episcopal Church in its adoption of the catechism as a part of the Prayer Book—to summarize the theology we have found in the liturgy.

Human Nature

The principal claim of Christian anthropology is that God created human nature in God's own image, and that human nature is something which God shared in the Incarnation. This claim is succinctly made by the collect for the Second Sunday after Christmas, which is also used after the first lesson at the Great Vigil of Easter (the story of creation):

O God, who wonderfully created, and yet more wonderfully restored, the dignity of human nature: Grant that we may share the divine life of him who humbled himself to share our humanity, your Son Jesus Christ our Lord. (BCP: 288)

The primary liturgical source for theological anthropology, however, is found in the thanksgiving for creation in the Great Thanksgiving of the eucharist. The Prayer Book refers to it specifically in Eucharistic Prayers C and D. Eucharistic Prayer C says:

From the primal elements you brought forth the human race, and blessed us with memory, reason, and skill. You made us the rulers of creation. But we turned against you, and betrayed your trust; and we turned against one another. (BCP: 370)

The comparable passage in Eucharistic Prayer D says:

You formed us in your own image, giving the whole world into our care, so that, in obedience to you, our Creator, we might rule and serve all your creatures. (BCP: 373)

Creation of the human race in the image of God involves endowing it with memory, reason, and skill, and giving to it the rule of the created world. But humanity abused this gift and rebelled: "our disobedience took us far from [God]," and we fell into the "power of death" (BCP: 373). This doctrine of the creation and fall is, of course, "contained in" the first three chapters of the Book of Genesis, and it is expounded in the questions and answers of the first section of the catechism (BCP: 845). It is the beginning of the human story, and that story is liturgically expounded in the recital of salvation history in the Great Thanksgiving of the eucharist. It is surprising that there is no celebration of creation in the cycle of the liturgical year. However, since the mystery of creation—as the one collect we quoted from the Great Vigil of Easter indicates—

leads so directly to the mystery of redemption and rec-
reation in Christ—the main theme of the entire liturgical year—creation becomes a sort of sub-theme in all
the great festivals of redemption. This is reflected in
the catechism itself, which concludes its first section by
asking, "How did God first help us?" (BCP: 845).

Interestingly and importantly, this question, too, is
answered in the Great Thanksgiving: "In your mercy
you came to our help, so that in seeking you we might
find you. Again and again you called us into covenant
with you, and through the prophets you taught us to
hope for salvation" (BCP: 373). Eucharistic Prayer C
(BCP: 370) answers the catechism question with almost
the same words as does Eucharistic Prayer D. And
Eucharistic Prayer B also answers the question when it
speaks of God's "goodness and love . . . in the calling
of Israel to be [God's] people" and "in [God's] Word
spoken through the prophets" (BCP: 368). The liturgical year celebrates the preaching of the prophets as a
theme of the Advent season, both directly in the reading of the prophetic material in the liturgy, and in the
collect for the Second Sunday of Advent. The latter
calls God's messengers, the prophets, and their preaching of repentance a preparation for the salvation given
us in Jesus Christ (BCP: 211). The progression of ideas
is the same as that in the eucharistic prayers.

The dignity of humanity, the gifts which constitute
the *imago Dei* in the human race, and the rebellion of
human sin—sufficiently important truths in themselves
—are the principal statements about human nature that
the liturgy proclaims. But the liturgy proclaims them in
the context of the even more wonderful truths of God's
action in the face of human sin to redeem humanity,
both through the covenant with Israel and the ministry
of the prophets, but chiefly and climactically in Jesus
Christ.

God the Father

The fatherhood of God is so frequently proclaimed in the liturgy that it would be both endless and unnecessary to document it. The witness of the opening words of the Lord's Prayer, "Our Father," should suffice. Again, it is the thanksgiving for creation in the Great Thanksgiving which proclaims the *meaning* of this divine fatherhood: God alone is "God, living and true, dwelling in light inaccessible from before time and for ever." Yet God is also addressed in these words: "fountain of life and source of all goodness, you made all things and fill them with your blessing; you created them to rejoice in the splendor of your radiance." Finally, the prayer also states that "your [God's] mighty works reveal your wisdom and love" (BCP: 373). The more modern phrases of Eucharistic Prayer C concerning galaxies, suns, and planets (BCP: 370) are saying the same thing. Creation itself is a reflection of the goodness and love of God. Creation and redemption both are grounded in the love of God.

"Creator" and "Father" are not synonyms, however. Only in the context of our union with God the Son and of Jesus' command and example can we properly speak of God as Father. It is both by creating and by saving us that God is revealed as our Father. Eucharistic Prayer B gives thanks for God's goodness and love revealed in creation, in the calling of Israel, in the preaching of the prophets, "and above all in the Word made flesh, Jesus, your Son" (BCP: 368). To reduce God the Father to God the Creator is to leave out a part of the proclamation.

It is important to say at the same time that the use of the title "Father" or of any other human term to describe God is metaphorical, or at least analogical. We dare not avoid personal terms and substitute abstractions lest the personhood of God seem to be denied and

God appear to be an impersonal force. To say that God is personal, having memory, reason, and skill as well as love and knowledge is unquestionably a part of what we mean by saying that we are made in God's image. Since we do not properly attribute to God other human characteristics, such as having a body, we need to beware of seeming to attribute sexual characteristics to the Godhead. Our available personal pronouns in the English language fail as badly as do our nouns. We call God "he" in the liturgy, because to say "it" would deny that God was personal or even living. Jesus was a man, but God, as God, has no sex, any more than God has height, color, weight, or race. To say that there is a problem in speaking of God in human language is to say nothing new; but contemporary English has created a new problem for theologians by its loss of grammatical gender as distinguished from sexual specification. Therefore, we need to be always on guard against any use of language, particularly in the prayers of the liturgy, which can appear to suggest that God is, if not an old man with a long beard, at least a male person. We have no terms to describe God as a *person* without sex, but all human language used of God is always analogical. As has been often said, we cannot speak of God by speaking of human beings in a loud voice. For some people, these caveats are sufficient to permit them to use traditional language about God without embarrassment. Others are still concerned to search for a more accurate way to speak of God in nonsexist terms, but that search has not yet produced universally acceptable results.

The Old Covenant
and The Ten Commandments

The liturgy's most obvious witness to the Old Covenant is its use of Old Testament readings both in the office and in the eucharist, and its significant references to the

New Covenant. The Lectionary's inclusion of the Old Testament, in which the covenant with Israel is found (BCP: 847), witnesses to its importance for the Church. It is also a significant part of the salvation history recounted in Eucharistic Prayer D—"Again and again you called us into covenant with you. . . " (BCP: 373) —and, by implication, in the other eucharistic prayers.

The Prayer Book clearly sets forth the decalogue as a standard for self-examination (BCP: 317), particularly in preparation for communion; and for the same purpose, the Ten Commandments may also form a part of the Penitential Order at the beginning of the eucharist (BCP: 317f, 350). The entire subject of sin and repentance is, however, broader than the acceptance of the decalogue. Thus, the Prayer Book makes it clear that proclaiming the ethical implications *of the Gospel* is a duty of preachers. The Lectionary includes ethical passages not only from the Old Testament but from the teachings of Jesus, which demand exposition in the sermon. The summary of the Law is included in Rite One of the eucharist (BCP: 324) and in the Penitential Order of both rites (BCP: 319, 351). In all of these ways, the standards of moral behavior and the ethical demands of the Gospel are brought before the people of God.

Sin and Redemption

The various rites of penitence and reconciliation—in the eucharist, the Ash Wednesday liturgy, and the Reconciliation of Penitents—all bring the Christian worshiper face to face with the fact of human sin and the need for repentance. The "redemption of the world by our Lord Jesus Christ" (BCP: 58) is such a pervasive idea in the liturgy that it is difficult to find a place where it is not manifested. It is central to the thanksgiving in all the eucharistic prayers. Eucharistic Prayer A may be taken as typical:

> . . . when we had fallen into sin and become subject to evil and death, you, in your mercy, sent Jesus Christ, your only and eternal Son, to share our human nature, to live and die as one of us, to reconcile us to you, the God and Father of all.

> He stretched out his arms upon the cross, and offered himself, in obedience to your will, a perfect sacrifice for the whole world. (BCP: 362)

The section of Chapter Six entitled "Thanksgiving for Redemption" expounded at length the central place and significance of the atonement in Christian faith and practice. The redeeming work of Christ, as we said there, is not confined to his death, but includes the entire Christ event from the annunciation through the sending of the Holy Spirit. This truth stands at the center of faith and worship and is explicitly declared in the sacraments, the prayers of the daily offices, the liturgical year, and in all we do when we come together. Thanksgiving for redemption as God's response to human sin is a primary motive for Christian worship. The Paschal Mystery is the mystery of redemption.

God the Son

The liturgy does not make dogmatic statements about the nature of the second person of the Trinity. We do, however, find such statements in the Chalcedonian definition (BCP: 864), and in the Nicene Creed.

> We believe in one Lord, Jesus Christ, the only Son of God, eternally begotten of the Father, God from God, Light from Light, true God from true God, begotten, not made, of one Being [*homoousios*] with the Father. Through him all things were made. For us and for our salvation he came down from heaven: by the power of the Holy Spirit he became incarnate from the Virgin Mary, and was made man. For our sake he was crucified under Pontius Pilate; he suffered death and was buried.

On the third day he rose again in accordance with the Scriptures; he ascended into heaven and is seated at the right hand of the Father. He will come again in glory to judge the living and the dead, and his kingdom will have no end. (BCP: 358-59)

Although not integral to the liturgy, the Nicene Creed is a part of the Sunday and Holy Day liturgy and therefore has some liturgical status apart from its formal dogmatic acceptance. Nevertheless, it is in the text of its prayers, and particularly in the eucharistic prayers, that the liturgy most characteristically proclaims its theology.

Eucharistic Prayer D parallels much of the language of the creeds in prayer form. The Son is sent "in the fullness of time" to be our Savior. He is "incarnate by the Holy Spirit, born of the Virgin Mary," and lives "as one of us, yet without sin." He proclaimed the Gospel, and "to fulfill [God's] purpose he gave himself up to death; and rising from the grave, destroyed death, and made the whole creation new" (BCP: 374). After proclaiming God's sending the Son, Eucharistic Prayer A adds the phrase "to share our human nature" (BCP: 362).

The meaning of God's sending the Son for our redemption is discussed in detail in Chapter Six in the section "Thanksgiving for Redemption." That section also points out the contributions of the proper prefaces of the season to Christology and soteriology. The proper preface for Trinity Sunday can also be cited as stating the relationship among the divine persons of the Trinity:

For with your co-eternal Son and Holy Spirit, you are one God, one Lord, in Trinity of Persons and in Unity of Being: and we celebrate the one and equal glory of you, O Father, and of the Son, and of the Holy Spirit. (BCP: 380)

The Son is co-equal, co-eternal, and one in being with
the Father and the Holy Spirit. This is the faith proclaimed in the recitation of the *Gloria Patri* and the
Gloria in excelsis. The traditional liturgical pattern of
addressing prayer to the Father, through the Son, and
in communion of the Holy Spirit, found in the eucharistic prayers and in most collects, was used by the Arians
in the fourth century as evidence that their Christology
was that of the Church's liturgy.[5] The effect of this was
the introduction of prayer addressed directly to Christ
in the liturgy. Such prayers are not common today, but
they are significant: Form V of the Prayers of the People is addressed to "you, Lord Christ" (BCP: 390); after
its opening Trinitarian petitions, the Great Litany continues, "Remember   not,   Lord   Christ,   our
offenses. . . " (BCP: 148); and the Prayer Book also
contains collects addressed to God the Son, such as
"Lord Jesus Christ, you said to your apostles. . . "
(BCP: 395).

The second section of the *Te Deum*, beginning "You,
Christ, are the king of glory," is another major liturgical proclamation of the Christology of the liturgy.
Christ is called the eternal Son who "became man to set
us free" and in so doing "did not shun the Virgin's
womb." He "overcame the sting of death and opened
the kingdom of heaven to all believers." Now he is
seated at the right hand of the Father's glory and "will
come and be our judge," since he has bought us "with
the price of [his] own blood" (BCP: 96).

This section of the *Te Deum*, the Creed, and the preface of the Incarnation (BCP: 378) are the clearest references in the liturgy to the Virgin Birth. The
Incarnation preface says, ". . . by the mighty power of
the Holy Spirit, [he] was made perfect Man of the flesh
of the Virgin Mary his mother." The central mystery is
that of the Incarnation itself: Christ became a perfect
human being "so that we might be delivered from the

bondage of sin, and receive power to become [God's] children." However, there clearly is a reference here to the Virgin Birth, or more properly the virginal conception of Jesus, as recounted in Luke 1:26-38 and Matthew 1:18-25. This is not argued but is set forth as a part of the scriptural record on the Incarnation of the Son of God, for which thanks is given. No other doctrines are made to depend on the virginal conception, but it is clearly asserted as a part of the Church's affirmation concerning God the Son.

Finally, the celebration of the seasons of the liturgical year, with their lessons and collects, provides an even larger screen on which to display the mighty acts of God in Christ. This is the material from which theologians construct their secondary Christologies as they follow St. Anselm's quest for understanding the faith they profess. But this is not only data for theology; it is itself theology. It is the Church's own liturgical Christology to which we say "Amen" at the conclusion of the Great Thanksgiving and the other prayers. It is the traditional faith of the catholic Church, which *Quicunque Vult* warns us to keep whole and undefiled lest we "perish everlastingly" (BCP: 864).

The New Covenant

"The New Covenant" is defined by the catechism as "the new relationship with God given by Jesus Christ, the Messiah, to the apostles; and, through them, to all who believe in him" (BCP: 850). It is this New Covenant which Christ proclaimed in his blood at the Last Supper and to which reference is made in the Words of Institution over the cup, and into which we are baptized. The Baptismal Covenant (BCP: 304f) binds us to Christ in his saving death and resurrection, which inaugurated the New Covenant. The use of the Apostles' Creed as the central element of the Baptismal Covenant binds us to Christian faith, and the questions that follow it commit us to Christian life and action. Baptism is our initiation into the New Covenant, and the eucharist is our covenant meal. The New Covenant is a covenant "of reconciliation," which God established in the Paschal Mystery (BCP: 223). Our entry into this covenant is the central experience of the new life in Christ.

The catechism says, "What Christians believe about Christ is found in the Scriptures and summed up in the creeds" (BCP: 851). It is in the liturgy that the Scriptures are read and preached and the creeds recited. To live as a Christian is to live the baptismal life as it is expressed and experienced *in the liturgy*. It is in the liturgical context that the implications of the Gospel for contemporary life should be drawn out, through preaching and pastoral ministry. If the liturgy does not provide answers to contemporary questions, such as nuclear disarmament, world hunger, or abortion, it does provide the context in which these issues can be considered, and it proclaims the theological principles we must learn to apply to them.

The Creeds
and the Holy Scriptures

Enough has probably been said already concerning the creeds and the Scriptures, both in the previous section and throughout this chapter. The Apostles' Creed is an integral part of the celebration of baptism and is said in the daily offices as a renewal of the baptismal faith. The renewal of baptism vows, both at confirmation and at the Great Vigil of Easter, centers in the affirmation of the Apostles' Creed. The Nicene Creed, as we have said, is used at the Sunday eucharist. At the ordination of a bishop, it is led by the new bishop and introduced by the Presiding Bishop with the words "We therefore call upon you [the Bishop-elect], chosen to be a guardian of the Church's faith, to lead us in confessing that faith" (BCP: 519). The faith expressed in the Nicene Creed is the faith the bishop is to guard and the congregation to confess as "the Church's faith." The Athanasian Creed, or *Quicunque Vult,* is described in the catechism as "an ancient document proclaiming the nature of the Incarnation and of God as Trinity" (BCP: 852). We discussed this creed earlier in this chapter when we looked at the Historical Documents of the Church, and we referred to it again in this chapter's section on God the Son.

The Church expresses its belief about the Bible primarily by using it. Liturgical readings are taken from the Old and New Testaments and the Apocrypha and are a part of all public services. The Bible is the subject of a Sunday collect:

> Blessed Lord, who caused all holy Scriptures to be written for our learning: Grant us so to hear them, read, mark, learn, and inwardly digest them, that we may embrace and ever hold fast the blessed hope of everlasting life, which you have given us in our Savior Jesus Christ; who lives and reigns with you and the Holy Spirit, one God, for ever and ever. (BCP: 236)

In the ordination rites the ordinand declares, "I do believe the Holy Sciptures of the Old and New Testaments to be the Word of God, and to contain all things necessary to salvation" (BCP: 513, 526, 538).

The catechism explains that we call the Holy Scriptures the Word of God "because God inspired their human authors and because God still speaks to us through the Bible" (BCP: 853). The liturgy does not explain how or why the Scriptures are the Word of God, but it describes them as such at the conclusion of every scriptural reading at office or eucharist. The Scriptures are proclaimed. We listen and learn from them the Good News of Jesus Christ and "all things necessary to salvation." The bishop, at ordination, is charged to interpret the Gospel (BCP: 517). The Church itself, acting by the Holy Spirit, is the interpreter of the Scriptures (BCP: 853f). Scriptural interpretation is a primary function of the liturgical sermon, which immediately follows the liturgical readings.

The collect for St. Jerome in *Lesser Feasts and Fasts* contains the petition:

> . . . we pray that your Holy Spirit will overshadow us as we read the written Word, and that Christ, the living Word, will transform us according to your righteous will. (LFF: 333)

This is probably as close as the liturgy comes to explaining biblical inspiration. Fundamentalism is not taught in the liturgy. The function of the Church as the interpreter of Scripture is set forth, both in words in the ordination rites and in liturgical action in the way the Bible is used and preached in the Sunday liturgies. The statements of the catechism go further than the *lex orandi*, but they are consonant with it and form the basis for the Episcopal Church's position outlined there. God did not dictate the Bible, but inspired its human authors without overruling their human limitations. The Bible is not self-explanatory; it is interpreted by the Church.

The Holy Spirit

Eucharistic Prayer D includes the sending of the Holy Spirit in its thanksgiving for redemption:

> And, that we might live no longer for ourselves, but for him who died and rose for us, he sent the Holy Spirit, his own first gift for those who believe, to complete his work in the world, and to bring to fulfillment the sanctification of all. (BCP: 374)

This is the fullest liturgical expression of the work of the Holy Spirit as "Sanctifier of the faithful"

(BCP: 148). All of the Trinitarian references cited in the section on God the Son apply also to God the Holy Spirit, but there is particular mention of the work of the Holy Spirit throughout the liturgy.

The *epiclesis* of the Holy Spirit is a part of the Great Thanksgiving of the eucharist. The Spirit sanctifies us to be the people of God, and the bread and wine to be the Body and Blood of Christ. The power of the Holy Spirit sanctifies the water of baptism (BCP: 307); the baptizands are "sealed by the Holy Spirit" (BCP: 308); and confirmands are strengthened "with [the] Holy Spirit" (BCP: 309). Absolution is given to penitent sinners "through [the priest's] ministry by the grace of the Holy Spirit" (BCP: 448); the sick who are anointed receive "the inward anointing of the Holy Spirit" (BCP: 456). The new bride and groom "by the power of [God's] Holy Spirit" (BCP: 430), receive God's nuptial blessing. And the Holy Spirit is invoked in a hymn and given to the ordinands in the consecration prayer for bishops, priests, and deacons (BCP: 520f, 533, 544f). The Holy Spirit is active in *all* the Church's sacramental rites and is invoked in all its liturgical actions, as in all else the Church does.

The Incarnation preface witnesses to the role of the Spirit in the Incarnation: "[Christ], by the mighty power of the Holy Spirit, was made perfect Man of the flesh of the Virgin Mary his mother" (BCP: 378). The Feast of Pentecost celebrates both the sending of the Holy Spirit and the Spirit's work. Its collects speak of the Holy Spirit as opening the way of eternal life to every race and nation through the preaching of the Gospel, and giving to the Church "right judgment in all things" and "holy comfort" (BCP: 227). The collect for the Baptism of our Lord says that God anointed Jesus with the Holy Spirit (BCP: 214). Other collects speak of the Holy Spirit as gathering the Church together in unity (BCP: 232), directing and ruling the hearts and minds of Christians (BCP: 233), enlightening and strengthening us for God's service (BCP: 251), and abiding with us forever (BCP: 255). The Church is the sphere of the activity of the Holy Spirit, and the liturgy is filled with the action and power of the Spirit.

The Church

The doctrine of the Church is set forth throughout the Prayer Book. It is the Church's book, and the Church that uses it is reflected on every page, from "Concerning the Service of the Church," through the lectionary for the daily office. Thus, through its liturgy the Church is most clearly manifest.

The Church we find in the Prayer Book is first and foremost a worshiping community. The Church is most itself when it worships. That worship is grounded in the Paschal Mystery of the death and resurrection of Jesus Christ and our participation in it. The Church is therefore the baptismal community that calls men and women to Christ and incorporates—literally plunges—them into that mystery. The eucharistic community celebrates that mystery week by week as the people of God gather to hear the Word and to celebrate the *anamnesis* of the mystery in the eucharistic banquet, the meal of God's kingdom in which we eat the bread of life and drink the cup of salvation. The Church is the reconciling community in which men and women are reconciled to God and one another in the Paschal Mystery.

The Church is also a structured community in which different people fill different ministries. Lay persons, bishops, priests, and deacons all play their roles. The picture the Prayer Book paints is one of the assembled Church presided over by its bishop, surrounded by a group of presbyters, or priests, who are associated with the bishop in his ministry, and assisted by deacons and lay persons (BCP: 354), all acting in harmony to offer prayer and praise to God. The Church is a community that sees its vocation as showing forth the love of Christ for the world by the love it manifests among its members and also toward those who do not belong to it; but it is also a Church that knows it fails to live up to its own image because of the power of sin in the lives of its members and in society.

The Church is a sacramental sign of the presence and ministry of Jesus Christ in the world. It is the sphere of operation of the Holy Spirit who continues that work. The Church is holy because of the indwelling of the Holy Spirit, but it is also composed of fallible and ignorant human beings. As Church, we continually fail to manifest ourselves to be what Christ has declared us to be: the members of his Body, the royal and priestly people of God, one with the saints in glory, partakers of the resurrection—the One, Holy, Catholic and Apostolic Church. Just as the bread which is the sacramental sign of the Body of Christ can, because it is real bread, become stale or moldy or soggy, so, too, can we (the Church) who are the sacramental sign of the Body of Christ, because we are fallen human beings, become sinful and stupid and cause the whole Church to appear sinful and stupid. But like bread, we are only the human sign of Christ's Body. The Body of Christ is both head and members, and Christ is the head. Christ himself remains undiminished by the failure of the sign.[6]

The Prayer Book does not claim that the Church, either the Episcopal Church or the Catholic Church as a whole, is infallible, although it is led and guided into all truth by the Holy Spirit. Rather, the Prayer Book prays with Archbishop William Laud: "Where [the Church] is corrupt, purify it; where it is in error, direct it; where in anything it is amiss, reform it," as well as "where it is right, strengthen it; where it is in want, provide for it; where it is divided, reunite it" (BCP: 816). The Church's mission is to continue the work of Christ by the power of the Holy Spirit so that all the world may be united to God in Christ.

The Ministry

As Church, our primary ministry is to live out the baptismal life. Our life in the Body of Christ, bearing witness to him, and using the diverse gifts God has given us to "carry on Christ's work of reconciliation in the world" (BCP: 855), is the primary ministry of the Church. The rubrics of the eucharist and of the other services show specific ways in which lay people can exercise their baptismal priesthood in the context of worship.

The theology of the ordained ministry, which is found principally in the ordination rites, has been discussed in Chapter Eight. Some of its implications for ecclesiology have been discussed in the immediately preceding section of this chapter. The most important thing the ordination rites tell us is that ordained ministry is set firmly *within* with Church, in service to the Church, not separated from it or set over against it so that ordained ministers are to function apart from the body of the faithful as "freelance shamans." It is only within the Body of Christ that ordained Christian ministry has any meaning.

Prayer and Worship

The *Book of Common Prayer*, as its name implies, is a book of corporate worship, but it also includes some prayers for individual use. Daily Devotions for Individuals and Families (BCP: 136-140) are informal private devotions based on the structure of the daily offices. They are widely used by both clergy and lay people. The daily offices are themselves often used as private prayer by individual Christians who wish in this way to participate in the ongoing prayer of the Church. The Prayer Book also provides Prayers for Use by a Sick Person at the end of the Ministration to the Sick (BCP: 461).

In a much wider sense, the Prayer Book is the Church's tutor in prayer. Those whose liturgical and devotional life has been formed by the *Book of Common Prayer* will use its services and prayers as a pattern for their personal prayers. Many of the collects, the entire section called Prayers and Thanksgivings (BCP: 809-41), the psalms and canticles, and many of the prayers contained in the various services are regularly used in private prayer, both directly from the book and in adapted form to meet the needs of a particular situation.

The Lord's Prayer, which is a part of all public services, is also the heart of private prayer and the model for Christian prayer. It begins with praise and adoration: "Our Father, who art in heaven, hallowed be thy Name." It continues with petition and oblation: "Thy kingdom come, thy will be done, on earth as it is in heaven." We submit our own wills to the divine will so that God may bring in God's endless reign. "Give us this day our daily bread" is petition; it asks God to fulfill our most important needs. "Forgive us our sins [or trespasses] as we forgive those who sin against us" is penitence. "Lead us not into temptation, but deliver us from evil" returns to petition, and the prayer ends with praise and adoration in the doxology. The plural form of the prayer makes its petitions also intercession for the entire human family, and the entire prayer may be seen as a prayer of thanksgiving.

The Prayers of the People in the eucharist and the intercessions at the close of Morning and Evening Prayer also provide a balanced program of prayer for the congregation, who are encouraged to use them as models for their own devotions.

Private and corporate prayer are not different things but different aspects of one thing. Liturgical prayer provides the context for private prayer, and private prayer deepens and strengthens liturgical prayer. Traditional Anglican spirituality has been liturgically centered. Other forms of personal spirituality, whether the classic meditation or retreat, the cursillo, or the prayer meeting, have been seen as optional devotions. As we grow in our knowledge and love of God, we may or may not choose to avail ourselves of these optional prayer forms. But the prayer of the liturgy is essential; it is the core of all prayer.

The Sacraments

The Gospel sacraments of baptism and eucharist, and the other sacramental rites of confirmation, ordination, matrimony, reconciliation of a penitent, and unction are all included in the *Book of Common Prayer,* and we have discussed the theology of each in succession. There seems little purpose in repeating here what we have already said in detail. It is significant, however, to look at the sacramental principle at work in Christian life.

We have said that *anthropos,* the "man" who is created both male and female, is created in the image of God. We express our interiority through the external medium of our bodies. We cannot, in fact, communicate with one another except through our senses. External actions are the necessary means of expressing interior realities.[7] When God wished to be revealed to the human race, God took flesh and was embodied in Jesus. God used external bodily means, outward and visible signs, to reveal and convey God's inward and spiritual gifts and graces. We find this pattern of revelation not only in the sacraments but also in the Incarnation, in the Church, and in all that has been created in

God's image. The Paschal Mystery reveals God work-ing in just such a "sacramental" way, overcoming death and sin by dying and rising in the person of Jesus. The sacraments of the Church connect us to that saving "sacramental" act. Baptism, eucharist, and, in a differ-ent sense, reconciliation unite us most directly to that mystery. They link us to the very core of the Gospel of salvation and make possible our participation in it. The other rites are also related to the Paschal Mystery—not only the sacraments, but the daily offices and the liturgi-cal year: all are different ways of celebrating and pro-claiming that Mystery.

We have seen how this is true of the individual rites. We also need to recognize that this is a consistent pat-tern of God's action, which, as the catechism reminds us, is not limited to the sacraments, which are the princi-pal means through which God is made known to us and we are united to God. The *Book of Common Prayer* dis-plays precisely this pattern of sacramental religion. It is the traditional pattern of the Catholic Church of the ages, preserved and adapted to the use of men and women of the present day.

The Christian life is the resurrection life. It begins in baptism and is nourished through the eucharist. Confir-mation, matrimony, thanksgiving for the birth of a child, Christian vocation, whether to ordination or min-istry as a lay person, ministration in sickness, rites for the dying, and burial in sure and certain hope of the resurrection—all these mark the earthly progression of the Christian/resurrection life. Reconciliation stands as spiritual medicine for those wounded on the journey. The Christian year is marked by the celebration of redemption in the cycle of feasts and fasts. The Chris-tian week is crowned by the Lord's Day and the assem-bly for the eucharist, and is supported by daily prayer in common and in private. Such is the liturgical pattern of prayer, worship and life which the Prayer Book sets out.

It is more than a pattern of worship, for it sets standards for living in the light of that worship, for being the Body of Christ in the world. Therefore, the Prayer Book makes ethical demands on the community and on the individual so that the life of the Church may manifest the love of Christ for the world. It is the task of Christian ethicists and moral theologians to work out the implications of those demands. It is the task of the Christian prophet to proclaim them to the community which often does not wish to hear them. Both tasks flow directly from the sacramental life.

Such was our starting point in Chapter One. We have returned full cycle.

The Christian Hope

Eschatology is traditionally the final subject of a systematic presentation of theology. The Christian hope is union with God in Christ in the risen and unending life into which we are initiated in the waters of baptism, and which does not end with death. Baptism, the burial rites, and the season of Advent provide rich sources for the Christian theology of death and resurrection; so, too, do the Easter Vigil and the collects of the Easter season.

The theology of resurrection and its central place in Christian life and hope have been sufficiently discussed, but little has been said about the second Advent and final judgment.

The congregational acclamations in Eucharistic Prayers A and B both speak of the second coming of Christ (BCP: 363, 368), and the *anamnesis* of both Eucharistic Prayers II and D looks forward to Christ's coming again in glory (BCP: 342, 374). The Advent preface proclaims his coming again "in power and great triumph to judge the world" (BCP: 378). The collects for three of the Sundays in Advent mention the second

Advent, as does the first Christmas collect (BCP: 211f). The burial rite addresses Christ as "worthy and eternal Judge" (BCP: 492). The scriptural reference is to Matthew 25:31-46, the Gospel for the Last Sunday after Pentecost in Year A. The burial liturgy emphasizes the mercy and love of the Judge, salvation, not damnation, and participation in the resurrection, not eternal death. In fact, the rite makes no actual statement that anyone is damned or suffers eternal death, although prayers such as "Deliver us not into the bitterness of eternal death" (BCP: 492) seem to argue strongly that the possibility of damnation truly exists.

Still, the hope of Christians is not born of fear. It is not a hope for deliverance *from* damnation, but a hope *for* union with Christ in the risen life, in the communion or fellowship of saints. Although the communion of saints was discussed extensively in Chapter Two in the section concerning the Festivals of Saints, it is relevant here because the liturgy tells us that we are not united to Christ in an isolated way, but as members of a communion and fellowship which is not separated by death, and of which the Church Militant here on earth is a part. We are one with each other in the risen Christ, from whom nothing can separate us (BCP: 507).

The Theology of the Liturgy

We began by looking at the *Book of Common Prayer* 1979 and reflecting on its liturgy as an expression of the theology of the Episcopal Church as a province of the Anglican Communion within the Catholic Church. Our goal was not to bring theology to the Prayer Book but to let the *lex orandi* speak for itself and to reflect on what was in the worship, both in its words and its actions. The Church is a living tradition, and we come to its liturgy from within that tradition. The Church is the interpreter of its liturgy, as it is of its Scripture, and we

cannot interpret the liturgy correctly except from
within that tradition. That is why I have used the liturgy of the Episcopal Church, within which I am a priest
of the Catholic Church, as the source for my theology. I
believe that the *Book of Common Prayer* 1979 expresses
that theology in a way that men and women today can
believe, live, and teach to their children.

Systematic theologians may find this work too unsys-
tematic. I myself would have been more comfortable
summing up my conclusions under traditional systematic headings: theology, Christology, pneumatology,
anthropology, ecclesiology, sacramental, ascetic, pastoral, and moral theology. But these categories would
have had to be imposed on the material from without.
The topics of the catechism are at least printed with the
liturgy and can be used quasi-liturgically. But this volume is not a work of systematic theology. It is a reflection on *theologia prima*, and it will leave many
ambiguities. The ambiguities exist, not because the liturgy and its theology are confused—although a good
case can be made that its theology of confirmation is
confused at present and has been for centuries—but
because the theology of the liturgy is not really a system
and therefore can be systematized in different ways by
different schools of academic theologians without being
betrayed.

I have tried to show where the liturgy speaks clearly
and where it leaves room for different interpretations.
Origen, in a wonderful passage in the *Peri Archon*, said
that the apostles delivered some doctrines "in plainest
terms to all believers," while "the grounds of their
statements they left to be investigated by such as should
merit the higher gifts of the Spirit."[8] Although Origen
and most modern theologians would probably differ
over what those doctrines were, I believe that in the
liturgy we can see the sort of distinction Origen was

talking about. The liturgy says some things, the necessary things, plainly, but it leaves to those with "the higher gifts of the Spirit"—that is, the secondary theologians—the task of working the "ground" of the liturgy's statements into a coherent system of how God acts among us. The liturgy, I believe, does this so that the work of reflection can begin. That work is highly important, not only for the theologians themselves but for all those of philosophical temperament who need to understand, or at least try to understand, everything. However, that work is not necessary for the ordinary Christian, even for those of us whom Origen described as "somewhat dull in the investigation of divine knowledge." What is necessary, however, for ordinary Christians and for those with "higher gifts" alike, is participation in the liturgy. For in the liturgy we have the words and the means to address God and to be united with God. And union with God, not deeper understanding, is the only thing essential for new life in Christ.

Endnotes

Introduction:
The Religion of the Prayerbook

1. Two of my former colleagues in the Graduate Program in Liturgical Studies at the University of Notre Dame have had a considerable influence on my thinking on this subject: Robert J. Taft, S.J., whose "Liturgy as Theology," *Worship* 56 (1982): 113-17, summarizes views which I have heard him express formally and informally on many occasions; and Aidan Kavanagh, O.S.B., whose 1982 Hale Lectures at Seabury-Western (published as *On Liturgical Theology*, New York: Pueblo, 1984) gave form and structure to the idea he has so often voiced. Kavanagh's discussion of *lex orandi-lex credendi* in his response to Geoffrey Wainwright in "Response: Primary Theology and Liturgical Act," *Worship* 57 (1983): 321-24, includes this insight:

> The old maxim means what it says. One thing it does *not*, however, say or mean is that the *lex credendi* exerts no influence upon the *lex supplicandi*: only that it does not constitute or found the *lex supplicandi*. That is all. But it is a precious, because fundamental, insight, at least in my own estimation, and its implications for both primary and secondary theology are indispensable.

2. Kavanagh's statement of this point in "Primary Theology and Liturgical Act" (see note 1 above) is this:

> I think that the liturgical act . . . is in fact the primary and foundational theological act from

305

which all subsequent theological activity arises. The liturgical assembly is a theological corporation.

Taft in "Liturgy as Theology" (see note 1 above) makes the following related contribution:

> To think that a homily of John Chrysostom or John Calvin, or a book by Karl Rahner or Karl Barth, is worthy of the theologian's attention, and fail to understand how the ways and the prayers with which the same gentlemen along with some other millions have worshipped God is worthy of the same, is the prejudice of those so locked into a narrow concept of expression as to think that only words communicate anything theological. Christian faith is not a set of verbal propositions.

3. *The Book of Common Prayer and Administration of the Sacraments and Other Rites and Ceremonies of the Church Together with The Psalter or Psalms of David According to the Use of the Episcopal Church* (New York: Church Hymnal Corporation and The Seabury Press, 1979), pp. 864f. Hereafter, all references to this work will appear in the text as BCP without the specification of a date, but followed by the appropriate page number(s).

4. Geoffrey Wainwright, "A Language in Which We Speak to God," *Worship* 47 (1983): 309-21.

5. Leonel L. Mitchell, "Response: Liturgy and Theology," *Worship* 57 (1983): 325.

Chapter One:
The Service of the Church

1. Massey H. Shepherd, *The Worship of the Church*, The Church's Teaching Series 4 (Greenwich, Conn.: The Seabury Press, 1952), p. 4.

2. *A Parish Program for Liturgy and Mission* (Madison, Wis.: Associated Parishes, 1964), p. 1.

3. *Constitution on the Sacred Liturgy*, Austin P. Flannery, ed., *Documents of Vatican II* (Grand Rapids, Mich.: Eerdmans, 1975), p. 1.

4. This is the purpose of the Pan-Anglican Document, "The Structure and Contents of the Eucharistic Liturgy," prepared by a committee consisting of the Most Rev. Leslie W. Brown of Uganda, the Most Rev. H. H. Clark, Archbishop of Rupert's Land, the Rt. Rev. C. K. Sandsbury, Bishop of Singapore and Malaya, and the Rev. Massey H. Shepherd, Professor of Liturgics at Church Divinity School of the Pacific, pursuant to a resolution of the 1958 Lambeth Conference, and published for the first time in *Prayer Book Studies XVII: The Liturgy of the Lord's Supper* (New York: Church Pension Fund, 1966), pp. 58f, and again with corrections and commentary in Colin O. Buchanan, *Modern Anglican Liturgies, 1958-1968* (London: Oxford University Press, 1968), pp. 22-32. A Second Pan Anglican Document, "The Structure and Contents of the Holy Eucharist and the Daily Office," (Colin O. Buchanan, *Further Anglican Liturgies, 1968-1975* (Bramcote Notts: Grove Books: 1975), pp. 26-31), was prepared by Bishop Brown and Dr. Ronald Jasper of the Liturgical Commission of the Church of England at the request of a Liturgical Consultation after the 1968 Lambeth Conference. This document was a revision and expansion of the earlier one.

Chapter Two:
The Calendar, Times and Seasons

1. Louis Bouyer, *Liturgical Piety* (Notre Dame: University of Notre Dame Press, 1955), p. 185.
2. Ibid., p. 186.
3. Massey H. Shepherd, *Liturgy and Education* (New York: The Seabury Press, 1965), p. 99.
4. Josef Pieper, *In Tune with the World* (Chicago: Franciscan Herald Press, 1973), p. 19.
5. Justin Martyr, *I Apology 67*, in *Early Christian Fathers*, ed. Cyril C. Richardson (Phildelphia: Westminster, 1953), pp. 287f.
6. Significant studies of the history and theology of Sunday observance include: H. Boone Porter, *The Day of Light*

(Greenwich: The Seabury Press, 1960); Willy Rordorf, *Sunday* (Philadelphia: Westminster Press, 1968); A. Allan MacArthur, *The Evolution of the Christian Year* (London: SCM Press, 1953), pp. 1-31; Adolph Adam, *The Liturgical Year* (New York: Pueblo, 1981), pp. 35-56; and the collections of papers from two French conferences: one in Lyon in 1947 sponsored by Le Centre du Pastorale Liturgique, *Le Jour du Seigneur* (Paris: Robert Laffont, 1948) [in French]; and one in Paris, the 9th Week of Liturgical Studies sponsored by St. Sergius Institute, *Le Demanche*, Lex Orandi 39 (Paris: Editions du Cerf, 1965).

7. Yves Congar, "The Theology of Sunday," *Le Jour du Seigneur* (Paris: Robert Laffont, 1948), p. 153. (My translation.)

8. See Adolph Adam, *The Liturgical Year* (New York: Pueblo, 1981), pp. 30-1, 57-9; Thomas J. Talley, "History and Eschatology in the Primitive Pascha," *Worship* 47 (1973): 212-21. The opposing position is taken, almost single-handedly, by C. W. Dugmore, "Lord's Day and Easter," *Neotestamentica et Patristica in honorem . . . Oscar Cullmann* (Leiden: Brill, 1962), pp. 272-81.

9. *The Proper for the Lesser Feasts and Fasts together with The Fixed Holy Days*, 3rd edition (New York: Church Hymnal Corporation, 1980). Hereafter, this work will be referred to in the text as LFF, followed by the appropriate page numbers.

10. The primary source material is in John Wilkinson, *Egeria's Travels* (London: SPCK, 1971), pp., 132-9. A good discussion is found in J. G. Davies, *Holy Week: A Short History*, Ecumenical Studies in Worship II (Richmond: Westminster Press, 1963), pp. 9-38.

11. Massey H. Shepherd, *Liturgy and Education* (New York: The Seabury Press, 1965), p. 100.

12. Ibid., p. 99.

Chapter Three:
The Daily Office

1. The classic study of the origins of the Office is Juan Mateos, S.J., "The Origins of the Divine Office," *Worship* 41 (1967): 447-85. Other significant treatments are in Cheslyn Jones, et al., *The Study of Liturgy*, Chapter 5, "The Divine Office," (New York: Oxford University Press, 1978), pp. 350-492 by Geoffrey Cuming, W. Jardine Grisbrooke, J. D. Crichton, and David Tripp; Paul F. Bradshaw, *Daily Prayer in the Early Church* (New York: Oxford University Press, 1982); and Balthasar Fischer, "The Common Prayer of Congregation and Family in the Ancient Church," *Studia Liturgica*, 10 (1974): 106-24. See also Marion J. Hatchett, *Commentary on the American Prayer Book* (New York: The Seabury Press, 1980), pp. 89-97.

2. Robert Taft, S.J., "Thanksgiving for the Light: Toward a Theology of Vespers," *Diakonia* 13 (1978): 43-4.

3. This significant distinction is well explained by William G. Storey, "The Liturgy of the Hours: Cathedral Versus Monastery," in *Christians at Prayer*, edited by John Gallen, S.J. (Notre Dame: Univeristy of Notre Dame Press, 1977), pp. 61-82; and by W. J. Grisbrooke, "The Formative Period—Cathedral and Monastic Offices," included in Chapter 5 of *The Study of Liturgy* (cited in note 1 above).

4. Storey, "Liturgy of the Hours," p. 66.

5. It is undeniably true that in the 16th century "thou" was the second person singular, and "you" the plural form. Like the French "tu" and the German "du," "thou" was increasingly being considered an intimate form, not suitable for addressing kings and others who made use of the plural of majesty, calling themselves "we" and being addressed by others as "you." Therefore, it may be significant that Archbishop Cranmer and his colleagues in the production of the first (1549) and second (1552) Prayer Books chose to call God "Thou." This is, however, precisely the reverse of the argument usually heard today in favor of so addressing God, namely: that a special term used only for addressing God is dignified and proper. Jesus addressed God as "Abba," a child's name for his

father, and commanded us to do the same (Luke 11:2). Piety, tradition, and deep emotion may weigh heavily in our choice of address for God, but it is hard to find a theological argument for excluding either "You" or "Thou."

6. *The Taizé Office* (London: Faith Press, 1966), p. 9.
7. Canticles 1-7 are the Rite One versions of those above-mentioned canticles which appeared in the 1928 Prayer Book. Their content does not differ from that of the Rite Two canticles discussed in the text. No traditional language versions of canticles new to the 1979 Prayer Book are included.
8. *Constitution on the Sacred Liturgy*, Austin P. Flannery, ed., *Documents of Vatican II* (Grand Rapids, Mich.: Eerdmans, 1975), p. 25.
9. Taft, p. 46. (See note 2 above.)
10. *Taizé*, p. 11. (See note 6 above.)
11. *The Hymnal 1982* (New York: Church Hymnal, 1985), Hymns 60 and 41.
12. Inter-Lutheran Commission on Worship, *Lutheran Book of Worship* (Minneapolis: Augsburg, 1978), p. 435.

Chapter Four:
The Great Vigil of Easter

1. Dom Odo Casel, *The Mystery of Christian Worship and Other Writings*, ed. Burkhard Neunheuser, tr. I. T. Hale (Westminster, Md.: Newman Press, 1962), p. 52.
2. There are significant discussions of Casel's work (see note 1 above) in Joseph Jungmann, *Early Liturgy* (Notre Dame: University of Notre Dame Press, 1959), pp. 152-63; in Louis Bouyer, *Liturgical Piety* (Notre Dame: University of Notre Dame Press, 1955), pp. 86-98 and *Rite and Man* (Notre Dame: University of Notre Dame Press, 1963), pp. 123-50; in Ernest B. Koenker, *The Liturgical Renaissance in the Roman Catholic Church*, 2nd edition (St. Louis: Concordia Publishing, 1966), pp. 104-24; as well as in Charles Davis, "Odo Casel and the Theology of Mysteries," *Worship* 34 (1960): 428-38; in Leo M. McMahon, "Toward a

Theology of the Liturgy: Dom Odo Casel and the 'Mysterientheorie,'" *Studia Liturgica* 3 (1964): 129-54; and in Burkhard Neunheuser, "Odo Casel in Retrospect and Prospect," *Worship* 50 (1976): 489-503. Casel's influence on the Constitution on the Sacred Liturgy is expounded by Bouyer in *The Liturgy Revived* (Notre Dame: University of Notre Dame Press, 1964), pp. 11-47. Most recently Casel's views have been discussed, not uncritically, in David N. Power, *Unsearchable Riches: The Symbolic Nature of the Liturgy* (New York: Pueblo Publishing, 1983), pp. 114-24.

3. The version of *Lauda, Sion* in *The Hymnal 1982*, like that in *The Hymnal 1940* is highly abridged and tightly edited to avoid expressing the Thomistic doctrine, but cf.
   Dogma datur Christianis:
   Quod in carnem transit panis,
   Et vinum in sanguinem.
   Quod non capis, quod non vides,
   Animosa firmat fides,
   Praeter rerum ordinem.

   Sub diversis speciebus
   Signis tantum et non rebus,
   Latent res eximiae.
   Caro cibus, sanguis potus:
   Manet tamen Christus totus,
   Sub utraque specie.

   A sumente non concisus,
   Non confractus, non divisus:
   Integer accipitur.
   Sumit unus, sumunt mille:
   Quantum isti, tantum ille:
   Nec sumptus consumitur.

   Sumunt boni, sumunt mali:
   Sorte tamen inaequali,
   Vitae, vel interitus,
   Mors est malis, vita bonis:
   Vide partis sumptionis
   Quam sit dispar exitus.

Fracto demum Sacramento,
Ne vacilles, sed memento,
Tantum esse sub fragmento,
Quantum toto tegitur.
Nulla rei fit scissura:
Signi tantum fit fractura:
Quae nec status, nec statura
Signati minuitur. (*Missale Romanum*)

4. See Mircea Eliade, *Patterns in Comparative Religion* (New York: Sheed and Ward, 1958), p. 398. Such symbols are, in Eliade's phrase, multivalent, and the addition of new meanings to them by Christians does not destroy their pre-Christian significance. See also Leonel L. Mitchell, *The Meaning of Ritual* (New York: Paulist Press, 1977), pp. 15-7.

5. This point is driven home quite tellingly by Maurice Wiles in a chapter entitled "Lex Orandi" in *The Making of Christian Doctrine* (Cambridge: Cambridge University Press, 1967), pp. 62-93, especially in this passage from page 62:

   It is not always easy to remember that theologians say their prayers and take part in the worship of the Church. . . . Yet many of [the early Fathers] were bishops, not merely participants but leaders in the liturgical life of the Church. And the fiercer the controversy in which they were involved, the more important it is to recall the influence of the Church's worship upon their doctrinal beliefs. For it is often there that the key to understanding the fervour and the bitterness of the controversy lies. Men do not normally feel so deeply over matters of formal doctrinal statement unless those matters are felt to bear upon the practice of their piety. The close interrelation of doctrine and worship is an important element in explaining the desperate seriousness with which issues of doctrine were regarded in the early centuries.

6. The identification of the saving waters of baptism with the saving of Noah and his family in the ark is already found in 1 Peter 3:21-22 and has a prominent place in many baptismal liturgies. It was the central theme of a

prayer written by Martin Luther for his baptismal liturgy (*Taufbüchlein* 1523) and adapted by Cranmer for the *Book of Common Prayer*; F. E. Brightman, *The English Rite* (London: Rivingtons, 1921:II), pp. 726-28. The Drafting Committee, of which I was a member, included a reference to it in the Thanksgiving over the Water for the present Prayer Book, but it was removed by the Standing Liturgical Commission before the text was printed.

7. An interesting commentary on the Exodus story in its Christian and liturgical context is Gabriel Hebert, *When Israel Came out of Egypt* (London: SCM Press, 1961). The late Fr. Hebert, S.S.M., was one of the early leaders of the Liturgical Movement in the Church of England and a founder of the Parish Communion movement, as well as an Old Testament scholar concerned with biblical typology.

8. Peter J. Jagger, *Clouded Witness: Initiation in the Church of England in the Mid-Victorian Period, 1850-1875* (Pittsburgh Theological Monographs, New Series, Allison Park, Pennsylvania: Pickwick Publications, 1982), pp. 8-55, provides an extensive account of this controversy, establishing, among other things, that the phrase "baptismal regeneration" did not mean the same thing to all the participants.

9. *The Book of Occasional Services* (New York: Church Hymnal Corporation, 1979). Hereafter, this work will be referred to in the text as BOS, followed by the appropriate page numbers.

10. The oldest Latin sacramentaries are traditionally called Gelasian and Gregorian. The first collect is found in both. Dating either the sacramentaries or the material in them is difficult. The Gelasian Sacramentary is believed to go back to the 6th century, and the Gregorian to be of about the same age. How much older than the oldest manuscripts a given collect is cannot be definitively shown, although attempts can be made based on such things as cursus and linguistic analysis.

11. Aulen expressed his ideas in the 1930 Olaus Petri lectures, "The Christian Idea of the Atonement," an abridged version of which was published in England in

1931 under the title *Christus Victor,* New edition with a
Foreword by Jaroslav Pelikan (New York: Macmillan Publishing Co., 1969), translated from the Swedish by Fr. A.
Gabriel Hebert, S.S.M., the leader of the English Liturgical Movement mentioned in note 7 above. In the preface
to the new edition Aulen describes his work this way:
> The central idea of *Christus Victor* is the view of God
> and the Kingdom of God as fighting against evil
> powers ravaging mankind. In this drama Christ has
> the key role, and the title *Christus Victor* says the
> decisive word about his role. (p. ix)

12. Marion J. Hatchett, *Commentary on the American Prayer
Book* (New York: The Seabury Press, 1980), p. 179.
13. The problems in understanding the temporal references
in the Greek text, while of concern to New Testament
scholars, do not affect the liturgical use of the pericope.
No theological conclusions are drawn from the hour. It
simply sets the scene at a time roughly parallel to that in
which it is being read.

Chapter Five:
Christian Initiation

1. Mircea Eliade, *Rites and Symbols of Initiation* (New York:
Harper and Row, 1965), p. x.
2. The relationship of Christian initiation to other rites of
initiation is discussed in Leonel L. Mitchell, *The Meaning
of Ritual* (Wilton, Ct.: Morehouse Publishing, 1987), 8-17,
48-57, 83-94.
3. Many of these same ideas were presented earlier with a
slightly different approach in Leonel L. Mitchell, "The
Theology of Christian Initiation and *The Proposed Book of
Common Prayer*," *Anglican Theological Review* 60 (1978):
399-419.
4. The section of *The Book of Occasional Services* dealing with
Christian initiation was drafted by a sub-committee of the
Standing Liturgical Commission of which I served as
chair. The other members were the Rt. Rev. William A.
Dimmick (whose illness prevented him from attending

the meetings), the Rev. Michael Merriman, Capt. Howard E. Galley, C.A., and Dr. Ralph Keifer (an ecumenical member).

5. The earliest text of the baptismal liturgy is in *The Apostolic Tradition of Hippolytus.* The baptism itself is in section 21. (Bernard Botte, ed., *La tradition apostolique de Saint Hippolyte,* Liturgiewissenschaftliche Quellen und Forsungen 39, (Münster: Aschendorff, 1963); English trans. G. J. Cuming, *Hippolytus: a Text for Students,* Grove Liturgical Study 8 (Bramcote Notts: Grove Books, 1976). This tradition of administering baptism is found as late as the Gelasian Sacramentary. (L. C. Molhberg, ed. *Liber Sacramentorum Romanae Ecclesiae Anni Circuli ((Sacramentarium Gelasianum)),* Rerum Ecclesiasticarum Documenta, Series Maior 4 (Rome: Herder, 1960), p. 449; English trans. E. C. Whitaker, *Documents of the Baptismal Liturgy,* 2nd edition (London: SPCK, 1970), p. 188. The classic work on the history of the creed is J. N. D. Kelly, *Early Christian Creeds,* 3rd edition (New York: David McKay Co., 1972). Chapter II, "Creeds and Baptism," discusses the intimate relationship between the origin of the creed and the baptismal interrogations. The baptismal questions are apparently older than the declarative form of the creed which Kelly describes as "a by-product of the Church's fully developed catechetical system. . . . The catechetical instruction of which the declaratory creeds were convenient summaries was instruction looking forward to baptism. . . . So closely did the catechetical instruction dovetail into the ceremony of initiation which was to be its climax that the single word baptism, in an extended sense, could be used to cover them both taken together" (Kelly, *Early Creeds,* p. 51).

6. The classic mystagogical catecheses have been collected by Edward Yarnold, S.J., in *The Awe-Inspiring Rites of Initiation: Baptismal Homilies of the Fourth Century* (Slough, England: St. Paul Publication, 1971). They provide detailed instruction in the meaning of the rites of baptism and eucharist and are significant primary sources for both liturgists and sacramental theologians. The most extensive surviving homilies are by St. Ambrose of Milan (*De*

Sacramentis), St. Cyril of Jerusalem, St. John Chrysostom (describing the liturgy of Antioch), and Theodore of Mopsuestia.

7. Kelly, *Early Creeds*, p. 68. (See note 5 above.)

8. I have discussed this prayer in the context of other Western blessings of the font in "The Thanksgiving over the Water in the Baptismal Rite of the Western Church," Bryan D. Spinks, ed., *The Sacrifice of Praise*, Bibliotheca "Ephemerides Liturgicae" Subsidia 19 (Rome: CLV— Editioni Liturgiche, 1981), pp. 49-87. See Hatchett, *Commentary on the American Prayer Book*, p. 275: "The 1928 Book . . . strip[ped] the rite of all references to classical biblical archetypes. The primary allusions are restored in the new prayer drafted by the Rev. Leonel L. Mitchell."

9. Following the example of Cranmer and Luther, an allusion to Noah and the flood was included in the original draft, but it was removed during the editorial process.

10. For a thorough discussion, see Leonel L. Mitchell, *Baptismal Anointing*, Alcuin Club Collections 48 (London: SPCK, 1966).

11. Marion Hatchett, *Commentary on the American Prayer Book*, p. 277, notes that at the time of the English Reformation, the baptism was the time at which the name of the child was made known, and the author comments, "Since baptisms have ceased to be the time of publication of the name, and since only rarely is a person's name changed at baptism, there seems to be little merit in perpetuating this tradition and much merit in restoring the earlier, more catholic custom of presenting the candidate by name."

12. "As the bishop pronounces the words, *N. is baptized in the name of the Father and of the Son and of the Holy Spirit,* he plunges your head into the water and lifts it up again three times." John Chrysostom, *Baptismal Homily* II: 26; Yarnold, *Awe-Inspiring Rites*, p. 168.

13. "Chrysostom says, for example, 'He does not say, "I baptize N.," but rather, "N. is baptized." This shows that he is only a minister of the grace and merely lends his hand since he has been ordained for this by the Spirit.'" (*Baptismal Homily* II: 26; Yarnold, *Awe-Inspring Rites*, p. 169). The Western active form does not appear until the 8th-

century sacramentaries, but the explanation traditionally given is that it is as the minister of Christ that the priest presumes to say, "Ego te baptizo. . . ." St. Ambrose, whose baptismal rite used the threefold creedal questions as its baptismal formula, writes, "The priest comes, he says a prayer at the font, he invokes the name of the Father, the presence of the Son and Holy Spirit; he uses heavenly words. They are the words of Christ which say that we must baptize in the name of the Father and of the Son and of the Holy Spirit," *De Sacramentis* 2:14; Yarnold, *Awe-Inspiring Rites*, p. 114. The emphasis is upon the words and the actions of Christ, who is seen as the true actor.

14. *The Book of Common Prayer . . . according to the Use of the Protestant Episcopal Church in the United States of America* (New York: The Church Hymnal Corporation, 1928), p. 297. Hereafter, all references to this work will appear in the text as BCP 1928 with the appropriate page numbers.

15. L. C. Mohlberg, ed., *Sacramentarium Gelasianum*, Rerum Ecclesiasticarum Documenta 4 (Rome: Herder, 1963), p. 451; Jean Deshusses, *Le Sacramentaire Grégorien*, Specilegium Friburgense 16 (Fribourg, Switzerland: Editions universitaires, 1971), p. 376. See also Ambrose, *De Sacramentis* III: 8, "The spiritual seal follows. . . . For after the ceremonies at the font, it still remains to bring the whole to perfection. This happens when the Holy Spirit is infused at the priest's invocation: 'the Spirit of wisdom and understanding, the Spirit of counsel and strength, the Spirit of knowledge and piety, the Spirit of holy fear.' These might be called the seven 'virtues' of the Spirit" (Yarnold, *Awe-Inspiring Rites*, p. 125). The testimony of Ambrose identifies this prayer for the gifts of the Spirit with the "seal" (or "sealing") which takes place immediately "after the ceremonies of the font" as in the *Book of Common Prayer*. The confusion was caused by the later separation of "confirmation" from the rite of Christian initiation.

16. Charles Price and Louis Weil, *Liturgy for Living*, The Church's Teaching Series 5 (New York: The Seabury Press, 1979), pp. 121-30.

17. My own defense of this position is contained in "The Theology of Christian Initiation and *The Proposed Book of Common Prayer, Anglican Theological Review* 55 (1978): 399-419 and in "What Is Confirmation?" *Anglican Theological Review* 55 (1973): 201-12.
18. Price and Weil, *Liturgy for Living*, p. 127.
19. Ibid., p. 129.
20. World Council of Churches, *Baptism, Eucharist and Ministry*, Faith and Order Paper 113 (Geneva: World Council of Churches, 1982), p. 20. Hereafter, this work will be referred to in the text as WCC 1982 with the appropriate page number.
21. Mitchell, "Theology of Christian Initiation," p. 400.
22. Marion J. Hatchett, "The Rite of 'Confirmation' in *The Book of Common Prayer* and *Authorized Services 1973*," *Anglican Theological Review* 56 (1974): 292-310.
23. The question is discussed by Massey H. Shepherd, *The Paschal Liturgy and the Apocalypse*, Ecumenical Studies in Worship 6 (Richmond, Va.: John Knox Press, 1960), pp. 90-1 and by me in *Baptismal Anointing*, Alcuin Club Collections 48 (London: SPCK, 1966), pp. 19-20.
24. *Holy Baptism and A Form for Confirmation . . . Authorized for Trial Use during 1975-1976* (New York: Church Hymnal Corporation, 1975) contained the rubric "Those who have been baptized may receive the Holy Communion" (p. 18). It was not in *The Draft Proposed Book of Common Prayer* (New York: Church Hymnal Corporation, 1976) presented to the General Convention of 1976 and subsequently adopted, with revisions as *The Proposed Book of Common Prayer* (1976) and finally as *The Book of Common Prayer* (1979).
25. J. D. C. Fisher, *Christian Initiation: Baptism in the Medieval West*, Alcuin Club Collections 47 (London: SPCK, 1965), pp. 101-8, 124f. This work is the classic study of the disintegration of the Western rite of Christian initiation in the middle ages.
26. The General Convention resolved on October 21, 1970, that children might be admitted to communion before confirmation, subject to the direction and guidance of the ordinary (*Services for Trial Use*, New York: Church

Hymnal Corporation, 1971, p. 21), and the House of Bishops in the "Pocono Statement" of November 1971 stated, "Confirmation should not be regarded as a procedure of admission to the Holy Communion." (See Hatchett, *Commentary on the American Prayer Book*, p. 271.) See also the "Statement of Agreed Positions" stemming from the joint meeting of the Standing Liturgical Commission with the Theological and Prayer Book Committees of the House of Bishops in Dallas in December 1972: "The rite embodying such affirmations should in no sense by understood . . . as being a condition precedent to admission to the Holy Communion." See *Holy Baptism together with A Form for Confirmation or the Laying-on of Hands by the Bishop with the Affirmation of Baptismal Vows, Prayer Book Studies 26* (New York: Church Hymnal Corporation, 1973), p. 4. Hereafter, reference to this work will appear in the text as PBS 26 with the appropriate page number.

27. The heart of the confusion about Christian initiation in the 1979 Prayer Book turns on precisely this question of the meaning of confirmation. Some theologians, such as Dom Gregory Dix and J. D. C. Fisher have identified confirmation with the post-baptismal consignation. Fisher wrote, for example, "Renewal of vows—*pace* some of our Evangelicals—is not the essence of Confirmation; if it is, then Confirmation was invented by Luther. . . . The essence of Confirmation is the imparting of the Holy Spirit." (See M. Perry, ed., *Crisis for Confirmation*, London: SCM Press, 1967, p. 90.) Dix expressed his views in *"Confirmation, or the Laying on of Hands?"* (London: SCM Press, 1936) and in *The Theology of Confirmation in Relation to Baptism* (Westminster: Dacre, 1946). On the other hand, Lampe writes definitively: "There should be no thought of the gift or seal of the Spirit as a grace of Confirmation" (Lampe, *Seal of the Spirit*, p. 318).

There would, of course, be a certain logic in calling the post-baptismal consignation "confirmation" and using some different term, such as "affirmation," for this rite. This was, in fact, the approach taken by *Prayer Book Studies 18, Holy Baptism with the Laying-on-of-Hands* (New York: Church Pension Fund, 1970) and subsequently rejected.

See Mitchell, "What Is Confirmation?" and "The Theology of Christian Initiation and *The Proposed Book of Common Prayer*," and Hatchett, "The Rite of Confirmation in the Book of Common Prayer." For some theologians the quarrel is purely verbal. What is at issue is neither the substance of the rites nor their pastoral desirability, but whether the consignation or this rite should properly be called confirmation. Urban T. Holmes, *Confirmation: The Celebration of Christian Maturity* (New York: The Seabury Press, 1975) defends the position taken by the Prayer Book; Holmes was a member of the Christian Initiation Drafting Committee. See also Leonel L. Mitchell, "Christian Initiation, Rites of Passage, and Confirmation," Kendig Burbaker Cully, ed., *Confirmation Reexamined* (Wilton, Conn.: Morehouse-Barlow, 1982), pp. 81-92.

28. This rubric, added by the General Convention of 1976 to the text proposed to them in *The Draft Proposed Book of Common Prayer*, suggests that the observation of Peter Hinchcliff is relevant:

> In the field of initiation-rites the experts are attempting to reduce the confusion by producing forms which express a coherent understanding of the meaning of Baptism and Confirmation. . . . The committee is able to produce a rite which is neat, consistent and capable of being explained logically. The committee, however, seldom has the power to authorize the use of the rite. Modifications are introduced by those who have the authority but not the expertise: the pattern is destroyed once more. (Jones, Cheslyn, et al., eds., *The Study of the Liturgy*, New York: Oxford University Press, 1978, p. 137.)

> From the point of view of theological consistency, Hinchcliff is accurately describing the situation in the American Episcopal Church. Liturgies, however, are not composed by committees of experts or by bishops; they grow organically out of the life of the Church. The difficulty with the constitutional process of liturgical revision both in the Episcopal

Church and in most other churches is that it artificially prevents the natural evolution of the *lex orandi*. Revisions are proposed by experts on the basis of their understanding of Church tradition, or by pastors on the basis of what they perceive to be the needs or desires of their people, and changes which would occur naturally in the course of centuries are authorized by authority and introduced as soon as the books can be printed. This is probably inevitable in the modern world, but it does produce some anomalies.

29. See Godfrey Diekmann, "The Laying on of Hands: The Basic Sacramental Rite" (*Catholic Theological Society of America Proceedings*, 1974: 339-51), and the response by Edward J. Kilmartin, S.J. (357-66).

30. Holmes, *Confirmation*, p. 66. (See note 27 above.)

31. Price and Weil, *Liturgy for Living*, p. 128.

32. Ibid., p. 129f.

33. A new and interesting hypothesis about the origin and meaning of confirmation is found in Aidan Kavanagh, "Confirmation: A Suggestion from Structure," *Worship* 58 (1984): 386-95. Kavanagh suggests that confirmation is the bishop's *missa*, or formal dismissal of the neophytes from the baptistry to the eucharistic assembly of the faithful, comparable to other dismissals in the liturgy, such as that of catechumens before the prayers of the faithful. The implication of this is that the rite loses its meaning when it does not serve as a bridge between baptism and the immediately following eucharist.

Chapter Six:
The Holy Eucharist

1. Gregory Dix, *The Shape of the Liturgy* (Westminster: Dacre Press, 1945), pp. 743f.

2. The *First Apology* of Justin Martyr, written in Rome about the year 150, contains this description:

On the day called Sun-day an assembly is held in one place of all who live in town or country, and the records of the apostles or writings of the prophets are read for as long as time allows. Then, when the reader has finished, the president in a discourse admonishes [us] to imitate these good things.

Then we all stand up together and offer prayers; and . . . , when we have finished praying, bread and wine and water are brought up, and the president likewise offers prayers and thanksgivings to the best of his ability, and the people assent, saying the Amen; and there is a distribution, and everyone participates in [the elements] over which thanks have been given; and they are sent through the deacons to those who are not present. (*First Apology* 67: 3-5, trans. R. C. D. Jasper & G. J. Cuming, *Prayers of the Eucharist: Early and Reformed,* London: Collins, 1975, pp. 19f.)

3. *The Oxford Dictionary of the Christian Church* defines "collect" as "The short form of prayer, constructed (with many varieties of detail) from (1) an invocation, (2) a petition, and (3) a pleading of Christ's name or an ascription of glory to God."

4. The term *collecta* derives from the Gallican rites. The Roman rite, although making extensive use of the collect structure for the composition of compact, pithy prayers of great beauty and profundity, calls the prayer which precedes the lessons at the Eucharist simply *oratio.* The solemn collects in the Good Friday liturgy (BCP: 277-80) provide an almost perfect example of the most traditional use of collects. Prayer is bidden for a particular purpose. Silence is kept while the people pray. Then the celebrant "collects" their prayers in a collect. The prayers are a trialogue among the deacon who bids the prayers, the people who do the praying, and the priest (or bishop) who says the collect.

5. The Lambeth Conference of 1978 recommended "a common lectionary for the Eucharist and the Offices as a unifying factor within our communion and ecumenically" and drew attention to "the experience of those Provinces which have adopted the three year Eucharistic lectionary

of the Roman Catholic Church." *Report of the Lambeth Conference 1978* (London: CIO Publishing, 1978), Resolution #24. The major exception to Anglican use of this Lectionary is the Church of England, which has adopted a two-year Lectionary developed by the Joint Liturgical Group and also used by the Reformed Church of Great Britain. In North America, versions of the Lectionary are used (at least optionally) by Anglicans in the United States and Canada, Disciples of Christ, Lutherans, Methodists, Presbyterians, Roman Catholics, and members of the United Church of Christ and the United Church in Canada. A version has also been published by the Consultation on Church Union, which has made it generally available to a variety of Protestant churches.

Much supporting material has been published ecumenically. The most accessible discussion of the rationale of the Lectionary is in William Skudlarek, *The Word in Worship: Preaching in a Liturgical Context,* Abingdon Preachers Library (Nashville: Abingdon, 1981), pp. 31-44. A proposed revision of this Lectionary has been prepared by the ecumenical North American Consultation on Common Texts and is published under the title *Common Lectionary: The Lectionary Proposed by the Consultation on Common Texts* (New York: Church Hymnal Corporation, 1984).

6. The classic Anglican view of preaching is expressed by Richard Hooker in Book 5 of the *Ecclesiastical Polity*:

So worthy a part of divine service we should greatly wrong, if we did not esteem Preaching as the blessed ordinance of God, sermons as keys to the kingdom of heaven, as wings to the soul, as spurs to the good affection of man, unto the sound and healthy as food, as physic unto diseased minds. Richard Hooker, *Of the Laws of Ecclesiastical Polity,* Vol. 2, Everyman's Library 202 (New York: E. P. Dutton, 1907 [reprinted 1954]).

Hooker, and the whole Anglican tradition with him, however, insists, "The external administration of his word is as well by reading barely the Scripture, as by

explaining the same when sermons thereon be made"
(5:21; 1907: 80).

7. There is some discussion of the content of the creed in
Chapter Five in connection with the use of the Apostles'
Creed in baptism. A full discussion of the theology of the
Nicene Creed and its implications for Christian faith and
life would be a multi-volume work in itself, and a task
which we shall not undertake.

8. This form appeared following the confession at Morning
Prayer in the Prayer Book of 1552 and remained as an
option in that place through the American Prayer Book
of 1928. The primary scriptural references are to Ezekiel
33:11, John 20:22-23, and Mark 1:14-15.

9. See Edward Schillebeeckx, *Ministry: Leadership in the Community of Jesus Christ* (New York: Crossroad, 1981), pp.
38-52, and Paul Bradshaw, *Liturgical Presidency in the Early
Church*, Grove Liturgical Study 36 (Bramcote Notts:
Grove Books, 1983).

10. In *Ministry*, p. 1, Schillebeeckx interprets the patristic
dictum *"Ecclesia non est quae not habet sacerdotes"* ("There
is no church which does not have priests.") to mean
"There can be no church community without a leader or
team of leaders." He does not actually advocate lay presidency of the eucharist but rather says:

> The tension between an ontological-sacerdotalist
> view of the ministry on one hand and a purely func-
> tionalist view on the other must therefore be
> resolved by a theological view of the church's minis-
> try as a charismatic office, the service of leading the
> community, and therefore as an ecclesial Function
> within the community and accepted by the commu-
> nity. (*Ministry*, p. 70)

> The ancient church and (above all since Vatican II)
> the modern church cannot envisage any Christian
> community without the celebration of the eucharist.
> There is an essential link between the local *ecclesia*
> and eucharist. Throughout the pre-Nicene church it
> was held, evidently on the basis of Jewish models,
> that a community in which at least twelve fathers of

families were assembled had the right to a priest or community leader and thus to the eucharist, at which he presided. . . . According to the views of the ancient church a shortage of priests was an ecclesiastical impossibility. (*Ministry*, p. 72)

11. This question is discussed in *Lay Presidency at the Eucharist*, Trevor Lloyd, ed., Grove Liturgical Study 9 (Bramcote Notts: Grove Books, 1977) and by William S. Adams, "The Eucharistic Assembly: Who Presides?", *Anglican Theological Review* 64 (1982): 311-21.
12. Schillebeeckx, *Ministry*, p. 138.
13. Dix, *The Shape of the Liturgy*, p. 48.
14. Ibid.
15. Ibid., p. 50.
16. There is literally no direct evidence concerning this monumental liturgical change. My suggestions about it have been published in *The Meaning of Ritual* (New York: Paulist Press, 1977), pp. 67-76.
17. Kenneth W. Stevenson, *Gregory Dix—Twenty-Five Years on*, Grove Liturgical Study 10 (Bramcote Notts: Grove Books, 1977), p. 24.
18. See *The Alternative Service Book 1980: Services authorized for use in the Church of England in conjunction with the Book of Common Prayer together with the Liturgical Psalter* (London: Oxford University Press, 1980), p. 129; hereafter referred to as ASB 1980, with the appropriate page number. See also *The Sacramentary*, from the English translation of *The Roman Missal* © 1973, International Committee on English in the Liturgy, Inc. (New York: Catholic Book Publishing Company, 1974), p. 25, #49; hereafter referred to as *Sac.*, with the appropriate page number.
19. Dix, *The Shape of the Liturgy*, p. 111.
20. Ibid., pp. 117f.
21. Price and Weil, *Liturgy for Living*, p. 198.
22. See Joachim Jeremias, *The Eucharistic Words of Jesus* (Philadelphia: Fortress Press, 1966), pp. 174f, for a different interpretation of Jesus' actions. See the discussion of Dix's position in K. W. Stevenson, *Gregory Dix—Twenty-Five Years on*, Grove Liturgical Study 10 (Bramcote Notts:

Grove Books, 1977), p. 24, and in Paul Marshall's notes to Dix's *The Shape of the Liturgy*, new edition with additional notes by Paul V. Marshall (New York: The Seabury Press, 1982), pp. 769f. Colin Buchanan, *The End of the Offertory An Anglican Study*, Grove Liturgical Study 14 (Bramcote Notts: Grove Books, 1978), pp. 28-34, is a good example of the rejection of Dix's position by English Anglican evangelicals.

23. The title *canon* is really the proper name of the Roman eucharistic prayer, although it has sometimes been used in a generic way to refer to eucharistic prayers in general, so that one might speak of the Anglican canon. *Canon* means "rule," and the distinctive thing about the *canon Romanus* was that it was invariably used, in contrast to the alternative eucharistic prayers of other rites. To some extent the idea that the canon began after the Sanctus derives from the format of medieval missals. After the various proper prefaces, the invariable *canon missae* was begun on a right-hand page, the entire left-hand page being taken up with an illuminated capital T, the first letter of "Te igitur," made into a crucifix. This was the fixed point at which the unchanging prayer always began, while the preface came to have its modern meaning of something which precedes the actual text.

24. Yarnell, *Awe-Inspiring Rites*, p. 89.

25. See R. C. D. Jasper and G. J. Cuming, *Prayers of the Eucharist: Early and Reformed* (London: Collins, 1975), p. 142.

26. The placement holds true, for example, of the so-called Clementine liturgy of Apostolic Constitutions 8 and the liturgy of St. John Chrysostom, but not of the liturgy of St. James, which gives thanks for God in his own being before the Sanctus, and begins with thanksgiving for creation after the angelic hymn, or of the liturgy of St. Basil, which gives thanks for the creation of the human race only after the Sanctus. The texts are most readily available in Jasper and Cuming, *Prayers of the Eucharist* (see note 24 above).

27. Martin Luther, *Formula Missae*, in Jasper and Cuming, *Prayers of the Eucharist*, p. 123.

28. Yarnell, *Awe-Inspiring Rites*, p. 134.

29. Two excellent complementary studies provide a good statement of the *status quaestionis*: John H. McKenna, *Eucharist and Holy Spirit: The Eucharistic Epiclesis in 20th Century Theology (1900-1966)*, Alcuin Club Collections 57 (Great Wakering, England: Mayhew-McCrimmon, 1975) and Richard F. Buxton, *Eucharist and Institution Narrative: A Study in the Roman and Anglican Traditions of the Consecration of the Eucharist from the Eighth to the Twentieth Centuries*, Alcuin Club Collections 58 (Great Wakering, England: Mayhew-McCrimmon, 1976). The classic work on the institution narrative itself is Joachim Jeremias, *The Eucharistic Words of Jesus* (Philadelphia: Fortress Press, 1966).

30. There are no extant texts of the Jewish table blessings dating to the time of Jesus. In fact, it is not certain whether the texts themselves were as yet fixed in Jesus' time. The traditional form for the blessing of bread, "Blessed are you, Lord our God, King of the universe, who bring forth bread from the earth," is found in the Mishna. Although the Mishna mentions a thanksgiving after meals (*birkat ha-mazon*, the blessing said over the cup at the conclusion of the meal), the earliest text is from the 8th century. The eminent Jewish scholar Louis Finkelstein has proposed this reconstruction of the 1st-century text:

> Blessed are you, O Lord our God, King of the universe, who feed the whole world in goodness, kindness and mercy. Blessed are you, O Lord, who feed all.
>
> We give you thanks, O Lord our God, for giving us this good land for our heritage that we may eat of its fruits and be satisfied with its goodness. Blessed are you, O Lord our God, for the land and the food.
>
> Have mercy, O Lord our God, upon Israel your people and Jerusalem your city and Zion the dwelling-place of your glory and of your altar, and of your sanctuary. Blessed are you, O Lord, who build Jerusalem. ("The Birkat Ha-Mazon," *Jewish Quarterly Review* 19 [1928-9]:211-62.)

This thanksgiving over the cup is commonly considered to be the source of the Christian eucharistic prayer, recognizing always that there is no certainty about the actual words used at the Last Supper. Dix's classic reconstruction of the acts of Jesus at the Last Supper (*The Shape of the Liturgy*, pp. 50-8) introduces the current discussion of the origins of the eucharistic prayer. Four significant studies which provide a good picture of current scholarship on the question are: Louis Ligier, S.J., "From the Last Supper to the Eucharist," in *The New Liturgy*, ed., Lancelot Shepherd (London: Darton, Longman, & Todd, 1970), pp. 113-50 and "Origins of the Eucharistic Prayer: From the Last Supper to the Eucharist," *Studia Liturgica* 9 (1973): 161-85; and Thomas J. Talley, "From *Berakah* to *Eucharistia*," *Worship* 50 (1976): 115-37 and "The Literary Structure of the Eucharistic Prayer," *Worship* 58 (1984): 404-20.

31. See Joachim Jeremias, *The Eucharistic Words of Jesus* (Philadelphia: Fortress Press, 1966), p. 56, and Dix, *The Shape of the Liturgy*, pp. 54, 58.

32. Yarnell, *Awe-Inspiring Rites*, p. 91.

33. The clearest exposition of the medieval aspect of the "moment of consecration" controversy is in Nathan Mitchell, *Cult and Controversy: The Worship of the Eucharist Outside Mass*, Studies in the Reformed Rites of the Catholic Church IV (New York: Pueblo Publishing, 1982), 151-63. McKenna and Buxton (both cited in note 29 above) discuss the question of the moment of consecration in some detail.

34. John H. McKenna, *Eucharist and Holy Spirit: The Eucharistic Epiclesis in 20th Century Theology*, Alcuin Club Collections 57 (Great Wakering, England: Mayhew-McCrimmon, 1975), p. 187.

35. Dix, *The Shape of the Liturgy*, p. 55.

36. *Passover Haggadah*, ed. Nahum N. Glatzer (New York: Schocken Books, 1969), p. 51.

37. Major works which influenced the contemporary understanding of *anamnesis* include the discussion of Jeremias in

the section of *The Eucharistic Words of Jesus* entitled
". . . That God May Remember Me," pp. 237-55, and
the two volumes of Max Thurian, *The Eucharistic Memorial,* Ecumenical Studies in Worship 7-8 (Richmond: John
Knox Press, 1960 and 1961). Geoffrey Wainwright, writing in an ecumenical context, says of *anamnesis*:

> While scholars give different nuances to their expla-
> nations, there exists a rather widespread agreement
> that a "memorial" can properly be understood as a
> human action undertaken at God's command in
> order to put the ecclesial community in touch with
> the saving action of God which is being commemo-
> rated before God. This process is neither magical
> nor mechanical: it neither compels God to do some-
> thing he would otherwise be reluctant to do nor
> involves the use of a time-machine. It rests rather
> upon the constant purpose of the eternal God who
> has revealed himself for our salvation in Jesus
> Christ, the same yesterday, today and for ever, and
> who never ceases to work by the Holy Spirit for the
> completion of his kingdom. This provides an oppor-
> tunity to settle old arguments between Catholics and
> Protestants, or among Protestants, concerning both
> "the eucharistic sacrifice" and the presence of
> Christ. It also helps in the controversies between
> East and West about the relation between the roles
> of Christ and the Holy Spirit in the eucharist. (Max
> Thurian and Geoffrey Wainwright, eds., *Baptism
> and Eucharist: Ecumenical Convergence in Celebration,*
> Geneva: World Council of Churches, 1983, p. 104.)

38. The text of the Scottish eucharistic prayer of 1764 is in
W. Jardine Grisbrooke, *Anglican Liturgies of the Seventeenth
and Eighteenth Centuries,* Alcuin Club Collections 40
(London: SPCK, 1948), p. 434. The discussion of the
ceremonial practice is in F. C. Eeles, *Traditional Ceremonial and Customs Connected with the Scottish Liturgy,* Alcuin
Club Collections 10 (London: Longmans, Green and Co.,
1910), pp. 65f.

39. Massey H. Shepherd, *The Oxford American Prayer Book Commentary* (New York: Oxford University Press, 1950), p. 81.

40. Jasper and Cuming, *Prayers of the Eucharist*, p. 35.

41. *A Collection of the Principal Liturgies, Used by the Christian Church in the Celebration of the Holy Eucharist: Particularly the Ancient, viz. the* Clementine, *as it stands in the Book call'd* The Apostolic Constitutions; *the Liturgies of* S. James, S. Mark, S. Chrysostom, S. Basil, &c. *Translated into English by several hands with a Dissertation upon Them, Showing their Usefulness and Authority, and pointing out their several Corruptions and Interpolations. By Thomas Brett, LL. D.* (London, 1720), pp. 185-86.

42. Eucharistic Prayer D was drafted in 1974 by an ecumenical group of American liturgical scholars chaired by the Rev. Dr. Marion J. Hatchett and published as "A Common Eucharistic Prayer." Its sources were the 4th-century Alexandrian *Anaphora* of St. Basil and Eucharistic Prayer IV of the *(Roman) Sacramentary.* See L. L. Mitchell, "The Alexandrian Anaphora of St. Basil of Caesarea: Ancient Source of 'A Common Eucharistic Prayer'," *Anglican Theological Review* 58 (1976): 194-206.

43. There is a fuller discussion of sacrifice in Leonel L. Mitchell, *The Meaning of Ritual*, pp. 17-21, 26-48, 64-6. I share the opinion of Louis Bouyer (*Rite and Man*, Notre Dame: Notre Dame University Press, 1963, p. 82) that the most important discussion of the meaning of sacrifice for Christianity is Royden K. Yerkes, *Sacrifice in Greek and Roman Religions and Early Judaism* (London: Adam and Charles Black, 1953), the 1951 Hale Lectures delivered in that year at Seabury-Western Theological Seminary.

44. Louis Bouyer, *Liturgical Piety* (Notre Dame: Notre Dame University Press, 1955), p. 257.

45. Dix, *The Shape of the Liturgy*, p. 48.

46. Buxton, *Eucharist and Institution Narrative* (note 29 above) discusses the problem of supplementary consecration at length.

Chapter Seven:
The Pastoral Offices

1. Kenneth W. Stevenson, *Nuptial Blessing: A Study of Christian Marriage Rites* (New York: Oxford University Press, 1983), p. 135.

2. Kenneth Stevenson, *Nuptial Blessing* (see note 1 above) is a good history of the marriage rites "from Isaac and Rebecca onwards" which includes a discussion of both the English and American revisions.

3. Hatchett, *Commentary on the American Prayer Book*, p. 434.

4. The form of vows in the York Manual was:

> I take the N. to my wedded wyf, to haue and to holde, fro this day forwarde, for bettere for wors, for richere for pourcr, [one manuscript adds 'for fayrere for fowlere'] in sycknesse and in hele, tyll dethe vs departe, if holy chyrche it wol ordeyne, and therto y plight the my trouthe.

> I take the N. to my wedded houshounde, to haue and to holde, fro this day forwarde, for bettere for wors, for richere for pourer, in sycknesse and in hele, to be bonere and buxsom, in bedde and atte bord, tyll dethe vs departe, if holy chyrche it wol ordeyne, and therto y plight the my trouthe. (Stevenson, *Nuptial Blessing*, p. 79.)

5. A provocative contemporary discussion of sin and redemption based upon Paul Ricoeur's *The Symbolism of Evil* (Boston: Beacon Press, 1967) is in David Power, *Unsearchable Riches: The Symbolic Nature of the Liturgy.* (New York: Pueblo Publishing Company, 1984), pp. 98-105.

6. The theology of this section is heavily influenced by Karl Rahner's essay, "Forgotten Truths Concerning the Sacrament of Penance," *Theological Investigations* 2 (London: Darton, Longmans, and Todd, 1963), pp. 135-74. Although I firmly believe that the theology is in the rites themselves, Rahner's work has provided the key by which I have attempted to unlock it. Other significant contemporary theological treatments are Charles E. Curran,

"The Sacrament of Penance Today," *Worship* 43 (1969):
510-31, 590-619; 44 (1970): 2-19; Peter Fink, "Investi-
gating the Sacrament of Penance," *Worship* 54 (1980):
206-20; and Bernard Häring, *Shalom: Peace: The Sacrament
of Reconciliation* (New York: Ferrar, Straus, and Giroux,
1969). Anglicans will wish to consult Clark Hyde, *To
Declare God's Forgiveness: Toward a Pastoral Theology of Reconciliation* (Wilton: Morehouse-Barlow, 1984), the only
commentary on the reconciliation rites of the Prayer
Book which I have encountered.

7. Godfrey Diekmann has suggested that the imposition of
hands was originally the sacramental sign of all seven
sacraments. See his "The Laying on of Hands: The Basic
Sacramental Rite," *Catholic Theological Society of America
Proceedings*, (1974): 339-51. See also James Dallen, "The
Imposition of Hands in Penance: A Study in Liturgical
History," *Worship* 51 (1977): 338-45. The development of
the confessional with a grill separating the penitent and
confessor brought the use of the imposition of hands in
penance to an end in the Western Church. However, it
remained a part of Eastern practice, and it is being widely
revived in the Christian West.

8. The history of the rite of reconciliation is a tangled web,
filled with discontinuities. The serious work of investigat-
ing origins was done by Karl Rahner, *Penance in the Early
Church*, Theological Investigations 15 (New York: Crossroad, 1982). The classic history is Bernhard Poschmann,
Penance and the Anointing of the Sick (New York: Herder
and Herder, 1964). John Gunstone, *The Liturgy of Penance*
(London: Faith Press, 1966) presents the history from an
Anglican point of view.

9. The classic study of the history and theology of the ministry to the sick is the final chapter of Bernhard
Poschmann, *Penance and the Anointing of the Sick* (New
York: Herder and Herder, 1964), pp. 233-57, which stops
with the council of Trent. Charles W. Gusmer, *The Ministry of Healing in the Church of England: an Ecumenical-Litur-
gical Study*, Alcuin Club Collections 56 (Great Wakering,
England: Mayhew-McCrimmon, 1974) deals with the
development of the theology and ministry of healing in

the Church of England. The essay by Charles Harris, "Visitation of the Sick, Unction, Imposition of Hands and Exorcism," in *Liturgy and Worship,* ed. W. K. Lowther Clarke (London: SPCK, 1932), pp. 472-540, is not only an excellent and illuminating study of all aspects of ministry to the sick but also itself has been a significant influence on the subsequent direction of Anglican theological thought and liturgical revision.

10. Thomas J. Talley, "Healing: Sacrament or Charism?" *Worship* 46 (1972): 525f.

11. Talley's article (see note 10 above) is an important contribution to the theological discussion of the rites for the sick and deserves to be widely read.

12. This use of oil is implied in the blessing of oil in *Apostolic Tradition,* and is specifically recognized by Innocent I in a letter to Decentius of Gubbio which said that the anointing may be used not only by priests but by all Christians. The same point is made by Cacsarius of Arles, Martin of Tours and the Venerable Bede. The evidence is discussed in Poschmann (see note 9 above).

13. The Prayer Book burial liturgy is included in an historical survey of Christian funeral rites by Geoffrey Rowell, *The Liturgy of Christian Burial: An Introductory Survey of the Historical Development of Christian Burial Rites,* Alcuin Club Collections 59 (London: SPCK, 1977). The background material in an even more recent study of the reformed Roman Catholic rite is also of interest: Richard Rutherford, C.S.C., *The Death of a Christian: The Rite of Funerals* (New York: Pueblo Publishing, 1980).

14. Hatchett, *Commentary on the American Prayer Book,* p. 491.

15. Ibid., pp. 494, 497.

16. Ibid., pp. 497f.

17. James A. Pike and Norman Pittenger, *The Faith of the Church,* The Church's Teachings Series 3 (New York: National Council, 1951), p. 143.

18. *A Parish Program for Liturgy and Mission* (Madison, Wis.: Associated Parishes, 1964), p. 3.

Chapter Eight:
Ordination Rites

1. Paul F. Bradshaw, *The Anglican Ordinal: Its History and Development from the Reformation to the Present Day*, Alcuin Club Collections 53 (London: SPCK, 1971), p. 209.

2. Ibid., p. 211. Bradshaw's study was published in 1971, before either the 1979 *Book of Common Prayer* or *Alternative Services 1980* was completed. The "American revision" to which he refers is Prayer Book Studies 20, *The Ordination of Bishops, Priests, and Deacons* (New York: Church Hymnal Corporation, 1970), which is in his bibliography. These proposals were authorized for trial use by the General Convention of 1970 and included in *Services for Trial Use* (New York: Church Hymnal Corporation, 1971). They were generally used from 1971 until they were superseded by the present revised form of the rites, which appeared in *The Draft Proposed Book of Common Prayer* (New York: Church Hymnal Corporation, 1976). The text finally adopted in 1979 does not differ substantively from the rites which Bradshaw discussed.

3. Typical of the references to the threefold ministry in Ignatius are: "Let the bishop preside in God's place, and the presbyters take the place of the apostolic council, and let the deacons (my special favorites) be entrusted with the ministry of Jesus Christ" (*Magnesians* 6:1); "There is one bishop along with the presbytery and the deacons, my fellow slaves" (*Philadelphians* 4); and "It is essential, therefore, to act in no way without the bishop. . . . Rather submit even to the presbytery as to the apostles of Jesus Christ. . . . Those too who are deacons of Jesus Christ's 'mysteries' must give complete satisfaction to everyone. For they do not minister mere food and drink, but minister to God's Church" (*Trallians* 2:2-3). The *locus classicus* is *Smyrneans* 8:

> You should all follow the bishop as Jesus Christ did the Father. Follow, too, the presbytery as you would the apostles; and respect the deacons as you would God's law. Nobody must do anything that has to do with the Church without the bishop's approval. You

should regard that Eucharist as valid which is celebrated either by the bishop or by someone he autho-
rizes. Where the bishop is present, there let the
congregation gather, just as where Jesus Christ is,
there is the Catholic Church. Without the bishop's
supervision, no baptisms or love feasts are permitted. On the other hand, whatever he approves
pleases God as well.

The threefold pattern in Ignatius is not clearly
found either in the New Testament or in the other
apostolic fathers. *I Clement* and *Didache* both have
patterns in which the titles *episcopos* and *presbyter* are
not clearly distinguished, and it is possible that they
represent local Churches, in the case of *I Clement* the
Church of Rome, which did not have the Ignatian
"one bishop" but were ruled by a board of *episcopoi*
or *presbyteroi*. *I Clement* 42 says:
The apostles received the gospel for us from the
Lord Jesus Christ: Jesus, the Christ, was sent from
God. Thus Christ is from God and the apostles from
Christ. . . . They preached in country and city,
and appointed their first converts, after testing them
by the Spirit, to be bishops and deacons of future
believers.
I Clement mentions presbyters in chapter 44, but
they appear to be the same people already referred
to as *episcopoi*. The picture is simply not as clear as it
is in Ignatius.

(All quotations are from the English translation
of Cyril C. Richardson, *Early Christian Fathers*, The
Library of the Christian Classics I, Phildelphia:
Westminster Press, 1953.)

4. *I Clement* 40:5, for example, speaks of the different liturgical functions of the high priest, priests, Levites, and lay-
men as an introduction to a discussion of Christian
ministry; and *Didache* 13 identifies resident "prophets" as
"your high priests." Such usage becomes more common
by the third century.

5. Cyprian of Carthage wrote "Episcopatus unus est cuius a
singulis in solidum pars tenetur," (*De Catholicae Ecclesiae*

Unitate 5) which S. L. Greenslade translates, "The episcopate is a single whole, in which each bishop's share gives
him a right to, and a responsibility for, the whole." (See
Early Latin Theology, Library of Christian Classics 5 (Philadelphia: Westminster Press, 1956, p. 127.) Cyprian's view
of the one episcopate binding the Church together is
widely accepted within the Episcopal Church.

6. Throughout this section we have used the masculine pro-
noun to refer to the bishop both for convenience and
because at this writing all bishops of the Anglican Communion are men. The *Book of Common Prayer*, however,
carefully italicizes all such gender-specific pronouns and
words such as *"brother"* used to refer to the bishop,
thereby making it plain that the Episcopal Church permits and envisions the possibility of the ordination of
women as bishops, as it does their ordination as priests
and deacons.

There is no theological discussion, either here or elsewhere in the Prayer Book, of the case for the ordination
of women, as earlier Prayer Books contained no defense
of their exclusion from holy orders, nor indeed any statement that they were excluded. It must be assumed that
this question belongs to the discipline rather than the
doctrine of the Church and is controlled by canonical
legislation. There are churches within the Anglican
Communion which do not ordain women to the priesthood, and the Roman Catholic and Orthodox Churches
officially state that there are theological objections to the
priestly and episcopal ordination of women, although the
mention of a deaconess in the New Testament has usually
precluded the same objection's being raised to diaconal
ordination. These official positions are by no means
unanimously endorsed by the members of the different
Churches. There are many Roman Catholics who believe
their church's refusal to ordain women to be unjust, and
there are Episcopalians who consider the Episcopal
Church's willingness to do so a break with Catholic tradition. Theological objections to the refusal to ordain
women are also raised, contending that it denies the full

humanity of women and/or the reality of their baptismal priesthood and membership in the Church.

7. There is a translation and discussion of the prayer of consecration of the bishop in *The Apostolic Tradition of Hippolytus* in H. Boone Porter, *The Ordination Prayers of the Ancient Western Churches,* Alcuin Club Collections 49 (London: SPCK, 1967), pp. 1-11. Porter served as chairman of the committee which drafted the ordination rites for the 1979 Prayer Book. A more extensive discussion of the theology of the Hippolytan prayer in an ecumenical context is Geoffrey Wainwright's "Some Theological Aspects of Ordination," *Studia Liturgica* 13 (1979): 125-52, a paper read at the 1979 Congress of Societas Liturgica in Washington, D.C., of which the general theme was Ordination Rites. It appears also in a slightly revised form as Chapter VI, "Ordained Ministry" in his *The Ecumenical Moment: Crisis and Opportunity for the Church* (Grand Rapids: Eerdmans, 1983).

8. The Orthodox theologian Alexander Schmemann, for example, writes: "Nowhere is the truly universal, truly cosmic significance of the sacrament of Matrimony, as the sacrament of love, expressed better than in its liturgical similitude with the liturgy of Ordination, the sacrament of Priesthood. It is not the mere identity of ritual symbolism. Through it is revealed the identity of the Reality to which both sacraments refer, of which both are the manifestation. . . . Both are the manifestation of Love. The Priest is indeed married to the Church. But just as human marriage is taken into the mystery of Christ and the Church, and becomes the sacrament of the Kingdom, it is this marriage of the priest with the Church that makes him really *priest,* the true minister of that Love which alone transforms the world and reveals the Church as the immaculate bride of Christ." (See Alexander Schmemann, *For the Life of the World,* New York: National Student Christian Federation, 1963, pp. 68, 70.)

9. The phrase is used in the title, "A Traditional Reflection on Diaconate in Relation to 'Omnivorous Priesthood'," *Living Worship* 12:9 (November, 1976). Among Porter's insights are:

By the end of the Middle Ages, the priesthood had, in a sense, devoured the whole sacred ministry of the church. Lesser clerks were helpers and servants to priests; deacons and subdeacons were apprentice priests; bishops were super-priests with the power to ordain more priests. At the time of the Reformation the system came under criticism. The Reformers did not call for the ministry of the laity, they called for "the priesthood of all believers," for priesthood was what it was all about. . . . It is similar in the twentieth century with the debate over the ordination of women. This has not centered around the goal of ordination to the diaconate, nor over the remote and long-range goal of ordination to the episcopate, but over ordination to the presbyterate or priesthood. For women as for men, it is the priesthood that has come to represent "real ministry."

It is today increasingly evident that this fixation on the priesthood as the sole pattern of ordained or unordained ministry is not adequate, and certainly does not express the New Testament conception of various kinds of people doing various kinds of things for the life and ministry of the Body of Christ.
See also Aidan Kavanagh, "Christian Ministry and Ministries," *Anglican Theological Review*, Supplementary Series 9 (1984): 36-78, especially:
The upshot of all this is that the Western churches in the first half of this present and most egalitarian of centuries found themselves with a highly undiversified ministerial structure focused upon a "learned" and thus ineluctably hieratic and elite group of people who were now regarded by many as "first class Christians": a church of the chosen within a far larger church of the unchosen who constituted a baptized proletariat of Christians of the second, third, or even fourth kind. The effects of this are

presently all around us. The other Christian ministries, where they survived, have been presbyteral-
ized, and the rest of the church has been
deministerialized. (p. 38)
10. Shepherd, *Oxford Prayer Book Commentary*, p. 532.
11. See Porter, *Ordination Prayers*, p. 11. (See note 7 above.)

Chapter Nine:
The Theology of the Prayerbook

1. Hatchett, *Commentary on the American Prayer Book*, pp.
583-8, provides excellent brief introductions to each of
the historical documents.
2. Shepherd, *Oxford Prayer Book Commentary*, p. 601.
3. Ibid.
4. Ibid.
5. The most comprehensive study of this is Joseph
Jungmann, *The Place of Christ in Liturgical Prayer* (Staten
Island: Alba House, 1965). Part Two of the book deals
specifically with the effects of the Arian controversy on
liturgical prayer.
6. I am indebted to Robert Capon's fertile mind for this
simile which I encountered in a magazine interview in *The
Wittenburg Door*.
7. I have expressed my own understanding of this in the
introduction to *Meaning of Ritual*, ix-xvi.
8. Origen, *Peri Archon*, in J. Stevenson, *A New Eusebius*
(London: SPCK, 1968), p. 212.

Bibliography

The Alternative Service Book 1980: Services authorized for use in the Church of England in conjunction with the Book of Common Prayer together with The Liturgical Psalter. London: Oxford University Press, 1980 (abbreviated ASB).

Associated Parishes. *A Parish Program for Liturgy and Mission.* Madison: Associated Parishes, 1964.

Aulen, Gustaf. *Christus Victor: An Historical Study of the Three Main Types of the Idea of the Atonement.* Trans. A.G. Hebert, new edition with foreword by Jaroslav Pelikan. New York: Macmillan, 1969.

Bouyer, Louis. *Liturgical Piety.* Notre Dame: University of Notre Dame Press, 1955.

_____. *Rite and Man.* Notre Dame: University of Notre Dame Press, 1963.

Bradshaw, Paul F. *The Anglican Ordinal: Its History and Development from the Reformation to the Present Day.* Alcuin Club Collections 53. London: SPCK, 1971.

Brett, Thomas. *A Collection of the Principal Liturgies, Used by the Christian Church in the Celebration of the Holy Eucharist: Particularly the Ancient, viz. the* Clementine, *as it stands in the Book call'd* The Apostolical Constitutions; *the Liturgies of* S. James, S. Mark, S. Chrysostom, S. Basil, &c. *Translated into English by several hands with a Dissertation upon Them, Showing their Usefulness and Authority, and pointing out their several Corruptions and Interpolations. By Thomas Brett, LL. D.,* London, 1720.

Buxton, Richard F. *Eucharist and Institution Narrative: A Study in the Roman and Anglican Traditions of the Consecration of the Eucharist from the Eighth to the Twentieth Centuries.* Alcuin Club Collections 58, Great Wakering, England: Mayhew-McCrimmon, 1976.

Clarke, W. K. Lother, ed. *Liturgy and Worship*. London: SPCK, 1932.

Constitution on the Sacred Liturgy. Austin Flannery, ed. *Documents of Vatican II*. Grand Rapids: Eerdmans, 1975.

Congar, Yves. "The Theology of Sunday." *Le Jour du Seigneur*. Paris: Robert Laffont, 1948.

Dix, Gregory. *The Shape of the Liturgy*. Westminster: Dacre Press, 1945. New edition with additional notes by Paul V. Marshall. New York: The Seabury Press, 1982.

Eliade, Mircea. *Rites and Symbols of Initiation*. New York: Harper and Row, 1965.

Episcopal Church. *The Book of Common Prayer and Administration of the Sacraments and Other Rites and Ceremonies of the Church Together with The Psalter or Psalms of David According to the Use of The Episcopal Church*. New York: Church Hymnal Corporation and The Seabury Press, 1979 (abbreviated BCP without the specification of a date).

_____. *The Book of Common Prayer . . . According to the Use of the Protestant Episcopal Church in the United States of America*. New York: Oxford University Press [and other publishers], 1928 (abbreviated BCP 1928).

_____. *The Book of Occasional Services*. New York: Church Hymnal Corporation, 1979 (abbreviated BOS).

_____. *The Hymnal 1982*. New York: Church Hymnal Corporation, 1985.

_____. *The Proper for the Lesser Feasts and Fasts together with the The Fixed Holy Days*, 3rd edition. New York: Church Hymnal Corporation, 1980 (abbreviated LLF).

Fisher, John D. C. *Christian Initiation: Baptism in the Medieval West*. Alcuin Club Collections 47. London: SPCK, 1965.

Hatchett, Marion J. *Commentary on the American Prayer Book*. New York: The Seabury Press, 1980.

_____. "The Rite of 'Confirmation' in *The Book of Common Prayer* and *Authorized Services 1973*." *Anglican Theological Review* 56 (1974): 292-310.

Hooker, Richard. *Of the Laws of Ecclesiastical Polity*. Volume 2. Everyman's Library 202. New York: E. P. Dutton & Co., 1907.

Hyde, Clark. *To Declare God's Forgiveness: Toward a Pastoral Theology of Reconciliation.* Wilton: Morehouse-Barlow, 1984.

Jasper, R. C. D., and Cuming, G. J. *Prayers of the Eucharist: Early and Reformed.* London: Collins, 1975.

Jeremias, Joachim. *The Eucharistic Words of Jesus.* Philadelphia: Fortress Press, 1966.

Jones, Cheslyn, et al., eds. *The Study of Liturgy.* New York: Oxford University Press, 1978.

Kavanagh, Aidan. *On Liturgical Theology.* The Hale Memorial Lectures of Seabury-Western Theological Seminary 1981. New York: Pueblo, 1984.

_____. "Response: Primary Theology and Liturgical Act." *Worship* 57 (1983): 321-24.

Kelly, John N. D. *Early Christian Creeds.* 3rd edition. New York: David McKay, 1972.

Lampe, G.W.H. *The Seal of the Spirit.* London: Longmans, Green and Co., 1951.

McKenna, John H. *Eucharist and Holy Spirit: The Eucharistic Epiclesis in 20th Century Theology.* Alcuin Club Collections 57. Great Wakering, England: Mayhew-McCrimmon, 1975.

Mitchell, Leonel L. *Baptismal Anointing.* Alcuin Club Collections 48. London: SPCK, 1966.

_____. "Christian Initiation, Rites of Passage, and Confirmation." Kendig Brubaker Cully, ed. *Confirmation Re-Examined.* Wilton, Conn.: Morehouse-Barlow Co., 1982, pp. 81-92.

_____. *The Meaning of Ritual,* New York: Paulist Press, 1977.

_____. "Response, Liturgy and Theology." *Worship* 57 (1983): 324-5.

_____. "Theology and Praxis of the Daily Office." *Anglican Theological Review* 66 (1984): pp. 38-49.

_____. "The Theology of Christian Initiation and *The Proposed Book of Common Prayer.*" *Anglican Theological Review* 60 (1978): 399-419.

_____. "What Is Confirmation?" *Anglican Theological Review* 55 (1972): 201-12.

Pieper, Josef. *In Tune with the World*. Chicago: Franciscan Herder Press, 1973.

Pike, James A., and Pittenger, Norman. *The Faith of the Church*. The Church's Teaching Series 3. New York: National Council, 1951.

Price, Charles, and Weil, Louis. *Liturgy for Living*. The Church's Teaching Series 5. New York: The Seabury Press, 1979.

Porter, H. Boone. *The Ordination Prayers of the Ancient Western Churches*. Alcuin Club Collections 29. London: SPCK, 1967.

Poschmann, Bernhard. *Penance and the Anointing of the Sick*. New York: Herder and Herder, 1964.

Power, David. *Unsearchable Riches: The Symbolic Nature of the Liturgy*. New York: Pueblo, 1984.

Richardson, Cyril C., ed. *Early Christian Fathers*. The Library of the Christian Classics I. Philadelphia: Westminster Press, 1953.

Sacramentary, The. From the English translation of *The Roman Missal* © 1973. International Committee on English in the Liturgy, Inc. New York: Catholic Books Publishing Company, 1974.

Schillebeeckx, Edward. *Ministry: Leadership in the Community of Jesus Christ*. New York: Crossroad, 1981.

Shepherd, Massey H. *Liturgy and Education*. New York: The Seabury Press, 1965.

_____. *The Oxford American Prayer Book Commentary*. New York: Oxford University Press, 1950.

_____. *The Worship of the Church*. The Church's Teaching Series 4, Greenwich, Conn.: The Seabury Press, 1952.

Standing Liturgical Commission. *Holy Baptism together with A Form of Confirmation or the Laying-on of Hands by the Bishop with the Affirmation of Baptismal Vows, as authorized by the General Convention of 1973*. Prayer Book Studies 26. New York: Church Hymnal Corporation, 1973 (abbreviated PBS 26).

Stevenson, J. *A New Eusebius*. London: SPCK, 1968.

Stevenson, Kenneth W. *Eucharist and Offering: A Liturgical Study* (unpublished manuscript).

_____. *Gregory Dix—Twenty-Five Years on.* Grove Liturgical Study 10. Bramcote Notts: Grove Books, 1977.

_____. *Nuptial Blessing: A Study of Christian Marriage Rites.* New York: Oxford University Press, 1983. (Also Alcuin Club Collections 64. London: SPCK, 1982.)

Stevick, Daniel. *Supplement to Prayer Book Studies 26.* New York: Church Hymnal Corporation, 1973.

Storey, William G. "The Liturgy of the Hours: Cathedral versus Monastery." *The Prayer of Christians.* John Gallen, S.J., ed. Notre Dame: University of Notre Dame Press, 1977.

Taft, Robert, S.J. "Liturgy as Theology." *Worship* 56 (1982): 113-7.

_____. "Thanksgiving for the Light: Toward a Theology of Vespers." *Diakonia* 13 (1978): 27-50.

The Taizé Office. London: Faith Press, 1966.

Talley, Thomas J. "Healing: Sacrament or Charism?" *Worship* 46 (1972): 518-27.

Wainwright, Geoffrey. "A Language in Which We Speak to God." *Worship* 57 (1983): 309-21.

Wiles, Maurice. *The Making of Christian Doctrine: A Study in the Principles of Early Doctrinal Development.* Cambridge: Cambridge University Press, 1967.

World Council of Churches. *Baptism, Eucharist and Ministry.* Faith and Order Paper 133. Geneva: World Council of Churches, 1982 ("The Lima Document").

Yarnold, Edward, S.J. *The Awe-Inspiring Rites of Initiation: Baptismal Homilies of the Fourth Century.* Slough: St. Paul Publications, 1971.

Index

Sacramental Sign,
206-207
Sacramental Theology,
205-207
Redemption, 155-59,
281, 285-86
Red Letter Days, 31
Renewal of Baptismal
Vows
Baptism, 90, 99
Great Vigil, 82
Renunciation of Satan,
97-98
Reserved Sacrament, 185
Rite One, 11, 40, 132,
152, 180, 219, 223,
225, 229
Rite Two, 40, 132, 152,
180, 219, 224, 225,
229, 230
Roman Missal of Paul VI,
147
Roman Pontifical, 247

-S-

Sabbath
Saturday, 19
Sacrament
Prayer before, 172
Reservation of, 185
Sacramental principle,
Sacramentary. See
Roman Missal of Paul
VI.

Sacrifice
Eucharistic. *See* Eucha-
ristic Sacrifice
of Praise and
Thanksgiving,
173-74
St. James
Liturgy of, 152
St. Jerome
Collect, 292
St. Mark
Liturgy of, 152
St Philip and St. James
Collect, 32
Saints
Commemoration of,
173
Festivals of, 31
Prayers of, 33, 66
Sanctus, 155
Saturday
Sabbath, 19
Schillebeeckx, Edward,
144-45
Scottish Eucharistic
Prayer
Epiclesis, 169
Intercessions, 172
Oblation, 166
Structure, 152
Seal of the Confessional,
199-200
Seal of the Spirit
Baptism, 114
Second Prayer Book of
Edward VI, 113-14
Serapion of Thmuis, 170

Sermon
  Daily Office, 44
  Eucharist, 135-36
Shema, 35-36. *See also*
  Jewish worship
Shepherd, Massey, 5, 14,
  31, 34, 170, 262-63,
  276-77
Sick
  Communion, 213
  Ministry to, 207-16
  Anointing, 209-12
  Confession of Sin,
  209
  laying on of Hands,
  209, 211-12
Silence, 41, 65
Spiritual Communion. *See*
  Communion
Stevick, Daniel, 121
Structure
  Alexandrian *Anaphora*,
  152, 168
  Scottish Eucharistic
  Prayer, 152
  West Syrian *Anaphora*,
  152-53
Suffrages
  Evening Prayer, 52-53
  Morning Prayer, 49
Sunday of the Passion.
  See Palm Sunday
Supplication, 67
Surge illuminare, 47-48
Sursum corda, 15

Symbolum. See Baptismal
  Creed
Synaxis, 5, 51, 144

-T-

Taft, Robert, 36, 54
Taizé Office, 46, 55
Talley, Thomas J.,
  210-11, 227
Taylor, Jeremy, 231
Te Deum, 46-47, 133, 288
Thanksgiving
  for Creation, 153-54
  for Redemption,
  155-59
  over the Water,
  103-105
  PostCommunion, 181
Thanksgivings, 50
Theologia prima, 2, 3
Theophilus of Antioch,
  107
Thirty-nine Articles. *See*
  Articles of Religion
Thomas Aquinas, 69
Threefold Ministry, 236,
  238
Traditional language. *See*
  Rite One
Trinity Sunday
  Proper preface, 157
Trisagion, 133, 228